GLOBAL CHAMPIONS OF SUSTAINABLE DEVELOPMENT

The 17 Sustainable Development Goals (SDGs) embody the collective aspirations of the world's peoples: peace, freedom, development and sustainability. The challenges associated with the struggle for attainment of these goals and objectives are as diverse and complex as the variety of human societies, national conditions and natural ecosystems worldwide. The problems to be addressed range from extreme poverty and pandemics to racism and refugee crises. Some of the best strategies and solutions to these problems emerged from unlikely places, ranging from the corporate boardrooms and halls of administration to the fields of civic engagement and the vortices of crises. Often, a single person is the dauntless driving force behind these innovative programs and courageous experiments that made all the difference to the poorest and most disadvantaged social groups. Somehow, they were able to turn the abstract goals and principles of sustainability into concrete programs and effective action.

This book, the first of its kind, offers a platform that shares the individual experiences and personal studies of champions around the world that 'make sustainability work' in different contexts.

In the trenches of practice, results are far from guaranteed, while sacrifice and obstacles are inevitable. These champions forge the paths forward – advocating ideas, mobilizing support and exercising leadership – in diverse nations, organizations and communities. In their struggle, they develop plans and solutions that inevitably involve adaptation, sacrifice, trade-offs and compromises that address the concerns of competing groups.

Patricia M. Flynn is Trustee Professor of Economics and Management, Bentley University.

Milenko Gudić is Founder of Refoment Consulting and Coaching.

Tay Keong Tan is Director of International Studies and Leadership Studies, Radford University.

Principles for Responsible Management Education (PRME) series
Editors Milenko Gudić, Carole Parkes, Patricia M. Flynn, Kemi Ogunyemi, Amy Verbos

Since the inception of the UN-supported Principles for Responsible Management Education (PRME) in 2007, there has been increased debate over how to adapt management education to best meet the demands of the 21st-century business environment. While consensus has been reached by the majority of globally focused management education institutions that sustainability must be incorporated into management education curricula, the relevant question is no longer why management education should change, but how.

Volumes within the Routledge/PRME book series aim to cultivate and inspire actively engaged participants by offering practical examples and case studies to support the implementation of the Six Principles of Responsible Management Education. Books in the series aim to enable participants to transition from a global learning community to an action community.

Books in the series

Inspirational Guide for the Implementation of PRME
Learning to Go Beyond, 2nd Edition
Edited by Alan Murray, Denise Baden, Paul Cashian, Alec Wersun and Kathryn Haynes

Learning to Read the Signs
Reclaiming Pragmatism for the Practice of Sustainable Management, 2nd Edition
F. Byron (Ron) Nahser

Inspirational Guide for the Implementation of PRME
Placing Sustainability at the Heart of Management Education
Edited by the Principles for Responsible Management Education

Global Champions of Sustainable Development
Edited by Patricia M. Flynn, Milenko Gudić and Tay Keong Tan

GLOBAL CHAMPIONS OF SUSTAINABLE DEVELOPMENT

Edited by Patricia M. Flynn, Milenko Gudić and Tay Keong Tan

LONDON AND NEW YORK

First published 2020
by Routledge
2 Park Square, Milton Park, Abingdon, Oxon OX14 4RN

and by Routledge
52 Vanderbilt Avenue, New York, NY 10017

Routledge is an imprint of the Taylor & Francis Group, an informa business

© 2020 selection and editorial matter, Patricia M. Flynn, Milenko Gudić and Tay Keong Tan; individual chapters, the contributors

The right of Patricia M. Flynn, Milenko Gudić and Tay Keong Tan to be identified as the authors of the editorial material, and of the authors for their individual chapters, has been asserted in accordance with sections 77 and 78 of the Copyright, Designs and Patents Act 1988.

All rights reserved. No part of this book may be reprinted or reproduced or utilised in any form or by any electronic, mechanical, or other means, now known or hereafter invented, including photocopying and recording, or in any information storage or retrieval system, without permission in writing from the publishers.

Trademark notice: Product or corporate names may be trademarks or registered trademarks, and are used only for identification and explanation without intent to infringe.

British Library Cataloguing-in-Publication Data
A catalogue record for this book is available from the British Library

Library of Congress Cataloging-in-Publication Data
Names: Flynn, Patricia M., editor. | Tan, Tay Keong, editor. | Gudić, Milenko, editor.
Title: Global champions of sustainable development / edited by Patricia M. Flynn, Milenko Gudić, and Tay Keong Tan.
Description: First Edition. | New York : Routledge, 2020. | Series: Principles of responsible management education | Includes bibliographical references.
Identifiers: LCCN 2019039667 (print) | LCCN 2019039668 (ebook) | ISBN 9780815385943 (hardback) | ISBN 9780815385950 (paperback) | ISBN 9781351176316 (ebook)
Subjects: LCSH: Sustainable development. | Recycling industry. | Economic policy—Environmental aspects. | Strategic planning.
Classification: LCC HC79.E5 G5918 2020 (print) | LCC HC79.E5 (ebook) | DDC 304.2—dc23
LC record available at https://lccn.loc.gov/2019039667
LC ebook record available at https://lccn.loc.gov/2019039668

ISBN: 978-0-8153-8594-3 (hbk)
ISBN: 978-0-8153-8595-0 (pbk)
ISBN: 978-1-351-17631-6 (ebk)

Typeset in Bembo
by Apex CoVantage, LLC

 Printed in the United Kingdom by Henry Ling Limited

CONTENTS

List of contributors vii

Introduction 1
Patricia M. Flynn, Tay Keong Tan and Milenko Gudić

PART I
SDGs and the big picture: key issues that transcend organizations, industries and countries 7

1 What does it mean to be a Latin family?: Achievements on sustainability of the Multi-Latina Grupo Familia 9
Claudia Vélez-Zapata, Juan Alejandro Cortés and Al Rosenbloom

2 Champions of sustainable development in Africa: challenges, successes and lessons learned in Nigeria 20
Ijeoma Nwagwu

3 Global Champions of water and sanitation for all 33
Diane M. Kellogg

PART II
Sustainability in traditional industries 47

4 Making sustainability work in plantation agriculture: the story of a sustainability champion in the tea industry in Sri Lanka 49
A. D. Nuwan Gunarathne

5 Among the poorest of the poor: Tauhid's sustainability approach in Northern Bangladesh 64
Enrico Fontana

6 A good cup of coffee from EcoCafé Haiti 77
Timothy Ewest, Kacee A. Garne and Tom Durant

PART III
Championing education and gender equality 91

7 M is for Malala 93
Laura Jackson Young

8 Role of participatory community education in Ireland 105
Edgar Bellow

9 Men as gender allies: Verizon's Craig Silliman and Walmart's Alan Bryan 115
Paola Cecchi-Dimeglio

PART IV
Partnerships and programs that foster sustainable development 127

10 Champions of sustainable development: the university for the common good and Grameen Caledonian College of Nursing in Bangladesh 129
Alec Wersun

11 Paths to empowerment: a case study of local sustainability from rural Nicaragua 142
Michael B. Smith, Susan Kinne, and Grupo Fénix

12 Poverty eradication and political engagement: a case of sustainable entrepreneurship in China 155
Xuanwei Cao and Xiao Wang

13 Global Champions of sustainable development. Uaná Refugees Program: an opportunity to start over 167
Norman de Paula Arruda Filho

Concluding remarks 178
Patricia M. Flynn, Tay Keong Tan and Milenko Gudić

CONTRIBUTORS

Edgar Bellow
Edgar Bellow is Professor of Sustainable Business and International Management at NEOMA Business School in France. He is currently Academic and Research Representative for Corporate Social Responsibility and Sustainable Development Goals for the school. Dr. Bellow is Sustainability Consultant and Visiting Professor in various universities in Asia and in Europe. His research focus is on sustainability, public policy and geopolitics. Email: edgar.bellow@neoma-bs.fr

Xuanwei Cao
Xuanwei Cao is Associate Professor of Strategic Management and Sustainability at International Business School at Suzhou Xi'an Jiaotong-Liverpool University. Dr. Cao's research interests, which are at the intersection of strategy and sustainability, include corporate environmental strategy, corporate sustainability strategy, sustainable entrepreneurship and sustainable innovation. Email: xuanwei.cao@xjtlu.edu.cn

Paola Cecchi-Dimeglio
Paola Cecchi-Dimeglio is Chair of the Executive Leadership Research Initiative for Women and Minority Attorneys at the Center for the Legal Profession at Harvard Law School (HLS) and a Senior Research Fellow at HLS and at Harvard Kennedy School (Women and Public Policy Program). A behavioral scientist and lawyer, Dr. Cecchi-Dimeglio, in her research, relies heavily on big data and field experiments in organizations. Email: paola@paolacecchidimeglio.com or pcecchidimeglio@law.harvard.edu

Juan Alejandro Cortés
Juan Alejandro Cortés has a PhD in Management from the CEU San Pablo University of Madrid, Spain, He specializes in Human Development Management. He is Director of the Faculty of Management of Universidad

Pontificia Bolivariana and professor and researcher of Estudios Empresariales Group of the Universidad Pontificia Bolivariana of Medellín, Colombia. His research interests include change and organizational learning. Email: Juan.cortes@upb.edu.co

Norman de Paula Arrund Filho
Norman de Paula Arrund Filho is President of the Higher Institute of Administration and Economics (ISAE) Brazilian Business School. He is Head of PRME Latin America and the Caribbean Chapter and a member of the Global Compact Brazilian Committee. He is Professor of Sustainability in Organizations of ISAE's Governance and Sustainability Master's Program. As a Brazilian responsible-management-education enthusiast, he contributed to the task force that outlined the UN Principles for Responsible Management Education in 2006. Since then, he has been strongly supporting the dissemination of UN initiatives as well as the 2030 Agenda for Sustainable Development around the world. He served as the main motivator and supporter for the implementation of the Uaná Refugees Program. Email: norman@isaebrasil.com.br

Tom Durant
Working out of offices in Eugene, Oregon, Tom Durant oversees EcoCafé Haiti as the founder, fund-raiser and marketing director of the organization. Durant's background includes 40 years of industrial and entrepreneurial business experience, graduate and undergraduate degrees in business and a master's degree in theological studies. Additionally, Durant serves as a senior instructor at the University of Oregon and the Oregon State University teaching Entrepreneurship, Global Business and other management courses. Email: tewest@hbu.edu

Timothy Ewest
Tim is Visiting Research Scholar at Princeton University's Faith & Work Initiative. He is a member of the Academy of Management (AOM) and part of the AOM divisions on Organizational Behavior, Social Issues in Management and Management, Religion and Spirituality. Timothy actively researches and publishes on the impact of human values as expressed in religion and leadership within the workplace. Tim received a doctorate in Management from George Fox University. Email: tewest@hbu.edu

Patricia M. Flynn (lead editor)
Patricia M. Flynn, PhD, is Trustee Professor of Economics and Management at Bentley University, USA, where she was as Dean of the McCallum Graduate School of Business for 10 years. She has served on numerous corporate, mutual fund and nonprofit boards and testified before the US Congress on the impacts of technological change on jobs and workers. Since 2011, Pat has served as co-facilitator of the UN Global Compact PRME Working Group on Gender Equality and has written extensively on gender issues in business

schools, corporate boardrooms and executive suites. In 2016, she became the inaugural recipient of the Patricia M., Flynn Distinguished Women Leader in Business Education Award now given annually by the Women Administrators in Management Education at AACSB-International. In 2017, Pat received a PRME Pioneer Award for "Thought Leadership – Translating PRME into Action." Email: pflynn@bentley.edu

Enrico Fontana
Enrico Fontana is a postdoctoral fellow at the University of Victoria, Gustavson School of Business in British Columbia, Canada. His research lies within the organizational domain and takes an interdisciplinary approach to study the role of business in society. That includes corporate social responsibility and sustainable value chains, with particular reference to South and East Asia. Enrico has published his work in multiple journals. He usually presents at different international conferences, including the Academy of Management annual meeting. Before embarking on his PhD studies, Enrico worked six years as a practitioner in the fashion industry in Asia and Europe. Email: efontana@uvic.ca

Kacee A. Garner
Kacee has a Doctor of Arts in Political Science with a social science cognate in Anthropology from Idaho State University. Her research interests include American political campaigns, social entrepreneurship, public policy and the intersection of political science and anthropology. She works for the State University System of New York, Morrisville and at her local small-town library. Email: kaceegarner@gmail.com

Milenko Gudić (co-editor)
Milenko Gudić is Founding Director of Refoment Consulting and Coaching, Belgrade, Serbia, and visiting lecturer at University Donja Gorica, Montenegro. He has worked as a consultant, researcher and lecturer at the Economics Institute, Belgrade, as a visiting lecturer in several countries, and as a speaker in more than 30 countries. He has been engaged as a consultant to the Organisation for Economic Co-operation and Development, the United Nations Development Programme and the United Nations Industrial Development Organization, among others, and on various entrepreneurship, regional, rural and public management development projects. Milenko was Founding and Managing Director (2000–2014) of the International Management Teachers Academy, while also leading CEEMAN's major international research and educational leadership capacity building projects. He was program chair of EURAM 2008. Since 2008 he has been coordinating the PRME Working Group on Poverty: A Challenge for Management Education. He is a member of the PRME Advisory Committee UN Global Compact Working Group on Poverty: A Challenge for Management Education. In 2017, Milenko he received a PRME Pioneer Award for "Thought Leadership – Translating PRME into Action." Email: Milenko.gudic@gmail.com

A. D. Nuwan Gunarathne

A. D. Nuwan Gunarathne is a doctoral candidate at Griffith University, Australia, and a Senior Lecturer at the University of Sri Jayewardenepura, Sri Lanka. He is an associate member of the Chartered Institute of Management Accountants, UK, and of the Institute of Certified Management Accountants, Sri Lanka. He holds a bachelor's and a master's degree in Business Administration from the University of Sri Jayewardenepura. Nuwan is also a member of the Environmental and Sustainability Management Accounting Network (EMAN) Asia Pacific (AP) and country representative of the Sri Lanka Chapter of EMAN-AP. Email: nuwan@sjp.ac.lk

Diane M. Kellogg

Diane M. Kellogg, EdD, is Professor Emerita of Management at Bentley University in the United States and Managing Partner of Kellogg Consultants. Kellogg Consultants, a sustainable sanitation consultancy, has received grant support from the Dutch government, the Bill and Melinda Gates Foundation and Oxfam America to improve sanitation in urban poor households. Email: dianekellogg@gmail.com

Susan Kinne

Susan Kinne spent her first 20 adult years in Cincinnati, Ohio, in the United States, teaching and working as a technician in the semiconductor industry. In 1989, she moved to Nicaragua to join the National Engineering University (UNI) where she grew into a promoter of human dignity via sustainable use of resources particularly renewable energies. With her students, she co-founded Grupo Fénix and the Alternative Energy Program at the UNI. In recent years she has focused on co-creating a "Solar Community" in Totogalpa, Northern Nicaragua. Email: susankinnefenix@gmail.com

Ijeoma Nwagwu

Ijeoma Nwagwu is Centre Manager, Lagos Business School Sustainability Centre, in Lagos, Nigeria. She earned her Doctor of Juridical Science (SJD) and Master in Laws (LLM) degrees from Harvard Law School. Ijeoma is a researcher, a lecturer and a writer. She currently teaches corporate social responsibility, sustainability, strategy and social entrepreneurship at Lagos Business School. Email: inwagwu@lbs.edu.ng

Al Rosenbloom

Al Rosenbloom, PhD, is John and Jeanne Rowe Distinguished Professor at Dominican University in River Forest, Illinois, USA. He teaches international business and marketing. His research interests include emerging markets, poverty and sustainable development. Email: right1al@comcast.net

Michael B. Smith

Michael B. Smith teaches history and environmental humanities at Ithaca College in Ithaca, New York. In 2017, he was a Fulbright Scholar in Nicaragua as part of a collaboration with the nongovernmental organization Grupo Fénix and the National Engineering University. He is the past recipient of a U.S. government National Endowment for the Humanities grant exploring digital learning in history and is coeditor of the volume *Citizenship Across the Curriculum* (Indiana University Press, 2010). Email: mlsmith.ithaca@gmail.com

Tay Keong Tan (co-editor)
Tay Keong Tan is Director of International Studies and Leadership Studies and Associate Professor in the Department of Political Science at Radford University, USA. His research interests are on sustainable development and anticorruption. He headed public and nonprofit organizations in Singapore, Israel and the United States and has worked in development projects in more than 15 countries. He is a member of the PRME Working Groups on Sustainable Mindset, Anti-Poverty and Anti-Corruption. He has a master's degree and a doctoral degree in Public Policy from Harvard University. Email: ttan2@radford.edu

Claudia Vélez-Zapata
Claudia Vélez-Zapata, has a PhD in Management with European Mention from the San Pablo University-CEU, Madrid, Spain. She also has a Master of Science in Management degree from EAFIT University. Claudia is a Professor of the Faculty of Management of the Universidad Pontificia Bolivariana of Medellín, Colombia, and Researcher of the Estudios Empresariales Group. Her research interests include informal institutions, illegitimate institutions related to marketing, and management. Email: claudiap.velez@upb.edu.co

Xiao Wang
Xiao Wang is Lecturer of Innovation and Entrepreneurship at International Business School at Suzhou Xi'an Jiaotong-Liverpool University. Dr. Wang's research interests include social entrepreneurship, social innovation and strategic entrepreneurship. Email: xiao.wang@xjtlu.edu.cn

Alec Wersun
Alec Wersun is Associate Professor in strategy and corporate responsibility at Glasgow Caledonian University in the UK. He serves as Chair of the UK and Ireland Regional Chapter of the United Nations initiative, the Principles for Responsible Management Education. Email: a.wersun@gcu.ac.uk

Laura Jackson Young
Laura Jackson Young graduated in 2014 from the University of North Carolina at Chapel Hill in the United States with a PhD in Economics. She is Assistant Professor of Economics at Bentley University, USA. Her teaching, research and publications focus on empirical macroeconomics, econometrics and monetary policy. Email: ljackson@bentley.edu

INTRODUCTION

Patricia M. Flynn, Tay Keong Tan and Milenko Gudić

On October 25, 2015, the United Nations General Assembly adopted the declaration *Transforming Our World: The 2030 Agenda for Sustainable Development*, which lays out the 17 Sustainable Development Goals (SDGs) that embody the collective aspirations of the world's peoples: peace, freedom, development and sustainability. This intergovernmental agreement sets out the global development agenda for the 15-year period 2016 to 2030, building on the progress made by the Millennium Development Goals (MDGs) from 2000 to 2015. Operationalized into 169 specific, measurable and time-bound objectives and some 232 indicators, the SDGs address some of the most serious challenges facing humanity today. Governments, development agencies, corporations, educational and management development institutions, civil society and communities have been mobilized to work on the economic, social and environmental issues involved.

The 17 SDGs adopted by world leaders to mobilize global efforts on sustainable development are as follows:

1. Poverty – End poverty in all its forms everywhere.
2. Food – End hunger, achieve food security and improved nutrition and promote sustainable agriculture.
3. Health – Ensure healthy lives and promote well-being for all at all ages.
4. Education – Ensure inclusive and equitable quality education and promote lifelong learning opportunities for all.
5. Women – Achieve gender equality and empower all women and girls.
6. Water – Ensure availability and sustainable management of water and sanitation for all.
7. Energy – Ensure access to affordable, reliable, sustainable and clean energy for all.

8 Economy – Promote sustained, inclusive and sustainable economic growth, full and productive employment and decent work for all.
9 Infrastructure – Build resilient infrastructure, promote inclusive and sustainable industrialization and foster innovation.
10 Inequality – Reduce inequality within and among countries.
11 Habitation – Make cities and human settlements inclusive, safe, resilient and sustainable.
12 Consumption – Ensure sustainable consumption and production patterns.
13 Climate – Take urgent action to combat climate change and its impacts.
14 Marine ecosystems – Conserve and sustainably use the oceans, seas and marine resources for sustainable development.
15 Ecosystems – Protect, restore and promote sustainable use of terrestrial ecosystems, sustainably manage forests, combat desertification and halt and reverse land degradation and halt biodiversity loss.
16 Institutions – Promote peaceful and inclusive societies for sustainable development, provide access to justice for all and build effective, accountable and inclusive institutions at all levels.
17 Sustainability – Strengthen the means of implementation and revitalize the global partnership for sustainable development.

It was a great accomplishment for the nations of the world to agree on a single set of goals and to make public commitments to pursue them at the UN summit. The problems to be addressed range from extreme poverty to rising inequality and refugee crises. However, the 2030 Agenda remains a voluntary agreement with no legally binding obligation on the UN member states. The plethora of goals and objectives, coupled with the reliance on each country's national and regional plans and institutions for implementation, makes the realization of the goals a daunting task. The challenges associated with the struggle for the attainment of these goals are as diverse and complex as the variety of human societies, national conditions and natural ecosystems worldwide. The problems to be addressed range from extreme poverty to rising inequality and refugee crises.

The poorest countries of the world often face the greatest social, economic and environmental problems. Yet it is these areas that have the least financial and technical capacities to address these challenges. Developing country governments with little public revenue to spare are working to translate the SDGs into national legislation, develop multiyear plans of action, seek additional resources and forge new partnerships to advance the 2030 Agenda within their borders. Many of the nations, including those with advanced industrialized economies, will have to grapple with the inherent contradictions in long lists of absolutist goals and targets. They have to manage the imperatives of economic growth and industrialization with the need for environmental protection and redistribution for social equity.

Despite the many obstacles to achieving the SDGs, particularly in the developing world, the goals provide a unifying agenda across the globe. They also provide official recognition to a broad range of issues that must be tackled if humanity is to survive decades of economic growth, industrialization and unbridled exploitation of the earth's natural resources. Important concerns such as sustainability, gender equality, poverty eradication and participatory decision-making are strongly embedded in the global development agenda. Moreover, these SDGs also offer new opportunities for important stakeholders to make their contribution to sustainable development, be they entrepreneurs, public servants, corporate managers or civil society activists. What may be perceived as a weakness of the SDGs – the large number of ambitious goals and targets – has opened up "entrepreneurial space" for world citizens to play their part as champions for sustainable development.

This book chronicles the stories of some of these global leaders, activists and entrepreneurs who have overcome great odds to develop and implement programs and activities that embody solutions and best practices to enduring sustainability challenges. They emerged from a wide range of organizations, industries, sectors and countries. Their laboratories of practice range from corporate boardrooms and factory floors to schools and the hills of plantations. The lessons from their early successes, productive failures and personal practices are chronicled in the following chapters, written by authors from 14 countries.

Organization of the book

Global Champions in Sustainable Development provides inspirational stories on how individuals and organizations operating in a wide range of industries and sectors worldwide and in diverse economic, social and cultural contexts, can successfully champion the advancement of the SDGs.

The book is an edited collection of 13 chapters, organized into four parts:

- Part I. SDGs and the big picture: key issues that transcend organizations, industries and countries
- Part II. Sustainability in traditional industries
- Part III. Championing education and gender equality
- Part IV. Partnerships and programs that foster sustainable development

Part I. SDGs and the big picture: key issues that transcend organizations, industries and countries

The first section of the book contributes to a better understanding of the big-picture, SDG-related issues that transcend organizations, industries and countries. The first two chapters show that sustainability can be pursued either through specific business initiatives or by having sustainable development as a driver for the overall business strategy. The third chapter demonstrates that advancing the global goals opens the space and calls for the engagement of a wide spectrum of actors, from individuals and organizations to national governments and global institutions.

In Chapter 1, Vélez-Zapata, Cortés and Rosenbloom present the case of the Multi-Latina Grupo Familia in Colombia and its chief executive officer, Andrés

Gómez, who succeeded in making sustainable development the main driver of the company. Their inspiring triple-bottom-line strategic approach is illustrated by three initiatives that build inclusive markets by engaging bottom-of-the-pyramid (BoP) recyclers, respecting BoP consumers and empowering impoverished communities.

Chapter 2 by Nwagwu presents cases of three organizations championing change by driving sustainable development in Nigeria. Innovative strategies and business models in the areas of food security, financial inclusion and environmental sustainability are implemented to combat the challenges of poverty, inequality and climate change.

In Chapter 3, Kellogg addresses the complex issues related to ensuring the availability and sustainable management of water and sanitation for all. The chapter highlights the work of selected organizations, programs, individuals and governments working to advance SDG #6 (Clean water and sanitation) and identifies key challenges that lie ahead in dealing with these global issues.

Part II. Sustainability in traditional industries

There is a general perspective that emerging, technologically advanced and clean industries can and will greatly contribute to the advancement of the SDGs. This section demonstrates, however, that significant contributions can also be achieved through innovations, improvements and new approaches in traditional industries. This is particularly important given the prevailing context in which these industries operate, where the sustainability challenges and development problems can be extensive, complex and interrelated. The cases clearly show how the advancement in one of the SDGs consequently, if not simultaneously, can contribute to progress in several other SDGs as well.

Gunarathne in Chapter 4 showcases the notable work of Mahendra Peiris, who helped revitalize the collapsing Sri Lankan tea industry using novel, yet simple, innovative approaches to achieve productivity gains. A dauntless pioneer of many innovative programs, Peiris's actions led to economic success and preservation while also improving the working conditions and living standards of the plantation workers.

Chapter 5 by Fontana describes the sustainability approach of Md. Tauhid Bin Abdus Salam ("Tauhid"), the founder of Classical Handmade Products BD in Bangladesh, a firm operating as part of the global value chains in the supply of rugs and baskets. Tauhid's sustainability approach contributed to poverty alleviation, gender equality, decent work and economic growth, as well as to responsible consumption and production. A critical component of his success was his collaboration with non-governmental organizations (NGOs) and buyers in the inclusive engagement of rural communities and in worker empowerment.

In Chapter 6, Ewest and Garner, together with global champion Tom Durant, present the case of the social venture, EcoCafé Haiti, a business Durant built around the traditional coffee industry. EcoCafé simultaneously addressed environmental and social needs by reviving the cottage coffee industry; creating employment and making workers and their families food secure; while also restoring land in one of the most economically challenged countries in the Western hemisphere. This venture directly addresses five of the 17 SDGs, demonstrating that even with severe social, economic and ecological challenges, progress toward the SDGs is possible.

Part III. Championing education and gender equality

The chapters in this section show how interrelated the issues of education and gender equality are for children and for adults. They also demonstrate how these factors can impact several other SDGs.

In Chapter 7, Young features the inspiring story of Malala Yousafzai, who was awarded the Nobel Peace Prize for her efforts in promoting "the right of all children to education." Surviving the Taliban's attempts to silence her, Malala has become a global advocate for gender equality in education and in poverty reduction by allowing everyone, especially girls and young women, to actively contribute towards their own economic advancement.

Chapter 8 by Bellow presents the case of the Longford Women's Link (LWL), an Irish center for women's empowerment, community engagement and education established by Louise Lovett. The case demonstrates how community adult education can work especially well for female learners who have typically suffered from structural oppression and exclusion and obstacles presented by normative systems of hegemonic masculine education.

In Chapter 9, Cecchi-Dimeglio emphasizes the importance of having men as allies in the quest for gender equality. The stories of Verizon's Craig Silliman and Walmart's Alan Bryan in the United States showcase how managers and organizations can enhance the roles of men in gender-parity initiatives. Recommendations are provided for setting a long-term agenda that incorporates changes in attitudes and behaviors of both men and women.

Part IV. Partnerships and programs that foster sustainable development

While most of the book's chapters address various forms of partnerships, the four chapters in this section provide explicit examples of how collaboration among diverse actors at different levels can play a critical role in making progress towards the SDGs.

Chapter 10 by Wersun tells the story of how sustainability champions from Scotland (Pamela Gilles and Barbara Parfitt) and Bangladesh (Muhammad Ynus) joined forces to establish the Grameen Caledonian College of Nursing (GCCN), a social business "For the Common Good." The case illustrates how the vision, unwavering belief and entrepreneurial spirit of these global champions, working in the spirit of SDG #17 (Partnerships), have led to the GCCN contributing to the reduction of poverty, along with the advancement of health, well-being and gender equality in Bangladesh.

Chapter 11 by Smith and Kinne presents the case of Grupo Fénix, a local NGO in Nicaragua. The authors have been personally involved in this venture. Their ongoing collaboration with the local people and with dozens of international partners has created pathways out of poverty and dependency for many of the rural women. Several of the beneficiaries of these efforts have, in turn, become teachers themselves, thus promoting longer-term viability of these programs and benefits.

In Chapter 12, Cao and Wang address the importance of private-public partnerships in a context where the relationship between the two sectors is described as complex and paradoxical. The authors show how the entrepreneur, Hanyuan Liu, effectively utilized his active political engagement in addressing SDGs, such as poverty alleviation (#1) and affordable and clean energy (#7). The case demonstrates how Liu and his Tongwei Group Co., Ltd. transformed their solar energy business practices and simultaneously pursued economic viability, social equity and environmental stability.

Last, Chapter 13 by Norman de Paula Arruda Filho, president of Higher Institute of Administration and Economics Brazilian Business School, documents the institution's impressive response to the refugee crisis in Brazil. The Uaná Refugees Program is a volunteer training initiative promoted by the school's students, alumni, teachers and staff. Engaging several other stakeholders as well, the program provides refugees and migrants with the tools to facilitate their entry and empowerment in Brazilian labor markets.

Conclusion

The Concluding Remarks at the end of the volume summarize the main lessons learned from the cases and the global champions on how to best address the SDGs. The motivations driving the global champions are highlighted, as is the importance of actively engaging local individuals and organizations in implementing viable solutions to poverty and/or other sustainable development problems they may face.

PART I
SDGs and the big picture
Key issues that transcend organizations, industries and countries

PART I

1

WHAT DOES IT MEAN TO BE A LATIN FAMILY?

Achievements on sustainability of the Multi-Latina Grupo Familia

Claudia Vélez-Zapata, Juan Alejandro Cortés and Al Rosenbloom

Abstract

This chapter profiles the MultiLatina, Grupo Familia, located in Medellín, Colombia, and the leadership of its chief executive officer, Andrés Felipe Gómez Salazar (hereafter referred to as Andrés Gómez), in transforming Grupo Familia into a company in which sustainable development is its main strategic driver. Andrés Gómez's sustainable development leadership is illustrated in three case examples: (1) building inclusive markets by including bottom-of-the-pyramid (BoP) recyclers, (2) respecting BoP consumers and (3) empowering impoverished communities. Grupo Familia and Andrés Gómez provide examples of how triple-bottom-line thinking can be integrated into a company's enterprise strategy, with significant results. Grupo Familia's history and its product lines are also discussed.

Introduction

Value creation is the long-term goal for every organization (Porter & Kramer 2011; Schumpeter 1936) and is, in fact, a dynamic concept that changes over time. Climate change, zero-waste production processes, the circular economy and the impact of consumption on the environment are becoming part of the public discourse around sustainable development. As Senge (2011) noted, the centrality of sustainability development to the quality of life on earth creates a "profound shift in strategic context for corporations" (Stead & Stead 2014, 6) and thus, by extension, how corporations understand and create value.

Studies of chief executive officers (CEOs) have found that reframing their firm's future in light of sustainable development presents challenges. Executives have reported changes to their firm's business model in order to capture strategic market opportunities created by a focus on sustainable development (Kiron et al. 2013). "CEOs believe action will be required not only in reshaping a new architecture for corporate sustainability, but also in linking sustainability tangibly and quantifiably to value creation . . . [and] toward transformational change" (Hayward et al. 2013, 19).

CEOs' strategic interest in sustainability parallels a much larger commitment to sustainable development set forth by the United Nations. In 2015, the UN established its own agenda for creating a sustainable future for all individuals on earth when it ratified its 17 Sustainable Development Goals (SDGs). Lubin and Esty (2010) capture the problem and promise of corporate sustainable development by observing, "[It's] not because [CEOs] don't see sustainability as a strategic issue. Rather, it's because they think they're facing an unprecedented journey for which there is no road map" (Lubin & Esty 2010, 2).

This chapter focuses on Grupo Familia, a Medellín-based Multi-Latina, and serves as a counterpoint to Lubin and Esty's (2010) observation that many CEOs do not have road maps for "the sustainability journey." The chapter illustrates how a founder's values and continued leadership by the current CEO, Andrés Gómez, have worked to create a company firmly committed to sustainable value creation in every market it serves.

Grupo Familia

Grupo Familia was founded in 1958 in Medellín (Colombia) by John Gómez Restrepo and Mario Uribe. Initially, the company was called URIGO, from the combination of the surnames Uribe and Gómez. It was dedicated to importing Waldorf brand toilet paper, a product of Scott Paper Co., USA. In 1970, Grupo Familia opened offices in Bogotá, Cali and Barranquilla and, in 1982, expanded into Peru and Chile, at which point it became a Multi-Latina. A 1997 joint venture with the Swedish multinational Svenska Cellulosa Aktiebolaget (SCA) led to the distribution of Grupo Familia products throughout all Central America and most of South America (Grupo Familia, s.f.).

In 2017, Grupo Familia was ranked among the top 10 most-remembered Colombian brands by the *Dinero Top of Mind Study* and the consulting firm Invamer Gallup (March 27, 2017). It was first in sales in the Colombian market in hygiene products for home and personal care (Group Familia 2016). In 2018, Grupo Familia had seven leading brands (see Table 1.1) that were variously marketed in 22 countries in Latin America and the Caribbean. It employed approximately 5,300 individuals, which is equivalent to providing a livelihood to some 5,300 Latino families.

Who is Andrés Gómez?

"My hobby is my family," said Andrés Gómez (Gómez-Salazar, field notes, 2018), and his world has literally revolved around both his biological family (his wife and two daughters) and his professional family, the Familia. Born in Medellín, Andrés Gómez was the youngest of five children in his family. He attended Universidad Pontificia Bolivariana and graduated with a degree in mechanical engineering. Andrés Gómez soon joined Grupo Familia as a project engineer in 2002

TABLE 1.1 Grupo Familia brands and products

Brand	Line of Products
Familia®	Toilet paper, napkins, kitchen towels, tissues, air fresheners, wet cloths, microfiber kitchen towels, antibacterial gels
Pequeñín®	Diapers, baby wet cloths, baby protective creams, baby shampoos
Petys®	Pet wet cloths, odor eliminators, pet shampoo, flea repellent spray, dog absorbent mats, cat litter
Nosotras®	Sanitary towels and napkins, daily protectors/pants liners, tampons, wet cloths, intimate and body soap, women V-zone after-shave-care products line
Pomys®	Wet wipe makeup removers for normal, dry, oily and mixed skin types
Familia Institutional®	Workplace hygiene and grooming products: toilet paper, hand towels, soaps, antibacterial gels, napkins, cleaners, wet cloths, semidisposable cloths, tissues, air fresheners
TENA®★	Broad range of incontinence products for men and women.

Source: Compiled by the authors based on commercial information from the company.

★ Distributor only in Argentina, Bolivia, Colombia, Curacao, Cuba, Ecuador, Haití, Jamaica, Santa Lucía, Perú, Puerto Rico, Paraguay, the Dominican Republic and Surinam.

and advanced rapidly within the company. He assumed expanded responsibility for Grupo Familia's operations in Bogotá, Argentina, Ecuador and the Dominican Republic. In 2016 and in the middle of a crucial situation for Grupo Familia, the board of directors asked Andres Gómez to become interim CEO.

Reflecting on this appointment as CEO, Andrés Gómez has said,

> [The Board] asked me to accompany the company in the middle of a storm. They asked me to accompany them to navigate this boat. I started sailing this boat, first without touching anything; second without letting anything get lost. . . . That was a year of great learning. . . . Those may have been the years I grew the most professional, because no [academic program] prepares you to manage [situations like this].

Through his choice of words, Andrés Gómez provides insight into who he is as an individual and into his own distinctive worldview. Worldviews are important because they shape how individuals see the world and they thus become part of an individual's core identity (De La Sienra Servin, Smith, & Mitchell 2017; Rimanoczy 2014). Andrés Gómez has said,

> When I am in moments of difficult decision, in crossroads of life, I go to the most basic thing that are my values to make a decision. The question is not then what would God do in this case, or what Jesus would do in this case. The question is what would a good human being armed with basic values that would be found in multiple religions do.

Andrés Gómez is a humanist, who is, himself, grounded in deep, universal values, and it is these deeply rooted, humane values that frame his commitment to sustainability at Grupo Familia.

Sustainable development at Grupo Familia: the big picture

Table 1.2 outlines Grupo Familia's progress on selected economic, environmental and social dimensions of sustainable development (i.e., the triple bottom line), both before (2014–2015) and after (2016–2017) when Andrés Gómez became CEO. As indicated in Table 1.2, Grupo Familia continued to meet its economic target. Moreover, under Andrés Gómez's leadership, the economic value of the firm increased significantly (2016 and 2017), as did the number of individuals who benefited from Grupo Familia's social engagement.

Yet the data in Table 1.2 tell an incomplete story. Table 1.2 illustrates the numbers but not "the story" behind the numbers.

Grupo Familia's (2014) *Sustainability Report* described sustainability as an important element that connected all strategies and structures within the company (Grupo Familia 2014). In 2015, the company's sustainability strategy appeared as each dimension of the triple bottom line: economic, social and environmental (Grupo Familia 2015). In 2016, the first sustainability report with Andrés Gómez as CEO, Grupo Familia described sustainable development as having a top strategy status, aligning all teams, projects and activities of the organization. The same report also redefined what it meant to be an organization committed to sustainability based on two action axes: (1) reduce environmental impacts and (2) implement strategies that have positive social, economic and environmental effects on communities (Grupo Familia 2016b).

TABLE 1.2 Grupo Familia triple-bottom-line metrics

Sustainability Dimensions	2014	2015	2016	2017
ECONOMIC				
Added value created (USD millions)	$629	$704	$766	$774
ENVIRONMENTAL				
Waste recovery	79%	80%	95%	93%
Reduced water consumption	40%	40%	34%	35%
Reduced electric energy consumption	3.6%	7%	8%	7.3%
Reduction of biological oxygen demand	42%	55%	46%	–
Reduction of direct CO_2 emissions	39%	36%	38%	33%
SOCIAL				
Number of people who benefit from management's social programs (health, education and education and living place)	–	1069	1382	1588

Source: Compiled by the authors based on the Grupo Familia *Sustainability Reports*.

By 2017, the report declared "Sustainability as a Premise" (Grupo Familia 2017, 15), which meant that a market perspective, a sustainability perspective and an innovation focus were completely integrated to guide all corporate strategies. Andrés Gómez's executive leadership transformed sustainable development efforts from meeting operational targets to a core enterprise-level strategy that was embedded completely throughout the firm (Grupo Familia 2016b, 2017). Sustainable development was now the firm's strategic DNA. Three examples illustrate how Grupo Familia integrated totally the economic and environmental dimensions of a sustainable company with a strong commitment to bringing development, empowerment and prosperity to the communities within which it operated (the social dimension).

First action: building inclusive markets by including base-of-the-pyramid (BoP) recyclers

Production always produces waste. As often noted, sustainable development is concerned with not only rebalancing the relationship between renewable and nonrenewable resources in the environment (i.e., consume less and reuse, recycle, repurpose more; Ottman 2013) but also with the impact production decisions have on various stakeholders (UN Development Programme 2014). Susan Irwin, Grupo Familia's director of sustainability, has said, *"For Grupo Familia, being a paper company brings an important responsibility in recycling processes, that's why we use around 70 percent recycled paper in our production processes as a raw material"* (Centro 2017). Yet how does Grupo Familia acquire the 300 tons per day of recycled paper that it needs for production? Quite simply, it integrates a network of paper recyclers into its production process.

Recyclers can be defined "as individuals collecting, separating, classifying, and selling solid waste as a means of subsistence or supplementation of income" (Binion & Gutberlet 2012, 18). They can be found in every country and generally exist as part of that country's informal economy. Terms that describe recyclers can range from "Pepenadores, Catroneros and Buscabotes in Mexico; Basuriegos, Cartoneros; Traperos and Chatarreros in Colombia; Chamberos in Ecuador; Buzos in Costa Rica; and Cirujas in Argentina" (Wilson, Velis, & Cheeseman 2006, 798). It should be noted that many of these terms, while colloquial in the country, have derogatory connotations. In Colombia, Grupo Familia uses the descriptive, nonjudgmental term *recicladores* to identify recyclers.

Grupo Familia works with 1,382 recycling workers to integrate them into the production process. As with most informal paper recycling efforts, individuals in Colombia's informal economy walk the streets in major cities, collecting paper thrown into city garbage cans. The individual recycler sorts the paper (clean vs. dirty), bundles the paper together and brings it to a cooperative, which coordinates the collection and quality of material, weighs the paper and pays a reasonable rate per kilo. The "reciclador" must become a member of the cooperative. Grupo Familia buys the paper from those cooperatives and collaborates with them in developing social programs for the "recicladores" themselves, their families and even their pets.

Second action: respecting BoP consumers

Although Latin America has seen substantial growth in the middle class, significant income inequality still exists (Banco Interamericano de Desarrollo 2016). World Bank data define the middle class on a per capita basis as having household incomes of between US$10–US$50/per day on a purchasing power parity basis (Ferrerira et al. 2013). Applying this measure, a middle-class family of four would have an annual income of between US$14,600 and US$73,000. The World Bank also defines a "vulnerable segment" as households with incomes between US$4–$US10/day and a "very poor segment" as having incomes of less than US$4/day (Ferrerira et al. 2013). Throughout Latin America, the World Bank estimates the total population living in poverty, on less than US$4/day, is between 165 and 170 million people.

Research on BoP consumers describes a consumer segment that is family-oriented, focused on the present but optimistic about the future and is sophisticated and discerning in its purchases (Confederation of Danish Industries 2007). Approximately "70 percent of low income consumers buy leading brands for specific product categories because of the brand's reputation and reliability" (Robles, Wiese, & Torres-Baumgarten 2015, 78). These products may not be the cheapest in the market.

Reaching the BoP consumer in Latin America presents challenges. Many BoP consumers live in "barrios," which are unplanned neighborhoods located in the foothills bordering many Latin American cities also affected by problems of public order. Unlike middle-class consumers, who shop in traditional supermarkets, discount warehouses and convenience store chains, BoP consumers shop in small, independent grocery stores, kiosks and mom-and-pop stores. Thus, products targeted at BoP consumers must be delivered in smaller package sizes to a very large number of outlets in neighborhoods characterized by violence and vandalism.

As Table 1.1 indicates, every segment of society uses Grupo Familia's products. Under Andrés Gómez's leadership, Grupo Familia now markets the same products, with the same brand packaging and performance characteristics, across all market segments. The Grupo Familia product lines found in middle- and upper-class supermarkets are available in the corner stores in "barrios" without sacrificing quality or brand image. For example, the Nosotras brand intimate soap for women and body shower gel, as well as the brand Familia odor eliminator, have developed an innovative package design strategy to get corner stores in barrios to sell them. Grupo Familia has taken this successful BoP strategy and transferred it to middle- and upper-income market segments. By so doing, Grupo Familia demonstrates that high-quality products can reach all society levels, increasing the brands' penetration of new markets and channels.

Third action: empowering the community

One of the Group's main production plants is located in Guachené in the Department of Cauca, Colombia. This is a rural, impoverished and violent area that has seen many armed conflicts (Defensoría del Pueblo 2011). Guachené has 19,815 inhabitants, 99 percent of whom are African Colombian (Alcaldía de Guachené

2016). According to Guachené's Mayor's Office Report (2016), education has its own difficulties: It reaches only 13 percent of the population and is evaluated as being of low quality. There are high rates of drug and alcohol consumption, as well as high rates of domestic violence. The city's economy is 57 percent based on agriculture, primarily sugar cane. Unemployment is high because many jobs are in the informal sector, which means individuals work without social security coverage. Grupo Familia's decision to build a production plant in Guachené demonstrates the company's commitments to economic and human development.

Since building a production plant in Guachené, the area's social and economic indicators have steadily improved (Alcaldía de Guachené 2016, 44–45). In 2017, 65 percent of plant employees came from the town, thus creating economic stability for these individuals and their families. Grupo Familia also supported a housing project called Misión + Hogar (mission + home), which is a joint initiative of Fundación Grupo Familia, Fonade (Financial Fund for Development Projects) and the national government. The project's main goal is to improve the housing and living conditions of Guachené residents. In 2017, the project had reached 332 homes to ensure that they had improved hygiene and health conditions. Grupo Familia helped rebuild the local primary and secondary school, Jorge Eliécer Gaitán, that educates about 1,100 children (Grupo Familia 2017).

Grupo Familia and Andrés Gómez as sustainability champions

Grupo Familia's actions vis-à-vis sustainable development align well with many SDGs. As a well-being company that provides solutions to care, hygiene and cleanliness, Grupo Familia's mission firmly supports a number of mutually interrelated and interconnected SDGs. Its product line (see Table 1.1) provides mass-market products across the family life cycle, with an emphasis on innovation and high-quality products for infants and women (SDG #3: Good health and well-being). Promoting social programs through its brand Nosotras®, such as "Nosotras changed #Bullying for #Loving," aims to strengthen the security and confidence of girls and adolescent women (SDG #5: Gender equality). Developing distribution channels that bring Grupo Familia products into low-income barrios expresses Grupo Familia's dedication to BoP consumers as part of the firm's core business development strategy (SDG #1: No poverty). And by building a production plant in Guachené, Grupo Familia demonstrates responsible, economic development (SDG# 8: Decent Work and Economic Growth), that, when coupled with genuine community and other stakeholder involvement and partnerships (SDG # 17: Partnership for the goals) such as Misión + Hogar, can lead to improved education (SDG #4: Quality education), better health (SDG #3: Good health and well-being), reductions in hunger (SDG #2: Zero hunger) and environmental and industry goals (SDG #9: Industry, innovation and infrastructure). See Table 1.2.

Grupo Familia's strategy of incorporating "recicladores" into its supply chain represents the firm's commitment to building inclusive markets that simultaneously address

SDG #8 (Decent work and economic growth) that promote sustained, inclusive and sustainable economic growth) and SDG #1 (No poverty). Yet under Andrés Gómez's leadership, Grupo Familia has recognized that recicladores have struggled hard, over many years, to dignify what they do for the environment and society (Rodríguez López & Vergara Ángel 2015; Aluna Consultora Limitada 2011). By treating recyclers with dignity and by paying them a fair price for their services Grupo Familia acts in a responsible, sustainable way. This decency is expressed by Magda Barinas, who said,

> I am a recycler by trade; this has always been my job. Thanks to the support of [Grupo] Familia, recycling is recognized every day as a worthy job.
> *(Grupo Familia, Sobre la Fundación, n.d.)*

Andrés Gómez provides entrepreneurs and other firm leaders an example of what it means to be a sustainability champion: (1) take the long view because sustainable development is a process of continual improvement; (2) develop a corporate culture that is so completely committed to sustainable development that sustainability becomes the company's DNA; (3) build inclusive markets by employing community members, including those living in poverty, and integrate them into the company's value chain; and (4) respect BoP consumers by providing not only quality products but also social investment to their communities.

Yet Andrés Gómez has one more quality as a sustainability champion: He has the unique ability to take a technical, complex idea, sustainable development and given it a human face:

> We have declared in Familia that sustainability has a first name: There is financial sustainability, environmental sustainability and around the communities in which we operate, market sustainability and sustainability of people. When we give ["sustainability"] a surname, each surname detonates different initiatives. . . . Yet we [also] look for sustainability in people. We want people to develop personally and professionally, that have a long term and a shared vision of the company, that have an adequate balance of life and family.
>
> That complete equation is how we decode sustainability not only [in] financial terms, or the environmental person, but [to be] able to understand how to manage [all] the tensions . . . [because] the temptations of financial sustainability [can work] against the sustainability of the environment; [or] when the tensions appear [related to] people the temptation [is] to attack the community. The beauty of this game of leadership is how you manage that equation.

By describing sustainability in terms that are relatable, Andrés Gómez motivates all employees to commit to making sustainability the core of Grupo Familia's corporate strategy and daily operations. Grupo Familia and Andrés Gómez demonstrate that triple-bottom-line thinking *can* be achieved and that when sustainable development permeates an entire organization, a better, more responsible and profitable company emerges.

VI. Integrating lessons learned into teaching and learning

This case can be used in four courses found in most undergraduate and graduate/postgraduate business curricula: Organizational Theory and Design, Leadership, Business Ethics/Business and Society/Corporate Social Responsibility and Strategic Management.

In an Organizational Theory and Design course, the case can be used to explore the temporal nature of corporate culture: (1) the broad idea of corporate culture, (2) the current corporate culture and (3) the goal corporate culture. An important case question is, What did Andrés Gómez do as CEO to align these three elements of Grupo Familia's corporate culture? The case demonstrates that Andrés Gómez is activating teamwork through the identification of natural leaders in every process within Grupo Familia and is moving the organizational structure towards embedding innovation completely within the firm.

Within a Leadership course, the case can prompt discussion around the importance of soft skills and how those soft skills are expressed in leadership action. In Andrés Gómez, soft-skill development began growing up in a traditional loving family in Medellín and continued to develop as he advanced in his formal academic studies, this first job, his first Grupo Familia position and finally as CEO.

Specific attention can be given to the direct quotes from Andrés Gómez to develop a profile of him as a humane individual. Discussion can then link his ability to communicate, motivate and empathize with people and the corporate culture of Grupo Familia that he created. Students who have taken previously the Organizational Theory and Design now would have opportunities to add nuance to their understanding of corporate culture through a leadership lens – and vice versa if students took the Leadership course before the Organizational Theory and Design course.

The Grupo Familia case can contribute to several topics within a Business Ethics/Business and Society/Corporate Social Responsibility course. Stakeholder theory is clearly illustrated in the case, since consumers, distributors, employees, communities and serving the common good with society are all considered as part of the strategy development process. The case also illustrates the tangible benefits of successful stakeholder engagement: vital, flourishing communities; a strong corporate image of being an honest, responsible corporate citizen; markets that value their products; and employees who are sincerely dedicated to the firm's mission and vision – all of which collectively support Grupo Familia's strong financial performance. Also, Andrés Gómez can be discussed as a CEO who understood sustainability not only as a strategic issue but also as an inherent part of the corporation, having CSR as a component of social sustainability. Such discussion can then lead to viewing Grupo Familia as a successful example of triple-bottom-line thinking (Table 1.2): How dedication to planet (sustainability) and people (employees and BoP consumers) can lead to profitability.

Finally, within the Strategic Management course, the case can be used to illustrate the relationship between corporate culture and innovation as key drivers of an effective sustainable-development enterprise strategy. Yet, as the case also illustrates, any enterprise-level strategy can be achieved only if the commitment of top and middle management is aligned to the vision of the CEO. Furthermore, the case provides a clear example of how ongoing, strategic commitments to the BoP have produced significant financial returns to Grupo Familia. Triple-bottom-line thinking can also be revisited now from the perspective of the triple bottom line being an enterprise rather than an operational strategy.

References

Alcaldía de Guachené. 2016. *Plan de Desarrollo Municipal Guachené 2016–2019 Acciones de Gobierno con Sentido Social.* (Municipal Development Plan Guachené 2016–2019 Government Actions with Social Sense). http://guachene-cauca.gov.co/Transparencia/PlaneacionGestionyControl/PLAN%20DE%20DESARROLLO%20MUNICIPIO%20DE%20GUACHENÉ%202016-2019.pdf

Aluna Consultora Limitada. 2011. *Historia del reciclaje y los recicladores en Colombia.* (History of Recycling and Recyclers in Colombia). http://cooperativaplanetaverde.org/

Banco Interamericano de Desarrollo. 2016. *Aumenta clase media en América Latina y el Caribe pero continúan retos de desigualdad y pobreza infantil.* (24 Oct.) (Middle Class Increases in Latin America and the Caribbean But Inequality and Child Poverty Challenges Continue). www.iadb.org/es/noticias/comunicados-de-prensa/2016-10-24/clase-media-en-america-latina-alcanza-los-186-millones%2C11611.html

Binion, E., & Gutberlet, J. 2012. "The effects of handling solid waste on the wellbeing of informal and organized recyclers: a review of the literature." *International journal of occupational and environmental health*, 18(1): 43–52.

Centro, R. S. 2017. *Grupo Familia contribuye al país con sus programas sociales y ambientales.* (15 Aug.) (Grupo Familia Contributes to the Country with Its Social and Environmental Programs). http://centrors.org/grupo-familia-contribuye-al-pais-programas-sociales-ambientales/

Confederation of Danish Industries. 2007. *Working with the Bottom of the Pyramid: Success in Low Income Markets.* Copenhagen: Dansk Industri.

Defensoría del Pueblo. 2011. *Decimoctavo informe del defensor del pueblo al Congreso de la República de Colombia.* (Eighteenth Report of the Ombudsman to the Congress of the Republic of Colombia). Bogotá: Imprenta Nacional.

De La Sienra Servin, E. E., Smith, T., & Mitchell, C. 2017. "Worldviews, a mental construct hiding the potential of human behaviour: A new learning framework to guide education for sustainable development." *The Journal of Sustainability Education* (Mar.). www.susted.com/wordpress/content/worldviews-a-mental-construct-hiding-the-potential-of-human-behaviour-a-new-learning-framework-to-guide-education-for-sustainable-development_2017_04/

Ferrerira, F. H. G., Messina, J., Rigolini, J., López-Calva, L.-F., Lugo, M. A., & Vakis, R. 2013. *La movilidad económica y el crecimiento de la clase media en América Latina.* (Economic Mobility and the Growth of the Middle Class in Latin America). Washington: Banco Internacional de Reconstrucción y Fomento/Banco Mundial.

Grupo Familia (sf). www.grupofamilia.com.co/es/inversionistas/DTLCentroDocumentos/informes-gestion/Informe-gestion-grupo-familia-2016.pdf (About the Foundation). www.grupofamilia.com.co/es/fundacion/Paginas/sobre-la-fundacion.aspx

Grupo Familia (sf.). *Grupo Familia en la historia.* (Family Group in History). www.grupofamilia.com.co/es/grupo/Paginas/historia-grupo-familia.aspx

Grupo Familia. 2014. *Informe de sostenibilidad 2014*. (Sustainability Report 2014). Medellín: Grupo Familia. www.grupofamilia.com.co/es/sostenibilidad/DTLCentroDocumentos/informe-sostenibilidad-2014.pdf

Grupo Familia. 2015. *Informe de sostenibilidad 2015*. (Sustainability Report 2015). Medellín: Grupo Familia. www.grupofamilia.com.co/es/sostenibilidad/DTLCentroDocumentos/Informe-sostenibilidad-2015.pdf

Grupo Familia. 2016a. *Informe de Gestión*. (Management Report). Medellín: Grupo Familia. www.grupofamilia.com.co/es/inversionistas/DTLCentroDocumentos/informes-gestion/Informe-gestion-grupo-familia-2016.pdf

Grupo Familia. 2016b. *Informe de sostenibilidad 2016*. (Sustainability Report 2016). Medellín: Grupo Familia. www.grupofamilia.com.co/es/sostenibilidad/DTLCentroDocumentos/Informe-sostenibilidad-2016.pdf

Grupo Familia. 2017. *Informe de sostenibilidad 2017*. (Sustainability Report 2017). Medellín: Grupo Familia. www.grupofamilia.com.co/es/sostenibilidad/DTLCentroDocumentos/Informe%20de%20sostenibilidad%20Grupo%20Familia%202017.pdf

Hayward, R., Lee, J., Keeble, J., McNamara, R., Hall, C., Cruse, S., Gupta, P., & Robinson, E. 2013. "The UN Global Compact-Accenture CEO study on sustainability 2013." *UN Global Compact Reports*, 5(3): 1–60.

Invamer Gallup. 2017. *Top of Mind 2017: Las marcas más recordadas por los Colombianos*. (27 Mar.) (Top of Mind 2017: The most remembered brands by Colombians). Revista Dinero. Edición 516.

Kiron, D., Kruschwitz, N., Reeves, M., & Goh, E. 2013. "The benefits of sustainability-driven innovation." *MIT Sloan Management Review*, 54(2): 69–73.

Lubin, D. A., & Esty, D. C. 2010. "The sustainability imperative." *Harvard Business Review*, 88(5): 42–50.

Ottman, J. 2013. *Las Nuevas Rreglas del Marketing Verde*. (The New Rules of Green Marketing). Bogotá: Norma.

Porter, M., & Kramer, M. 2011. "Creating shared value: Redefining capitalism and the role of the corporation in society." *Harvard Business Review*, 89(1/2): 62–77.

Rimanoczy, I. 2014. "A matter of being: Developing sustainability-minded leaders." *Journal of Management for Global Sustainability*, 2(1): 95–122.

Robles, F., Wiese, N., & Torres-Baumgarten, G. 2014. *Business in Emerging Latin America*. New York: Routledge.

Rodríguez López, L. K., & Vergara Ángel, R. A. 2015. "Condiciones sociales y culturales de los recicladores en Colombia." ("Social and cultural conditions of waste pickers in Colombia"). *Revista Ensayos*, 8(8): 101–115.

Schumpeter, J. 1936. *Theory of Economic Development*. Cambridge, MA: Harvard University Press.

Senge, P. 2011. "Educating Leaders for a Sustainable Future." *AACSB Conference on Sustainability*. Charlotte, NC. (June 17).

Stead, J., & Stead, W. 2014. *Sustainable Strategic Management* (2nd ed.), Armonk, NY: M. E. Sharpe.

United Nations Development Program. 2014. *Stakeholder Response Mechanism: Overview and Guidance*. www.undp.org/content/undp/en/home/librarypage/operations1/stakeholder-response-mechanism.html

Wilson, D. C., Velis, C., & Cheeseman, C. 2006. "Role of informal sector recycling in waste management in developing countries." *Habitat international*, 30(4): 797–808.

2

CHAMPIONS OF SUSTAINABLE DEVELOPMENT IN AFRICA

Challenges, successes and lessons learned in Nigeria

Ijeoma Nwagwu

Abstract

In view of the sustainable development issues facing Africa today, there is an urgent need to develop innovative strategies to combat major challenges, including those related to poverty, inequality and climate change. This chapter presents illustrative case analyses of three organizations championing change in Nigeria, using unique approaches to drive sustainable development in the key areas of food security, financial inclusion and environmental sustainability. The respective models, impacts, successes and challenges of these sustainable development "champions" are highlighted to increase the understanding of their experience and dynamics.

Introduction

Addressing the challenge of sustainable development is of critical importance. The world is increasingly experiencing crises of poverty, inequality and climate change. Unless there is a change in course, the crises will continue and even worsen (Ahenkan & Osei-Kojo 2014; Denis 2008; Sachs 2015). As businesses, technologies, people and ideas move across boundaries with unparalleled speed and intensity, so do epidemic diseases, conflicts and economic exclusion. Furthermore, globalization creates linkages in which issues that affect one part of the world matter in other parts (Denis 2008; Sachs 2015).

Sub-Saharan Africa's sustainable development challenge

Several authors (e.g., Ahenkan & Osei-Kojo 2014; Gitahi 2017; Goodland 1995; United Nations Economic Commission for Africa [UNECA] 2011) assert that before sustainable development can be achieved along any dimension, the challenge of poverty must be tackled. According to the United Nations Economic Commission on Africa (UNECA; 2011), Africa is the only region in the world where poverty has increased in absolute and relative terms. Adding to this, Gitahi (2017) states that while the world's average rate of poverty reduction is at 68 percent, Africa's stands at 28 percent. Aside from poverty, other problems threatening the economic, social and environmental development of Africa include land and water degradation, biodiversity loss, climate variability, droughts and floods, high disease burden, malnutrition, unemployment, violent conflicts and weak institutional capacities (Denis 2008; Goodland 1995; UNECA 2011, 2017).

Countless failed efforts at advancing sustainable development, and its discourse globally has been linked to the lack of the necessary global public literacy to develop solutions to intimately connected issues such as climate change and food security (Folke et al. 2002; Hopwood, Mellor, & O'Brien 2005; Sachs 2015). Furthermore, the slow pace of accelerating sustainable development has been linked to the exclusion of members of disadvantaged communities from the development of knowledge and solutions informing remedial policies and programs (Nwankwo, Chacharbaghi, & Boyd 2009; Okolie 2003). Nwankwo, Chacharbaghi, and Boyd (2009) also claim that discourses on sustainable development presented for adoption in developing world communities coming straight out of the developed world may reflect values, philosophies and challenges faced in such developed regions but that are likely to be different from those faced by the developing world.

Scope

This chapter explores the sustainable development landscape in Nigeria, a country in sub-Saharan Africa. It sheds light on the efforts of organizations to drive progress in key areas of food security, financial inclusion and environmental sustainability, areas critical to the actualization of sustainable development in the region.

While exploring challenges, philosophies and perspectives around sustainable development in sub-Saharan Africa, the chapter presents illustrative case analyses of three sustainable development "champions." The activities of these champions cut across several of the 17 United Nations Sustainable Development Goals (UN SDGs). These three Nigerian ventures are Diamond Beta, Babban Gona (of Doreo Partners) and Wecyclers. The chapter includes analyses of these organizations in terms of the particular UN SDGs they address. Diamond Beta tackles SDG #1 (No poverty), SDG #5 (Gender equality), SDG #8 (Decent work and economic growth) and SDG #10 (Reduced inequalities). Babban Gona advances SDG #1 (No poverty), SDG #2 (Zero hunger), SDG #3 (Good health and well-being) and SDG #12 (Responsible consumption and production). Finally, Wecyclers addresses SDG #1 (No poverty), SDG #6 (Clean water and sanitation), SDG #13 (Climate action), SDG #15 (Life on land) and SDG#17 (Partnership for the goals).

Methodology

Adopting a qualitative approach, research for this chapter was conducted through semistructured interviews, surveys and document review, as well as reviews of media and scholarly articles. Further interviews were conducted with key personnel within the case organizations.

Table 2.1 presents the UN SDGs that the three illustrative case organizations address. These goals are contrasted with related goals from Africa's 2063 development agenda (UNECA 2017).

Diamond Bank's Diamond BETA is promoting gender equality and consequently economic development by enabling women to fully participate in, and

TABLE 2.1 Sub-Saharan Africa's SDGs addressed by case organizations

Agenda 2030 Goals (SDGs)	Agenda 2063 Goals
1 No poverty	5 Modern agriculture for increased productivity and production
	7 Environmentally sustainable climate-resilient economies and communities
	17 Full gender equality in all spheres of life
2 Zero hunger	3 Healthy and well-nourished citizens
	4 Transformed economies and job creation
	5 Modern agriculture for increased productivity and production
	7 Environmentally sustainable climate-resilient economies and communities
3 Good health and well-being	3 Healthy and well-nourished citizens
	7 Environmentally sustainable climate-resilient economies and communities
	17 Full gender equality in all spheres of life
5 Gender equality	17 Full gender equality in all spheres of life
6 Clean water and sanitation	1 A high standard of living, quality of life and well-being for all
	7 Environmentally sustainable climate-resilient economies and communities
8 Decent work and economic growth	4 Transformed economies and job creation
	7 Environmentally sustainable climate-resilient economies and communities
	17 Full gender equality in all spheres of life
10 Reduced inequalities	4 Transformed economies and job creation
	7 Environmentally sustainable climate-resilient economies and communities
	20 Africa takes full responsibility for financing her development
12 Responsible consumption and production	4 Transformed economies and job creation
	5 Modern agriculture for increased productivity and production
	7 Environmentally sustainable climate-resilient economies and communities
13 Climate action	5 Modern agriculture for increased productivity and production
	7 Environmentally sustainable climate-resilient economies and communities

Agenda 2030 Goals (SDGs)	Agenda 2063 Goals
15 Life on land	7 Environmentally sustainable climate-resilient economies and communities
17 Partnerships for the goals	4 Transformed economies and job creation
	7 Environmentally sustainable climate-resilient economies and communities
	20 Africa takes full responsibility for financing her development

Source: Adapted by the author from UNECA (2017) and UN SDGs (2015).

contribute effectively to, the nation's economic life. By engaging in sustainable agricultural practices, Babban Gona of Doreo Partners is addressing food insecurity and malnutrition (UNECA 2011, 2017). And Wecyclers is promoting and advocating for the stability of biological and physical systems (UNECA 2011).

The subsequent segments of this chapter address Africa's finance, agriculture and environmental sustainability issues and the solutions the three case organizations are providing to these challenges.

A. The Diamond BETA case

Africa's finance – issues

Africa's financial systems are characterized by very limited outreach to the clientele of their financial services (World Bank 2007). Although financial inclusion is not a distinct SDG, because formal financial systems have such profound effects on the environment, economy and social order, it is a critical part of any movement toward sustainable development (Horrigan, Lawrence, & Walker 2002; UN Capital Development Fund [UNCDF] 2018). It is believed that exclusion from the formal financial system is one of the causes and evidence of the continued divide between the rich and poor (David-West 2016; Donovan 2012; Radcliffe & Voorhies 2012). The absence of accounts with financial institutions continually perpetuates the cycle of poverty as poor households remain limited in their ability to save, repay debts and manage risks responsibly (Amaeshi et al. 2007; Radcliffe & Voorhies 2012).

This absence of representation within formal financial systems for the poor does not mean they lack financially active lives. However, certain barriers (e.g., documentation requirements, costs, access to financial services, literacy and inadequate infrastructure) restricting their entry into the formal financial systems propagate their continued participation in informal systems (David-West 2016; Donovan 2012). Optimism grows as advances in banking technology and mobile cellular service access provide new opportunities for social and financial inclusion (David-West 2016; Donovan 2012). This case study explains how Diamond Bank through its Diamond BETA package is addressing financial inclusion challenges and why its efforts matter.

The Diamond BETA solutions for financial inclusion

Diamond BETA is an initiative of the Diamond Bank Plc, Nigeria. The BETA account is a savings account targeted at women small-business owners, encouraging them to save on a daily basis. The initiative leverages the informal financial system structure of "Alaajo" and "Esusu" (daily contributory) programs. While it mimics informal system structures, it links to the *convenience* of formal financial services (banking services are delivered to customers' shops, accounts are opened in the field via mobile phones, debit cards are issued and activated in field and deposits and withdrawals are possible in the field via mobile phones) and to *security* (the security the formal financial system provides its customers). The package also promises *affordability* (absence of restriction on deposit and withdrawal amounts), *flexibility* (access to multiple channels: bank branches, ATMs and BETA Friends, sales and service agents) and *access* to loan services (Diamond BETA 2018).

Diamond BETA provides a savings account with no minimum balance and no transaction fees. A network of agents, known as BETA Friends, assists customers with their transactions. Compensated on an incentive basis, the BETA Friends create their own portfolio of customers (International Financial Corporation [IFC] 2014). At the end of the six-month pilot program, the bank had 38,600 new accounts of which 40 percent were held by women; 1.5 million USD in savings had been gathered with approximately 74 percent of customers transacting at least once a month (IFC 2014). The Diamond BETA package is targeted at fighting poverty (SDG #1), promoting gender equality (SDG #5) and economic growth (SDG #8) and reducing inequality (SDG #10).

Figure 2.1 shows how the numbers of Diamond BETA customers have grown between 2013 and 2017. Figure 2.2 illustrates the respective changes in the customers' gender distribution.

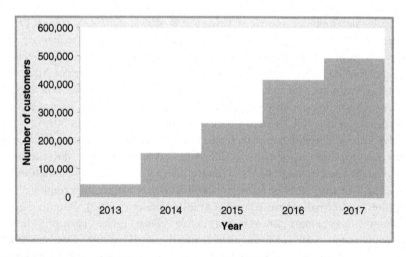

FIGURE 2.1 Growth of BETA customer base, 2013–2017

Source: AFI (2017).

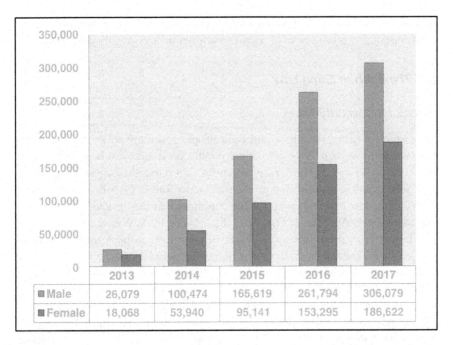

FIGURE 2.2 Gender distribution of BETA customers, 2013–2017

Source: AFI (2017).

According to UNCDF (2018), access to a formal savings account has the potential to reduce the likelihood of women selling their assets to address health emergencies, to stabilize their incomes in times of economic shocks and to provide greater control of their funds. A report by Alliance for Financial Inclusion (AFI), tells the story of Ime Akpan Isaacs, a petty trader, who because of Diamond BETA was able to save on a regular basis (AFI 2017). As a result, she has expanded her business significantly, supports her husband and seven children and hopes to fund her children's education.

Challenges of the Diamond BETA initiative

In the course of the Diamond BETA scheme, numerous challenges have been encountered. One was that the average account balance of many of the participants fell far short of the expectations of the bank. The reason for this was that some of the women being accustomed to their traditional contributory saving schemes were slow to adapt to the new products. Hence, using the excuse of not wanting to "put all their eggs in one basket," they split savings between their BETA accounts and their traditional savings schemes.

Also, KYC (know-your-customer) restrictions have imposed some regulatory limits on the scheme. Although the Central Bank of Nigeria established a tiered KYC requirement, which made it possible to open a simple savings account without identity documents, the lack of identity and address verification documents limits customers from engaging in certain types of transactions given by KYC regulations (AFI 2017).

B. The Babban Gona case

Africa's food security issues

While food security remains a global challenge, it is more so in African countries, where more than 39 percent of the population is malnourished (Pretty 1999; Webersik & Wilson 2009). African countries face diminished agricultural stocks, high food prices and decreasing productivity (Ahenkan & Osei-Kojo 2014; Pretty 1999). This does not bode well for the continent that has agriculture as its economic mainstay (Ahenkan & Osei-Kojo 2014; Webersik & Wilson 2009).

Africa's agricultural challenge includes the continent's inability to produce more to feed its inhabitants because of the rudimentary and labor-intensive tools and equipment, the low level of inputs used and the unavailability of credit (Ahenkan & Osei-Kojo 2014; UNECA 2017). At the same time, ecological viability is being lost; soil quality and fertility, water and biodiversity are being adversely affected and agricultural practices are threatening human and animal health (Horrigan, Lawrence, & Walker 2002; Reganold, Papendick, & Parr 1990; Webersik & Wilson 2009). Hence, sustainable agriculture is no longer an option but a critical part of the movement toward sustainable development (Horrigan, Lawrence, & Walker 2002; Reganold, Papendick, & Parr 1990).

The Babban Gona, Doreo Partners model

Babban Gona is an agricultural franchise developed by the Nigerian impact investment firm Doreo Partners. It provides support to smallholder farmers, who constitute more than 70 percent of Nigeria's working population in the informal agricultural space and are the weakest link in the value chain. Babban Gona helps enable them to turn their subsistent farming practices into profitable ventures. It does this by partnering with these farmers. It offers them training, provides high-quality inputs (high-yield seeds, fertilizers, etc.) on credit and supports them in warehousing, marketing and distributing their produce. Moreover, the Babban Gona initiative makes financial loans available to these smallholder farmers (Doreo Partners 2018).

This initiative, partly owned by the smallholder farmers (28 percent of the business) through a members trust, is present in 3 of the 19 northern states in Nigeria. It has empowered approximately 3,000 smallholder farmers who sustainably cultivate staple crops such as corn, rice and soybeans on more than 5,000 hectares of land. Indirectly, it has empowered 21,000 farmers and their families. It has also successfully granted 6,000 profitable loans and recorded 99.9 percent repayment rates for these loans (Babban Gona 2015). Baban Gona through its innovative business model is tackling poverty among smallholder farmers (SDG #1), addressing the challenge of food insecurity (SDG #2) and advancing good health and well-being (SDG #3) by promoting sustainable agriculture (SDG #12).

Babban Gona as a case in sustainable agriculture

"Sustainable agriculture" combines traditional conservative farming methods with technology and the consideration of environmental soundness, economic viability and social justice (Reganold, Papendick, & Parr 1990). Babban Gona achieves this by training farmers to ensure they attain optimal levels of productivity and product quality while minimizing negative environmental impact. Also, Babban Gona provides facilities and technology that make harvesting, packaging and storage of produce quicker and cheaper. The company also helps farmers sell the produce to big buyers at premium prices, after which they then pay the farmers via a quarterly dividend payment.

Impact of Babban Gona

Babban Gona's unique business model has advanced the production of healthy food (e.g., maize free from aflatoxins), boosted the income of smallholder farmers, improved the living standards of rural dwellers and provided employment for youth and reduced their vulnerability to the lure of extremism and violent conflicts. Storrs (2014) sheds light on the footprint of Babban Gona on the rural dwellers: "Some have been able to buy cars and put new roofs on their homes. One is preparing to buy a tractor for his fellow members to share. Another is sending his children to private school." Also, Naomi Michaels, a rural farmer who prior to joining Babban Gona had experienced extreme poverty due to very poor yields and low income shares her success story: "Joining Babban Gona has caused poverty to flee and thanks to Babban Gona, I can now reap my reward here on earth." (Babban Gona 2018).

Babban Gona's challenges

As Babban Gona keeps growing and extending its reach to touch more smallholder farmers and communities, its major challenge is in identifying and attracting the talent and institutional resources needed to support the organization in actualizing its goals. This challenge is particularly acute in the context of Nigeria's shortage of skilled labor as well as its pronounced infrastructural challenges.

C. The Wecyclers case

Africa's environmental issues

Taiwo (2009) asserts that the fragile balance between development and the limited stock of natural resources must be sustained as these natural resources belong to future generations and not the present. The environment that was considered a means of achieving development objectives is becoming a major constraint on human progress (Goodland 1995; Hughes et al. 2012; Omisore 2017). Africa is widely viewed as the most vulnerable to global environmental change and the least able to adapt (Webersik & Wilson 2009). Significant progress will not be made on the SDGs until environmental issues are given a deserved priority by concerned stakeholders. Among the numerous environmental issues that Africa contends with is the pervasive problem of waste management (Omisore 2017; Annepu 2016).

Waste management is a major challenge in developing countries (Taiwo 2009). Sub-Saharan Africa today is in the midst of a dramatic urban transition. Between 2010 and 2035, Africa's urban population is expected to more than double from approximately 298 million to 697 million (UN 2014). While urbanization has the potential to act as an engine of economic growth and human development, it also comes with enormous challenges, not least among these is that of effectively managing waste.

Wecyclers's solutions to waste management in Nigeria

Wecyclers is a waste recycling social enterprise that provides waste collection infrastructure in the form of "low-cost cargo bikes." A fleet of cyclists pedal custom-made cargo tricycles door to door every week, down narrow, unpaved, streets where trucks cannot easily reach, to collect and to weigh recyclable waste from registered households. The aim is to raise awareness of recycling and the environmental and health importance of proper waste disposal. According to the founder, Bilikiss Adebiyi-Abiola, "Wecyclers has a very special mission in Nigeria – to empower Africa to be the recycling leader in the World" (Oluruonbi 2017).

The pioneering work of Wecyclers in the environmental sustainability space is very significant as a case of addressing poverty (SDG #1), sanitation issues (SDG #6), climate change (SDG #13) and environmental degradation (SDG #15) and of enacting multisector stakeholder collaboration (SDG #17). Wecyclers works with the poor to address the problem of waste in the urban communities and implements a rewards system that gives poor people some benefit in joining the effort to rid the urban environment of plastic waste. Plastic waste contributes to fatal flooding incidents in the densely populated city of Lagos (a megacity of more than 20 million, with infrastructure designed only for 3 million). In this effort, Wecyclers brings together in partnership, the state government and its numerous agencies, beverage companies (multinationals), development sector actors, universities (as technical partners) and, most critically, the local community. Its partnership model and recycling program prefigure the collaborative effort required to champion development at scale (Wecyclers 2018).

Annepu (2016) posits that 3 billion people (approximately 40 percent of the world's population) lack access to safe waste-disposal facilities. Poor waste-disposal practices have the tendency to cause blocked drainage systems and create

PHOTO 2.1 Wecyclers in action

Source: Nwagwu and Onuzo (2018).

breeding grounds for mosquitoes. These blocked drainage systems, in turn, have the tendency of leading to flooding, land degradation and diseases, such as malaria (Annepu 2016; Taiwo 2009). The target of Wecyclers is to build a low-cost waste collection infrastructure while raising general awareness on the importance of recycling to enhance environmental sustainability, social welfare and public health (Wecyclers 2018).

Challenges for the Wecyclers group

Wecyclers seeks to mitigate the waste challenge in Lagos and demonstrates that waste can be managed in an environmentally friendly and economically profitable way. The organization is poised to improve its services and expand coverage across the country. The organization faces challenges, such as difficulty in generating sufficient funds to drive its expansion, the unavailability of constant electricity to power its operations and the incorrect perspectives of many residents that working with waste is a dishonorable job. However, through collaboration and partnership, the company has been able to get support from other organizations, including the Lagos state government, and it seeks to enter into more of such partnerships.

Lessons learned and the way forward

The pioneering approaches of each of the three case organizations in solving key sustainable development issues on the continent are exemplars of possibilities for corporate engagement in social advancement. Vital lessons can be gleaned from each of these champion organizations.

First, these champion organizations exemplify the need for entrepreneurs irrespective of their industry to develop locally appropriate business models and processes that holistically address the fundamental problem of poverty (SDG #1) – a catalyst to other problems and a major constraint to sustainable development in other facets. By using locally appropriate business processes that specifically meet the needs of local people and by developing low-cost business tools that cater to the customers at the bottom of the pyramid while still ensuring a healthy profit margin, businesses can significantly contribute to reducing poverty. Tackling the problem of poverty also goes a long way in catalyzing the attainment of other SDGs (Ahenkan & Osei-Kojo 2014; Gitahi 2017; UNECA 2011). For example, while Babban Gona tackles food insecurity (SDG #2) by promoting sustainable agriculture (SDG #12), it models its business in such a way as to improve the livelihoods of farmers (SDG #1) and promote health and well-being (SDG #3). It also tackles youth unemployment by making agriculture attractive to youth, thereby reducing their tendency to be instruments for propagating crime and violence. When more organizations in Africa adopt similar approaches, the attainment of the SDGs will be greatly accelerated.

Another important lesson that resounds throughout the success stories of these "champions" is that multistakeholder collaboration, partnerships and joint efforts are the foundation necessary to break through sustainable development challenges and establish sustainable development in any sector (SDG #17). This is vital because the challenges Africa currently faces are complex, multifaceted and rooted across different sectors, hence the need to mobilize knowledge, skills, finance and other resources from diverse angles. Added emphasis needs to be placed on partnership approaches (Webersik & Wilson 2009).

Furthermore, continuously taking into account Africa's unique context and realities will enable sustainable development efforts to be more customized and more effective in battling the continent's sustainability challenges (Nwankwo, Chacharbaghi, & Boyd 2009). To ensure success in attaining the SDGs in Africa, corporations, governments, civil societies, academics and other individuals must join forces to champion change and confront the prevailing social, economic and environmental challenges with renewed efforts.

References

Ahenkan, A., & Osei-Kojo, A. 2014. "Achieving sustainable development in Africa: Progress, challenges and prospects." *International Journal of Development and Sustainability*, 3(1): 162–176.

Alliance for Financial Inclusion (AFI). 2017. *Bank on Her: Diamond Bank Enhances Opportunities for Nigeria's Low-Income Women to Save*. AFI FIS Working Group Publication.

Amaeshi, K. M., Ezeoha, A. E., Adi, B. C., & Nwafor, M. 2007. Financial exclusion and strategic corporate social responsibility: A missing link in sustainable finance discourse? University of Nottingham *ICCSR Research Paper Series* ISSN 1479-5124 No. 49-2007.

Annepu, R. 2016. "Coconuts for compost and bicycling recycling: Two new solutions to waste management." *Appropriate Technology*, 43(4): 50–51.

Babban Gona. 2015. *Babban Gona BMGF Grant-Annual Report 2015*. Nigeria: Babban Gona-Doreo Partners.

Babban Gona 2018. 2016. *Harvesting and Threshing*. Accessed 23 Oct. 2018. www.babbangona.com/2016-babban-gona-harvest-threshing-gallery/

Babban Gona 2018. *Number of Times Naomi Michael Saw Her Income Increase in 2013*. Accessed 12 Feb. 2019. www.babbangona.com/naomi-michael/

Casat Reports (2018, February). *Diamond Bank – BETA Savings Account & New Features*. Retrieved from http://www.casatreports.com.

David-West, O. 2016. "The path to digital financial inclusion in Nigeria: Experiences of Firstmonie." *Journal of Payments Strategy & Systems*, 9(4): 256–273.

Denis, J. 2008. "The challenge of environmentally sustainable development in Africa." *Africare* (11 Apr.). Accessed 12 Apr. 2018. www.africare.org/the-challenge-of-environmentally-sustainable-development-in-africa/

Donovan, K. 2012. "Mobile money for financial inclusion." *Information and Communications for Development*, 61(1): 61–73.

Doreo Partners. 2018. *Welcome*. Accessed 12 Apr. 2018. www.doreopartners.com/

Folke, C., Carpenter, S., Elmgyist, T., Gunderson, L., Holling, C., & Walker, B. 2002. "Resilience and sustainable development: Building adaptive capacity in a world of transformations." *AMBIO: A Journal of the Human Environment*, 31(5): 437–440.

Gitahi, G. 2017. "Africa in the era of sustainable development." *Elsevier* (19 Apr.). Accessed 12 Apr. 2018. www.elsevier.com/connect/africa-in-the-era-of-sustainable-development

Goodland, R. 1995. "The concept of environmental sustainability." *Annual Review of Ecology and Systematics*, 26: 1–24.

Hopwood, B., Mellor, M., & O'Brien, G. 2005. "Sustainable development: Mapping different approaches." *Sustainable Development*, 13: 38–52.

Horrigan, L., Lawrence, R. S., & Walker, P. 2002. "How sustainable agriculture can address the environmental and human health harms of industrial agriculture." *Environmental Health Perspectives*, 110(5): 445–456.

Hughes, B. B., Irfan, M. T., Moyer, J. D., Rothman, D., & Solórzano, J. 2012. "Exploring future impacts of environmental constraints on human development." *Sustainability*, 4: 958–994.

International Finance Corporation (IFC), 2014. *Banking on the Market, Gender & Digital Financial Services Working Paper*, Washington, DC, IFC. Retrieved from https://www.ifc.org

Nwagwu, I., & Onuzo, N. 2018. *Partnering for Social Good: Creating Value from Waste: The Wecyclers Model of Social Entrepreneurship*. Unpublished manuscript, Pan Atlantic University, Lagos, Nigeria.

Nwankwo, S., Chacharbaghi, K., & Boyd, D. 2009. "Sustainable development in sub-Saharan Africa: Issues of knowledge development and agenda setting." *International Journal of Development and Sustainability*, 8(2): 119–133.

Okolie, A. 2003. "Producing knowledge for sustainable development in Africa: Implications for higher education." *Higher Education*, 46: 35–260.

Oluruonbi, R. 2017. "Wecyclers founder relinquishes leadership, names Olawale Adebiyi new CEO." *The Nigerian Tribune* (2 Oct.). www.tribuneonlineng.com/113541/

Omisore, A. G. 2017. "Attaining sustainable development goals in sub-Saharan Africa: The need to address environmental challenges." *Environmental Development*, 25: 138–145.

Pretty, J. 1999. "Can sustainable agriculture feed Africa? New evidence on progress, processes, and impacts." *Environment, Development and Sustainability*, 1: 253–274.

Radcliffe, D., & Voorhies, R. 2012. *A Digital Pathway to Financial Inclusion*, Bill and Melinda Gates Foundation Policy Paper. Seattle: Bill and Melinda Gates Foundation.

Reganold, J. P., Papendick, R. I., & Parr, J. F. 1990. "Sustainable agriculture." *Scientific American*, 262(6): 112–115.

Sachs, J. 2015. *The Age of Sustainable Development*. New York: Columbia University Press.

Storrs, F. 2014. "The solution to the global food crisis just might come from Nigeria." *Harvard Business School Alumni Magazine*. Accessed 25 Aug. 2018. www.alumni.hbs.edu/stories/Pages/story-bulletin.aspx?num=3264

Taiwo, A. A. 2009. "Waste management towards sustainable development in Nigeria: A case study of Lagos state." *International NGO Journal*, 4(4): 173–179.

UNECA. 2017. *Africa Sustainable Development Report: Tracing Progress on Agenda 2063 and the Sustainable Development Goals*. Addis Ababa, Ethiopia.

United Nations (U.N.). 2014. *Urbanisation Challenges, Waste Management, and Development*. ACP-EC Joint Parliamentary Assembly (12–14 Feb.), Mauritius.

United Nations (U.N.). 2018. *Financing for Development: Progress and Prospects*, Retrieved from the website of the UN Inter-Agency Task Force of Financing for Development, http://www.developmentfinance.un.org

United Nations Capital Development Fund. 2018. *UNCDF and the SDGs*. Accessed 12 Apr. 2018. www.uncdf.org/financial-inclusion-and-the-sdgs

United Nations Economic Commission for Africa (UNECA). 2011. *Sustainable Development Report on Africa: Managing Land-based Resources for Sustainable Development*. Addis Ababa, Ethiopia.

Webersik, C., & Wilson, C. 2009. "Achieving environmental sustainability and growth in Africa: The role of science, technology and innovation." *Sustainable Development*, 17: 400–413.

Wecyclers. 2018. *About Us*. Accessed 12 Apr. 2018. http://wecyclers.com/

World Bank. 2007. *Finance for All? Policies and Pitfalls in Expanding Access*. Washington, DC.

3
GLOBAL CHAMPIONS OF WATER AND SANITATION FOR ALL

Diane M. Kellogg

If you want to go fast, *go* alone; *if you want to go far,* go together.
— *African Proverb*

Abstract

"Ensure availability and sustainable management of water and sanitation for all" is the mandate of Sustainable Development Goal (SDG) #6. This strengthened global emphasis was the result of advocacy work of "global champions" of water and sanitation. After touching on the history of the planet's water and sanitation problem, this chapter highlights the work of selected organizations, individuals and governments working to advance SDG #6. After summarizing what can be learned from the work of these champions, the conclusion identifies key challenges that lie ahead if we are to provide access to clean water and safe sanitation for all people.

Introduction

The UN Sustainable Development Goals (SDGs) are ambitious. Some say too ambitious given the 2030 deadline. Nonetheless, achieving sustainable development is critical not only to the health and well-being of people but to sustaining the planet itself. Much of the life-sustaining water on the planet is polluted and hence threatens our future. The work of generations will be needed to clean up the rivers, lakes and aquifers that have been polluted by human, industrial and agricultural waste over the last two centuries.

SDG #6, to "ensure availability and sustainable management of water and sanitation for all," includes attention to managing all sources of waste and the preservation of the earth's water supply. This chapter focuses on four specific

SDG #6 targets: 6.1, 6.2, 6.a and 6.b. After noting that clean water and sanitation are the foundation for all sustainable development, the chapter summarizes how SDG #6 is linked to the other SDGs and why international cooperation is so critical.

The chapter discusses the work of "global champions" of water and sanitation by highlighting the laudable work of three nongovernment organizations (NGOs), one professional association, one individual and one government. Each of the six examples features international cooperation and focus on the work done in the developing world. The chapter concludes with an analysis of what can be learned from the successes and failures of the ongoing global struggle to achieve clean water and safe sanitation for all.

SDG #6

The mandate of SDG #6 is water, sanitation and hygiene (WASH), which have always been critical to life itself. People need water daily to survive. More often than once a day, people need a place to relieve themselves without polluting their own habitat. We rely on the water resources in mountains, forests, wetlands, rivers, aquifers and lakes to meet the needs of the growing population. According to the *Sustainable Development Goal 6 Synthesis Report 2018 on Water and Sanitation*: "Fresh water, in sufficient quantity and quality, is essential for all aspects of life and sustainable development" (UN Water 2018). Thus, achieving SDG #6 is the foundation for achieving all the SDGs. See Figure 3.1 for more details on the interlinkages between SDG #6 and the other SDGs.

Water and sanitation targets and indicators

Each of the SDGs includes targets related to the specific sustainable development need, as well as targets that call for international cooperation with implementation. This chapter addresses targets 6.1 and 6.2 as well as the associated SDG objectives 6.a. and 6.b., the two targets related to international cooperation, specified as follows:

> Target 6.1: By 2030, achieve universal and equitable access to safe and affordable drinking water for all.
> Target 6.2: By 2030, achieve access to adequate and equitable sanitation and hygiene for all and end open defecation, paying special attention to the needs of women and girls and those in vulnerable situations.
> Target 6.a: By 2030, expand international cooperation and capacity-building support to developing countries in water-and sanitation-related activities and programmes, including water harvesting, desalination, water efficiency, wastewater treatment, recycling and reuse technologies.
> Target 6.b: Support and strengthen the participation of local communities in improving water and sanitation management.

Water and sanitation for all   35

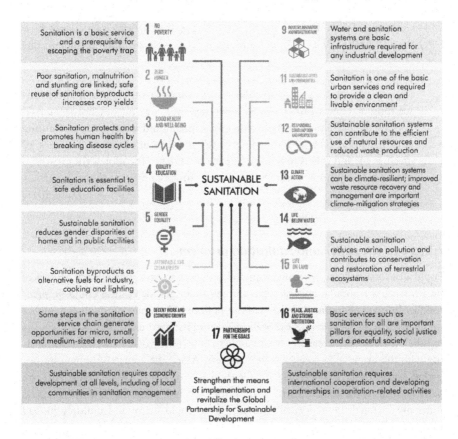

FIGURE 3.1 Sustainable Sanitation and the SDGs

The "indicator" that will measure progress on Targets 6.1 and 6.2, as published in the SDG agreements, is "the proportion of population using safely-managed drinking water and sanitation services." Safely managed water is defined as "located on premises, available when needed and free from contamination." Safely managed sanitation is defined as "excreta safely disposed of in situ or treated off-site" (UN 2015).

Water and sanitation as the foundation for sustainable development

Roland Schertenleib, professor emeritus of Swiss Federal Institute of Aquatic Science and Technology (Eawag), led a team of people from multiple WASH organizations to analyze the relationship between SDG #6 and the other SDGs. The result was a much-consulted reference document that guides action: "Sustainable Sanitation and the SDGs: Interlinkages and Opportunities" (SuSanA 2018). Figure 3.1 is an excellent visual summary of the connection between SDG #6 and several other sustainability goals.

For example, Susan Davis, founder of Improve International, articulates how SDG #6 and health (SDG #3) and education (SDG #4) are interdependent. She says,

> Improper practices related to solid waste management, sanitation and handwashing at clinics puts patients, especially mothers and newborns, at risk. Faecal contamination of the home environment and water leads to stunting and diarrhoea, which is a leading cause of death in children. The lack of clean water and toilets in schools impacts attendance for adolescent girls, who sometimes stay home for a few days each month to manage their period.
>
> (Davis 2018)

History of the water and sanitation problem

Populations naturally congregate around clean water sources. In the early history of humankind, the population was small enough that open defecation could be practised by humans and animals alike, without polluting the water supply they counted on. The earth and ecosystems of local organisms processed urine and faeces, returning the nutrients to the earth. Oceans and rivers had their own ecosystems for dealing with the urine and faeces of water dwellers. Along the course of human history, people began using water bodies for the discharge of human waste. Nutrients and pathogens intended for the earth were introduced into water bodies, where excess nutrients changed the ecosystem and pathogens could thrive and multiply instead of dying off.

The story of Rome is instructive. The original city was built on the Tiber River, which provided a good supply of clean water. The aqueducts we so admire today became necessary because of "utter environmental mismanagement" (Narain 2017). The first sewers, built between 800 and 735 BC (Farnsworth 1940), were originally for draining stormwater, which did not have a negative impact on the quality of water in the river. Unfortunately, household latrines were eventually connected to the sewers, leaving the river water too polluted to be used for drinking. The aqueducts for bringing clean water to the city were the remedy for a problem Rome created for itself.

Cities across the planet face similar dilemmas today: solutions to one problem can sometimes create new problems. To better understand the current water and sanitation situation globally, UN organizations monitor progress on 6.1 and 6.2 and publish statistical reports that are widely used and accepted by the WASH sector.

Progress on drinking water, sanitation and hygiene

The Joint Monitoring Program (JMP) monitors progress on SDG #6. A collaboration between the World Health Organization (WHO) and the United Nations International Children's Emergency Fund (UNICEF), called the "Progress on

Drinking Water Sanitation and Hygiene 2017" (WHO/UNICEF 2017) is also referred to as JMP 2017. The 2017 report states that three out of ten people do not have access to safely managed water services. Further, six out of ten people are without access to safely managed sanitation. Other statistics from JMP 2017 also show how serious the situation is:

- 844 million people lack even a basic drinking water service
- 2.3 billion people lack even a basic sanitation solution
- 892 million people rely on open defecation

Financing water and sanitation

The Global Analysis and Assessment of Sanitation and Drinking Water (GLAAS) report is a collaboration between UN Water and WHO to analyse financing of SDG #6. The overarching conclusion of GLAAS 2017 is that

> [a] large financing gap has been identified as one of the greatest barriers to achieving these targets. To meet Targets 6.1 and 6.2, capital financing would need to triple to US$ 114 billion per annum and operating and maintenance costs need to be considered in addition.
>
> *(UN Water/WHO 2017)*

The main findings are delicately framed, to present some good news with the bad. To paraphrase three of those findings: (1) National WASH budgets are increasing but not enough; (2) development assistance is increasing, but future investments are uncertain and (3) extending WASH services to the poor is a policy priority, but implementation is lagging. Statistics backing up these conclusions include the following:

- 80 percent of countries report insufficient financing to meet national WASH targets.
- Over 50 percent of countries say household tariffs are insufficient to recover operation and maintenance costs, leading to an increase in disrepair and service failure.
- While international aid spending on WASH increased from US$6.3 billion to US$7.4 billion between 2012 and 2015, future commitments declined from US$10.4 billion to US$8.2 billion in the same period.

(UN Water/WHO 2017)

The role financing will have in the success and failure of the SDGs cannot be overstated. However, the goal of this chapter is to highlight work done by organizations, individuals and governments. The chapter does not go into detail on the financing, past or future, of SDG #6.

Global champions of SDG #6

Selections for who and what to highlight in this chapter were guided by an interest in (1) touching on work being done in both water and in sanitation, (2) paying special attention to work in developing countries and (3) choosing projects that involve international cooperation and strengthened participation of local communities called for by SDG #17.

Stockholm International Water Institute

Each year in late August, the Stockholm International Water Institute (SIWI) hosts a week-long conference in Stockholm. World Water Week (WWW) is an important gathering place for the WASH sector. In 2018, 3,600 people attended, representing 133 countries from around the globe. (SIWI 2018) WWW facilitates information exchange, networking and global-scale planning as water-related organizations gather. SIWI uses its well-established convening power to foster international cooperation in support of SDG #17. The conference alone would justify naming SIWI as a global champion of SDG #6.

However, in addition to managing the logistics and preparation for WWW, SIWI has, since 1991, encouraged innovation and commitment by awarding the prestigious Stockholm Water Prize (SWP) to "women, men and organizations who have made outstanding contributions to the sustainable use and protection of the world's water resources" (SIWI 2018). Taken together, WWW and the SWP are significant contributions SIWI makes to the community or practitioners working on SDG #6.

Two organizations that won the SWP (the Centre for Science and Environment in 2005 and WaterAid in 1995) and one individual (Peter Morgan in 2013) are highlighted in this chapter. In addition, it highlights one government (India) and one professional organization (the Sustainable Sanitation Alliance) for important work being done in the WASH sector.

Centre for Science and Environment

Dr. Sunita Narain, the current director of the Centre for Science and Environment (CSE), was also the director in 2005 when the SWP was awarded to CSE. Under Sunita's leadership, CSE was honoured for work in rejuvenating traditional systems of rainwater harvesting, which relied on "the supply in the sky."

The SWP citation was also for "excellence in public education and policy advocacy" and for helping to "spawn a rediscovery of this practical, traditional and inexpensive technique to capture rainwater" (SIWI 2018). Two books helped promote CSE's ideas: *Dying Wisdom: Rise, Fall and Potential of India's Water Harvesting System* (1997) and *Making Water Everybody's Business* (2001). According to the SWP citation, CSE distinguished itself among other NGOs for its "insistence on hard facts before rhetoric" (SIWI 2018).

One might wonder why advocating for traditional approaches to water management was prize-worthy, since many traditional systems were abandoned. Put differently, if traditional technologies did not stand the test of time, why return to traditional approaches now?

Sunita points out (Narain 2017) that it was not the traditional solutions that failed; it was emerging political systems that failed. Take the example of a village near Biklar, India. Sunita tells the story of driving along a dusty road when the Kheji trees abruptly stopped, giving way to what looked like an upside-down flying saucer. A local resident explained: "It is our water system . . . we pave the ground with lime and make it drain to the middle." From there the water goes through a channel to a covered well where it is stored without risk of contamination. Villagers are naturally motivated to maintain the system and the expertise is passed on.

Unfortunately, governing bodies wanting to centralize water provision sometimes take over from local communities. Those attempts to centralize are not always as successful as the local option in the long term. Moreover, they often last long enough for the expertise needed to maintain traditional systems to be lost (Narain 2017).

The advantages of returning to decentralized water management were a key finding of extensive research CSE did in India when it investigated how water was managed. The research findings led to recommendations for returning control to local populations, especially in rural areas. This is consistent with WaterAid's experiences in advocating for community control over water management decisions.

WaterAid

During the Thirsty Third World Conference of 1981, companies attending from the U.K. water industry joined forces to establish WaterAid as a charity to improve water access in the less developed world. The first projects were in Zambia and Sri Lanka. In 1992, U.K. water companies began a practice that continues to this day: monthly water bills include an appeal inviting customers to donate to WaterAid. This funding strategy, along with WaterAid's down-to-earth approach to collaborating with villages, was the basis for the SWP in 1995. That year, 23 million households received the appeal. In fiscal year 2017–18, more than £14 million (US$18 million) was generated for WaterAid. More than £178 million (US$228 million) has been raised since the original appeal in 1992 (Benjamin 2018).

WaterAid's approach was to collaborate with villagers and with water and health ministries to find the most practical and least expensive water sources and sanitation solutions. Meetings were convened in villages to set up water committees, employ supervisors and pump technicians and educate villagers about best practices in hygiene and water conservation. WaterAid currently has teams in 35 countries. A primary goal is to reduce the distance people (usually women) have to go to retrieve clean water.

Jon Lane was the newly appointed director of WaterAid in 1994 when news of the SWP award came. He thought his predecessor, David Collett, should go to Stockholm to receive the award, since David had led WaterAid since 1981. Nonetheless, both David and the trustees insisted that Jon receive the award on behalf of WaterAid. As Jon Lane wrote in a personal reflection in July 2018,

> I didn't feel I earned the SWP, however, it gave me exposure and kudos in a much wider world than I had previously experienced. In return I felt – and still do feel – strongly motivated to repay that good fortune by working hard to promote the importance of water supply and sanitation for the world's poorest people.
>
> *(Lane 2018)*

The prize money went to a new program Jon proposed then implemented at WaterAid: a dedicated research policy and advocacy department to provide evidence-based work at country and international levels.

Peter Morgan

Dr. Peter Morgan was awarded the prestigious SWP in 2013 for "protecting the health and lives of millions of people through improved sanitation and water technologies" (SIWI 2018; Zimbabwean 2013). Prior to that, he received the 2009 AfricaSan Award for Technical Innovation in Sanitation from the African Ministers' Council and the 2012 Rural Water Supply Network Award for Lifetime Services to Rural Water Supply.

It may have been a commitment to Zimbabwe that motivated him and his first-hand experience with the cultural context that made his designs so valuable. However, it was his personal commitment to public sharing of knowledge that resulted in his work being adopted in many other countries.

Between 1972 and 1993, Peter was a medical research officer and later an advisor to the Ministry of Health at the Blair Research Laboratory in Zimbabwe, where he is a naturalized citizen, having moved there (from the United Kingdom) at the age of 25 to do research. Peter's innovative and simple designs improved latrines and water pumps, and his research impacted how water was supplied and how human waste was processed. The international acceptance of his designs and international recognition came later.

The toilet he designed was originally named the Blair Pit Latrine and became known globally as the VIP (Ventilated Improved Pit) latrine when it was renamed by the World Bank. He invented several novel water-lifting devices and restyled the earlier national hand pump of Zimbabwe, calling it the B-type Bush Pump. His design was simpler and had fewer working parts, yet the pump remained very robust. The revised design has been the national standard in Zimbabwe since 1989 and has been accepted as a public domain pump with international specifications.

In the 1980s, Peter initiated the Upgraded Family Well Program long before the term *self-supply* was officially adopted by the WASH sector in 2004 (Olschewski 2016). He promoted the concept of family-owned water supplies for rural areas after implementing some simple changes to the design of wellheads and then doing scientific research to confirm the safety of "self-supply." His research resulted in more Zimbabweans, and sector professionals, accepting traditional practices as a safe option. Research published in 2016 showed that the cost of self-supply (as promoted by the Centre for Environment and Science as well as Peter Morgan) is 50 per cent less than the cost of providing public water systems (Olschewski 2016).

Dr. Sasha Kramer, keynote speaker for the 2018 Urine Diversion Summit sponsored by the Rich Earth Institute, acknowledged Peter for his early research on recovering the nitrogen from urine for use as a fertilizer. "Peter Morgan was my mentor, and many of us are indebted to him for his groundbreaking work." Recovering and recycling "toilet resources" is a theme many WASH organizations are working on right now, which is another credit to Peter's lasting impact.

India's Swachh Bharat Mission

Possibly the largest and most ambitious water and sanitation effort of its kind was initiated by the country of India before the SDGs were affirmed. In October 2014, Prime Minister Narenda Modi set a vision for a Clean India (Swachh Bharat), calling for clean streets and an end to open defecation by 2 October 2019, the 150th anniversary of the birth of Mahatma Gandhi. Attesting to India's commitment to the goal is the US$30 billion the government has committed to constructing 90 million toilets in rural India (Modi 2018).

As part of the campaign, Swachhagrahis (ambassadors of cleanliness) promote indoor plumbing in villages. Bollywood got in on the Swachh Bharat Mission (SBM) campaign by producing what turned out to be a very popular movie titled *Toilet: A Love Story*. It features India megastar Akshay Kumar, who plays a man who builds a toilet to win back his wife.

The SBM website (Swachh Bharat 2018) features "live updates" on the number of toilets installed. Whether those toilets are used or not will be a matter of what may be a much longer process of cultural and behavioural change. Understandably, rural citizens may prefer having plenty of space and open air to a confined, sometimes smelly, small enclosure. Counting the number of toilets and focusing only on "installation" is a problem. Critics of India's plans raise the concern that the broader system is not being addressed. What about the whole sanitation value chain? Are there enough businesses for maintaining those toilets, for withdrawing the contents of pit latrines, for safely processing and disposing of waste? Nonetheless, India has become a model for the positive impact governments can have when they make a major commitment to SDG #6.

The Sustainable Sanitation Alliance

Christine Werner of Deutsche Gesellschaft für Internationale Zusammenarbeit (GIZ) and Arno Rosemarin of the Stockholm Environment Institute (SEI) initiated the Sustainable Sanitation Alliance in 2008 to act as a consultative body to advise the UN in regard to the International Year of Sanitation 2008 (Kellogg 2017). The Sustainable Sanitation Alliance (SuSanA) membership grew from the original 40 to more than 10,000 in just 10 years. SuSanA was influential in getting water and sanitation on the SDG agenda. SuSanA has either initiated or supported a number of sector-wide projects that have been foundational for the work of WASH practitioners all over the globe. The following examples required cooperation across multiple organizations working in multiple countries. Each contributes to the foundation for a large-scale change that is needed to meet the goal of water and sanitation for all.

Compendium of sanitation systems and technologies

The first *Compendium of Sanitation Systems and Technologies* was published in 2008, with a second edition published in 2014 (Tilley et al. 2008, 2014), both with support from SuSanA. This effort met a need to standardize terms and provide decision-makers with a catalogue of tried-and-tested technologies to guide sanitation programs. In 2018, the *Compendium of Sanitation Technologies in Emergencies* (Gensch 2018) was released. Eawag was the initiating organization for the first *Compendium* in 2008 along with the Water Supply and Sanitation Collaborative Council. The International Water Association joined the project for the second edition. The German WASH Network and the Global WASH Cluster were added as collaborators for the *Emergency Compendium*.

Importantly, the *Compendiums* call for a systematic approach to decision-making by guiding attention to not only the technological decisions but also the broader societal, governmental, environmental and cultural contexts that must be considered before technology decisions are made. The *Compendiums*, with translations to multiple languages, are available online and utilized for training and capacity-building efforts related to Targets 6.1 and 6.2.

Shit-Flow Diagram tools

The Shit Flow Diagram (SFD; Panesar et al. 2018) is an analytic tool that makes it possible to follow the flow of human waste from its point of origin to its point of disposal or reuse. Daniela Krahl, deputy head of the water, urban development and mobility division at the German Federal Ministry for Economic Development and Cooperation preferred "excreta flow diagram," when she pointed out that the SFD project addresses the SDGs "in a holistic manner, thus going beyond SDG 6"(Panesar et al. 2018). The SFD Portal (which guides people to make an SFD for a specific neighbourhood or city) is publicly available on www.susana.org and is a result of the collaboration of 10 different organizations.

Bill Gates used an SFD graphic in 2016 as a basis for a conversation with India's prime minister, Narendra Modi, to explore where to focus efforts to alleviate India's urban sanitation crisis. SFDs can also be used to identify "waste to value" opportunities whereby "toilet resources" (human waste) could be recovered and converted into something of value for re-sale, such as fertilizer or energy.

Sanitation Wikipedia – a public education initiative

Elisabeth von Muench, a sanitation consultant with a PhD in Chemical Engineering, initiated "Sanitation Wikipedia" in 2014 (Sanitation Wikipedia 2018). The project uses the SuSanA platform to promote the importance of Wikipedia as a public education tool and to recruit SuSanA members to update and improve articles to assure they are accurate, complete and easy to understand.

As the fifth-most-used website on the internet, Wikipedia gets 15 billion views per month (Wikipedia Analytics 2018). The Wikipedia article on the SDGs gets more than 3,000 views per day and has had 11 different authors working on the article. Editors on the Sanitation Wikipedia team get an email anytime anyone makes a change to any of the 600 sanitation-related articles, assuring that the quality of articles is constantly monitored.

Keeping the public educated is important to achieving SDG 6, as public pressure can influence public policy and budget decisions and even what kind of off-grid toilet a rural family might choose to buy. Sanitation Wikipedia helps make sure research published in professional journals is added to Wikipedia articles and made accessible to average readers.

Summarizing lessons of the past

A strength of the sanitation sector is its history of cooperation and collaboration, as evidenced by the *Compendium* series, the SFD Portal and other multilateral efforts that provided infrastructure-like support to all WASH projects. It took collaboration and compromise to agree on the strengths and weaknesses of various technologies, knowing this "Bible-like" reference guide would impact decisions globally. This is consistent with the "international cooperation" called for by SDG #17 (Partnerships).

Also related to SDG #17 is the value placed on "local participation" in the work on SDG #6. This learning accrued from the work of both the Centre for Science and the Environment and WaterAid. Both valued working closely with local leaders – formal leaders and opinion leaders – to develop sustainable options for water provision. Technical experts based in NGOs and in private sector companies have come to appreciate that the "best" technology is not, in fact, the best if it is not acceptable to local users.

From Peter Morgan's early work in Zimbabwe to India's current SBM, the sector has increasingly recognized how vital it is to have support from local, regional and national governing bodies. Peter's inventions were officially adopted as countrywide standards, giving a better chance for widespread implementation. An example of what happens if there is not support from government actors is illuminating. A project in Accra, Ghana, intended to increase the number of household toilets in urban poor homes did engage local officials from the beginning. They signed formal agreements to market toilets to landlords and enforce existing laws requiring a toilet in every dwelling. Grant money was spent on improving the manufacturing facility of the toilet company. However, inadequate staffing in the local government office made enforcing laws difficult, and the grant did not fund the resources necessary for enforcement. This failure also illustrates the need for attention to, and appropriate funding for, the broader system.

The theme of a 2017 conference held in Uganda was "Using a Systems Approach." For example, many regions have learned the hard way that isolated programs for installing latrines can fail for inattention to the whole supply chain that is required to support sanitation. Businesses that withdraw contents of full latrines are required. Water treatment facilities must have adequate capacity to receive sewage from pipes or trucks. Laws, and law enforcement, are needed to prevent businesses from dumping untreated sewage. Even the lack of solid-waste garbage pick-up service affects how successful latrines installation projects are. How? Families resort to using the pit for disposing of all kinds of garbage if there aren't formal arrangements for solid waste. Furthermore, vacuum tubes meant for withdrawing liquid get clogged if latrines are used as garbage pits.

As Arne Panesar of GIZ put it (Panesar 2018), "[w]e weren't talking about the whole value chain ten years ago. Now we are: we know how important it is to pay attention to the broader system." Taking a systems approach requires attention and expertise along the whole supply chain related to sanitation as well as attention and expertise to the broader political and sociocultural environment. In conclusion, the WASH sector can be credited with promoting interorganizational cooperation, applying appropriate traditional and new technologies, increasing the participation of local decision-makers, seeking the support of government and taking a systems approach to change to assure sustainability.

Key challenges

Consistently applying the lessons of the past has been a challenge that requires better knowledge sharing processes and easier access to relevant information. The tendency to publish and post success stories (to appease and attract funders) works against the sector's ability to learn from mistakes and missteps.

Securing government support will continue to be a challenge, given budget constraints and the frequent turnover brought about by political appointments at the local and national levels. Even if support is in place, it can be disrupted by elections and new appointments.

Creating a marketplace for water and sanitation products is difficult. There is general agreement, however, that market-based solutions are more sustainable than reliance on funding and technical assistance by foundations and donated goods and services. However, people living at the base of the pyramid do not have the disposable income to spend in the newly emerging sanitation marketplaces. It is challenging enough to create a market for toilets when the competing product (i.e., open defecation) is perceived to be free. The long-term health costs are not immediately relevant when you have a choice to make today: Should I buy food for my family, or should I save that money so I can eventually buy a toilet?

This final example circles us back to the original section about the interlinkages between all the SDGs. Reducing poverty by improving employment leads to better outcomes for health and education and makes it possible for families to save money to invest in clean water and sanitation. The interdependence of the SDGs makes it clear that achieving any of the SDGs requires that we care about all the SDGs.

Bibliography

Aquamor. 2018. Accessed Sept. 2018. www.aquamor.info/Zimbabwe-b-type-bush-pump.html

Benjamin, C. 2018. Email correspondence with the author dated 31 July.

Davis, S. 2018. Author's interview notes, Aug.

Farnsworth Gray, H. 1940. "Sewerage in ancient and medieval times." *Sewage Works Journal*, 12(5): 939–946.

Gensch, R., Jennings, A., Rengglis, S., & Reymond, P. 2018. *Compendium for Sanitation Technologies in Emergencies*. Accessed Sept. 2018. www.susana.org/en/knowledge-hub/resources-and-publications/library/details/3145

Kellogg, D. 2017. "The global sanitation crisis: A role for business." In M. Gudić, T. K. Tan, & P. M. Flynn, eds. *Beyond the Bottom Line: Integrating Sustainability into Business and Management Practice*. UK: Greenleaf Publishing: 120–130.

Lane, J. 2018. Email correspondence with the author dated 26 June.

Modi, N. 2018. "Satyagraha to Swachhagrah: Narendra Modi addresses rally in Champaran." *Business Standard* (10 Apr.).

Narain, S. 2017. *Conflicts of Interest: My Journey through India's Green Movement*. Penguin Books.

Olschewski, A. 2016. *Supported Self-Supply: Learning from 15 Years of Experiences*. Peer reviewed paper for the 7th Rural Water Supply Network (RWSN) Forum "Water for Everyone", Abidjan, Côte d'Ivoire, 29 Nov.–2 Dec.

Panesar, A. 2018. Author's interview notes, Sept.

Panesar, A., Walther, D., Kauter-Eby, T., Bieker, S., Rohilla, S., Dube, R., Augustin, K., & Schertenleib, R. 2018. "The SuSanA platform and the shit flow diagram: Tools to achieve more sustainable sanitation for all." In L. Trowbridge, ed. *A Better World*, Volume 3. London: Tudor Rose: 40.

Rose, J. G. 2015. "Water, sanitation and the millennium development goals: A report card on global progress." *Water Quality and Health Council*. https://waterandhealth.org/safe-drinking-water/drinking-water/water-sanitation-millennium-development-goals-report-card-global-progress/

Sanitation Wikipedia. 2018. Accessed Sept. 2018. https://en.wikipedia.org/wiki/Wikipedia:WikiProject_Sanitation

Schertenleib, R. 2018. Author's interview notes, Aug.

SuSanA. 2018. "Sustainable sanitation and the SDGs: Interlinkages and opportunities." *SuSanA Secretariat, Eschborn, Germany*. Accessed Sept. 2018. www.susana.org/en/knowledge-hub/resources-and-publications/library/details/2859

Swachh Bharat. 2018. Accessed Sept. 2018. http://swachhbharatmission.gov.in/sbmcms/index.htm

Tilley, E., Lüthi, C., Morel, A., Zurbrügg, C., & Schertenleib, R. 2008. *Compendium of Sanitation Systems and Technologies*, 1st ed.

Tilley, E., Ulrich, L., Lüthi, C., Reymond, P., & Zurbrügg, C. 2014. *Compendium of Sanitation Systems and Technologies Revised*, 2nd ed. Accessed Sept. 2018. www.wsscc.org/resources-feed/compendium-of-sanitation-systems-and-technologies-2nd-edition/

Toilet Board Coalition. 2018. Accessed Sept. 2018. www.toiletboard.org/sanitation-economy

United Nations (UN). 2015. *Sustainable Development Agenda*. Accessed Sept. 2018. www.un.org/sustainabledevelopment/development-agenda/

United Nations Water. 2018. *Sustainable Development Goal 6 Synthesis Report on Water and Sanitation*. Accessed Sept. 2018. www.unwater.org/publication_categories/sdg-6-synthesis-report-2018-on-water-and-sanitation/

United Nations Water/WHO. 2017. *UN Water Global Analysis and Assessment of Sanitation and Drinking Water (GLAAS): Financing Universal Water, Sanitation and Hygiene under the SDGs*. Accessed Sept. 2018. www.who.int/water_sanitation_health/publications/glaas-report-2017/en/

WHO/UNICEF Joint Monitoring Program. 2017. *Progress on Drinking Water, Sanitation and Hygiene: 2017 Update and SDG Baselines*. Accessed Sept. 2018. https://washdata.org/

Wikipedia Analytics. 2018. Accessed Sept. 2018. https://analytics.wikimedia.org/dashboards/reportcard/#pageviews-july-2015-now

Zimbabwean. 2013. "Peter Morgan: An unsung legend." *The Zimbabwean* (20 June). Accessed Sept. 2018. www.thezimbabwean.co/2013/06/peter-morgan-an-unsung-legend/

PART II
Sustainability in traditional industries

4

MAKING SUSTAINABILITY WORK IN PLANTATION AGRICULTURE

The story of a sustainability champion in the tea industry in Sri Lanka

A. D. Nuwan Gunarathne

Abstract

This chapter showcases the notable work of a sustainability champion, Mahendra Peiris, in the collapsing Sri Lankan tea industry, an individual who has become a dauntless pioneer of many innovative programs. Despite its economic, environmental and social importance, in the recent past, the tea industry in Sri Lanka has faced serious sustainability challenges on many fronts. These require urgent productivity improvements leading to economic success and ecosystem preservation while improving the working conditions and living standards of the plantation communities. The sustainability champion introduced many novel, yet simple, innovative approaches. These focused on controlling the weeds through biological means by boosting ecosystem immunity instead of using weedicide chemicals, low-cost productivity improvements that need minimum use of synthetic agricultural inputs such as fertilizer, preservation of the ecosystem and enhancement of the income level and well-being of employees in the century-old tea industry. However, his campaign was met with criticism, scepticism and rejection. Nevertheless, his dauntless struggle to make sustainability work offers interesting lessons for aspiring sustainability champions around the world.

Agriculture and its contribution to sustainable development

Agriculture has strategic importance for the achievement of the UN Sustainable Development Goals (SDGs) owing to its significance as a source of livelihood and employment, a supply of food, a source of revenue from international trade, inputs to other industries and contribution to economic development and human health. More precisely, agriculture is a main contributor to ending hunger, achieving food security and improving nutrition (SDG #2) while its impact is also evident in many other SDGs, such as good health and well-being (SDG #3), managing climate change (SDG #13) and ecosystem management (SDG #15) (UN Development Programme [UNDP] 2018; Farming First 2018).

The ever-diminishing availability of land and water resources for farming and the rising cost of energy and labour pose challenges to the industry (UN Environment Programme [UNEP] 2008). In achieving most of the relevant SDGs, sustainable agricultural practices and sustainable innovation are becoming crucial in many traditional agricultural industries, such as plantation agriculture. Plantation agriculture is the production of commodity crops by large-scale agribusiness organisations (Goldthorpe 1988). It is a form of commercial farming where crops are grown for profit such as beverage crops (e.g. tea, coffee and cocoa), rubber, palm oil, cotton, fruit (e.g. pineapples and bananas) and sugarcane (Geography 2012).

However, the lack of sustainability innovations in this industry is a major obstacle to realising the SDGs (Berdegue & Escobar 2002; Negny et al. 2012). Although this is pervasive worldwide, there are many fascinating, unheard of, innovative developments in different parts of the world. This chapter describes the work of a sustainability champion in the collapsing Sri Lankan tea industry: Mahendra Peiris, who has become a driving force behind many sustainable innovations. The chapter highlights his industry background, motivations and challenges, as well as some lessons for those who champion sustainability work in different cultural contexts and natural ecosystems.

The work of this sustainability champion is important for three reasons. First, Mahendra's innovations confirm the green–lean relationship in agriculture, one of the most significant industries for achieving sustainable development. These innovations are not only beneficial in economic terms but also in protecting the environment and ecosystem. Second, Mahendra's journey has been full of struggles through which he developed plans and innovative solutions to address the needs of different stakeholders in a community that has received little attention in the sustainable development process. Third, his courageous and out-of-the-box experiments that gave rise to these innovations benefit the majority of smallholder farmers in rural areas who depend heavily on agriculture amidst many constraints, such as the lack of scientific knowledge and capital investment.

The rest of the chapter is organised as follows: The next section provides the industry background in which these notable innovative sustainable agricultural practices were carried out in the tea industry while highlighting the industry challenges for sustainable development. This section also outlines the significance of this industry for inclusive economic development, environmental preservation and social well-being. The following section tells the story of the sustainability champion while highlighting his innovations. This section also discusses how these innovations are important in addressing the SDGs. Thereafter, the chapter focuses on the obstacles he faced and how he overcame them. The last section highlights the lessons for the future.

Industry background

From about 2700 BC, tea (*Camellia sinensis*) has been the most widely consumed manufactured drink in the world (Chang 2015). It is currently grown in more than 35 countries, the majority of which are developing countries. The tea industry in these countries is a major economic sector, providing a valuable source of employment and foreign exchange earnings (Forum for the Future 2014). At present, China, India, Kenya and Sri Lanka are the world's largest tea-producing and -exporting countries (Forum for the Future 2014). Among the various global sources of tea, Ceylon tea (tea produced in Sri Lanka, known as Ceylon in the past), always commands premium prices due to its high quality (Sri Lanka Tea Board (SLTB) 2016).

The first commercial tea plantations in Sri Lanka were established by the British in the mid-nineteenth century (SLTB 2014). Over the next one and a half centuries, the tea industry in Sri Lanka gradually became an important sector from economic, environmental and social perspectives. It now represents 1% of value added to the Sri Lankan economy while providing more than 1 million direct jobs and 2.5 million indirect jobs (Central Bank of Sri Lanka (CBSL) 2016). Sri Lanka has earned a global reputation for producing quality tea in the world due to its unique flavour and lower contamination levels with respect to agrochemical residues (Ali, Choudhry, & Lister 1997).

From an environmental perspective, this industry is important for Sri Lanka as most of the tea plantations are located mainly in the central highlands of the country where many rivers originate. The central highlands of Sri Lanka are also home to an extraordinary range of flora and fauna, including several endangered species such as giant tree ferns (*Cyathea gigantea*), the Sri Lankan highland slender loris (*Loris tardigradus nycticeboides*), the Sri Lanka whistling thrush (*Myophonus blighi*), Asanka's shrub frog (*Pseudophilautus asankai*) and the barred danio (*Devario pathirana*). Due to the significance of the natural ecosystems in the central highlands, the International Union for Conservation of Nature has declared this mountain region a "super-biodiversity hot spot" on the planet (ICUN 2017).

Despite its economic, environmental and social significance, the tea industry in Sri Lanka has faced serious challenges in the recent past. Among them, the rocketing cost of production due to rising labour costs and low productivity is important. This has resulted in most of the commercial tea plantations making losses in recent years. Plagued by losses the tea plantation companies are compelled to diversify crops especially by introducing other crops such as oil palm, which is widely criticised globally for its negative impact on the environment.

Further, the introduction of other alien crops in environmentally sensitive areas could threaten the natural ecosystems. Moreover, plantation companies tend to adopt unsustainable practices such as increasing use of agrochemicals to increase their production levels. Recently, the Government of Sri Lanka banned some weedicides, such as glyphosate, that cause widespread health and environmental problems. Worsening the existing industry problems, this policy has left the tea industry with few options for the management of weeds.

While many of the large plantation companies are struggling, there are also a large number of smallholder farmers who engage in tea cultivation without the necessary technical know-how and capital investment. Since their income level is low, the living conditions of these smallholder farmers have not improved. Moreover, the living conditions of the plantation employees and their communities have remained in a deplorable state, with fluctuating income levels, lack of proper health care, an unsafe working environment with constant seasonal bee attacks, malnutrition and a lack of education. There is, therefore, a tendency for the younger generations to leave the tea estates in search of better jobs and living conditions in the urban areas, creating labour shortages in the industry.

The primitive living standards of the plantation community have also created many environmental problems for the highly sensitive ecosystem in the hill country mainly due to improper waste management. Owing to these reasons, the future of the commercial tea industry in the country is uncertain unless there are real breakthroughs in productivity, environmental preservation and social development (Oxford Business Group 2016). This situation calls for the tea industry to urgently make productivity improvements leading to stronger economic success and better ecosystem preservation while providing better working conditions and living standards for the plantation communities. The next section provides a brief overview of the sustainability champion and his tireless efforts to address these industry challenges.

Story of the sustainability champion in the tea industry

The Sri Lankan tea industry needs visionary leaders and out-of-the-box thinkers who are ready to change century-old practices to spur innovation. Despite the urgent need for improvements and developments, changing these practices in the tea industry is laborious and often attracts criticism, scepticism and rejection. Innovators and change agents have to face not only various challenges but also personal attacks. This section presents an overview of the sustainability champion, Mahendra Peiris, who has become an unfaltering driving force behind many innovative programs aimed at delivering sustainable development outcomes for the collapsing tea industry in Sri Lanka.

Mahendra has a bachelor's degree in Agriculture and a master's degree in Biodiversity, Ecotourism and Environment Management, both from the University of Peradeniya, Sri Lanka, which is one of the oldest universities in the country. His academic background has given him a solid understanding to explore various innovative practices from a wider perspective. In his multifaceted role, he acts as a naturalist, a nature photographer and a science journalist. He has accumulated m 20 years of experience in the local tea industry by working in various positions, including research assistant at the Tea Research Institute of Sri Lanka, management trainee in tea tasting and tea brokering, tea buyer and blender and a superintendent of many tea estates.

Currently, he is serving as a manager of Compliance & Project Management of a leading tea plantation company in Sri Lanka. Recalling his journey, Mahendra had this to say:

> When you really look at nature for answers, you will have great success. Most of my [sustainability] innovations were inspired by looking at the intricate yet common relationships in nature. I am really happy [that] I have come a long way now. It was not easy most of the time. I had to face many challenges and I am still encountering them.

Mahendra's innovations earned him the "Presidential Green Award in 2016" for the best medium-scale sustainable farming model in Sri Lanka. He has also received two awards at the "Merrill J. Fernando Eco-innovation Awards 2016", presented by Dilmah Conservation, the corporate social responsibility initiative of the world-famous Dilmah tea company, for breakthrough technologies developed for the commercial tea industry. He was also nominated for the "Global Tea Sustainability Award 2016" at the North American Tea Conference, Ontario, Canada, by the Rainforest Alliance. He is featured in the 2017 Rainforest Alliance's General Inspirational Video, *We are the Rainforest Alliance*. In fact, the Rainforest Alliance recently called him an evangelist of the tea industry (Rainforest Alliance 2016).

Moreover, Mahendra has served as a Rainforest Alliance Trainer for "plantations on climate-smart agriculture and conservation awareness programs" conducted in all three languages (Sinhala, Tamil and English) spoken in Sri Lanka. In addition, he was a recipient of the Australian Department of Foreign Affairs and Trade–UNESCO grant for the promotion of women smallholder entrepreneurs in climate-smart agriculture practices. He has become a much sought-after speaker on innovative agricultural management practices, especially for smallholder farmers. The Rainforest Alliance Program coordinator in Sri Lanka explained how it got connected with Mahendra;

> [Smallholder tea] farmers were using herbicides, fertilizers and chemicals but still their yields were declining. We wanted to train them in herbicide free weed management and improve the harvest with sustainable agricultural practices. Then we saw what Mahendra was doing. He has been experimenting with what we really wanted to promote [i.e. sustainable agricultural practices]. His trials have improved our programs a lot.

Photo 4.1 shows a visit by a Rainforest Alliance team to observe Mahendra's experimental tea block to learn how to incorporate his herbicide-free agricultural practices into their smallholder tea farmer training programs.

Mahendra's innovations have focused on the non-use of weedicides and boosting ecosystem immunity for weed control, minimum use of other agrochemicals such

54 A. D. Nuwan Gunarathne

PHOTO 4.1 Rainforest Alliance team observing Mahendra's experimental tea block

as fertilizer, productivity improvements, preservation of the ecosystem, enhancement of income and the safety and well-being of employees in the century-old tea industry. The rest of this section describes his innovative approaches while linking their outcomes to the achievement of the SDGs. (See Table 4.1.)

Notes to Table 4.1:

- SSTB is a method that promotes a quick re-establishment of a bush canopy of tea bushes after periodic pruning by radial spreading of growing shoots using parallel stripes. This simple technique exposes a tea bush more to sunlight allowing it to grow larger and wider, forming a thicker and broader canopy over the ground. It increases resource use efficiency and yield, thus providing a better income for the employees while also reducing soil erosion and suppressing weed growth (see Gunarathne & Peiris 2017 for more details).
- HFIWM is a method that selectively controls troublesome weeds in tea lands while promoting the growth of naturally occurring harmless plants to form a ground cover without chemical weed control (see Peiris & Gunarathne 2015 for more details).
- FYWMS is a community-driven waste management system, whereby the organic content of domestic food waste is used as an input for home farming and the rest is sold for recycling.
- HBPLM involves the identification of factors disturbing giant honeybees (*Apis dorsata*) based on their behaviour and the development of a knowledge base and a strategy to avoid disturbing bees. It also involves the development of a highly effective antidote for bee venom.

TABLE 4.1 Notable innovative solutions developed by Mahendra Peiris

Problems Faced by Commercial Tea Industry	Possible Reasons	Innovative Solutions Developed	Significance/Outcomes of the Innovations	Contribution to Sustainable Development Goals (SDGs)
Declining yield	Variations in health and size of the tea bush canopy	Stripe-spreading of tea bushes (SSTB)	Approx. 30%–40% increase in crop Increased income for plantation workers	These innovative approaches are directly related to many SDGs, for example, SDG #12 (sustainable production, whereby the industries minimise the use or depletion of natural resources, the use of toxic materials used and the generation of waste and pollutants in their production process). Also, they are indirectly related to many other SDGs, such as SDG #6 (ensuring availability of clean water), SDG #8 (promotion of sustainable economic growth and improvement of the standard of living of plantation workers), SDG #14 (conservation of life below water) and SDG #15 (protection of terrestrial ecosystems and biodiversity).
Debilitation of tea bushes	Increasing use of herbicides	Herbicide-free integrated weed management (HFIWM)	Weedicides not used Healthy and toxic-free environment and clean drinking water for workers Cost savings	
Soil degradation and wastage of agricultural inputs polluting environment	Ground exposure to natural forces such as air, wind and sunlight the improper use of agrochemicals without risk awareness	Development of a standard operating procedure based on SSTB and HFIWM Identification of an antidote	Reduced soil erosion Productive use of agrochemical inputs	
Improper waste management in plantation communities	Lack of technical know-how	Food-yielding waste management system (FYWMS) for plantation households	Safe disposal of solid waste and the quick conversion of organic waste into food. Income for the community	This system is related to SDG #11 (making the plantation communities safe and sustainable), SDG #2 (achieving food security and improving nutrition) and SDG #1 (improving the income of plantation workers to end poverty).
Giant honey bee attacks on estate workers	Lack of knowledge about the giant honey bees	Honey bee proof living mechanism (HBPLM)	Safe and peaceful working conditions for employees. Improvement in health and well-being. Improved ecosystem health by promoting natural pollination.	This mechanism contributes to SDG #8 (by providing a safe and productive work environment for plantation workers) and SDG #3 (promotion of health and well-being.

Obstacles and strategies adopted

Some of Mahendra's innovative solutions such as herbicide-free weed management systems spurred immense industry pressures especially from multinational and local agrochemical companies as they were a clear threat to their business if accepted widely by the tea and other industries. Hence, these businesses took all possible actions to keep these innovations at bay as soon as they witnessed early signs of success. These chemical companies have a network of individual employees in the plantation companies, who, in turn, promote the use of chemicals. Furthermore, chemical companies have become smart enough to bribe some of the middle and top management of the plantation companies, who would then always suppress any innovative approaches that reduce the use of chemicals or fertilizer.

There are people who were upset by the innovative approaches propagated by Mahendra as they threatened their status quo, financial benefits and long-held belief systems. The chemical companies together with these individuals exerted immense pressure to suppress and sabotage Mahendra's innovative strategies. These included, but were not limited to, changing employment; sanctioning of research work, publications and statements to media on innovative practices; blocking national-level awards by influencing the relevant authorities; physically destroying research plots; and preventing the extension of training mechanisms.

Due to the uncertainty and negative propaganda, there was conflict and confusion among Mahendra's team members some of whom chose not to support him or otherwise impeded his innovations. These chemical companies and individuals then launched negative propaganda campaigns through the media and other tea industry partners to create suspicion and scepticism about the results and outcomes of the innovative approaches adopted. Even the other plantation managers and some smallholder tea farmers who voluntarily commenced practising Mahendra's work were threatened and forced to stop by the networks operated by agrochemical companies. The purpose of these actions was to reduce industry acceptance and adoption of innovative solutions.

Some of these obstacles were initially successful and were a real setback to the efforts taken by Mahendra. Understanding that resistance to change is inevitable and unsurprising, he had to take untrodden paths to achieve his objectives of contributing to the realisation of the SDGs in the tea industry. He therefore adopted many strategies to withstand and overcome these challenges. First, he had to prove the success of his innovations in addressing the challenges faced by the tea industry. He followed the accepted industry standards and scientific approaches not only when conducting his innovative experiments but also when communicating those results. This is where he partnered with academics and other scientific researchers in different disciplines in a bid to enhance the credibility of his research while also benefitting from their field of expertise. See Photo 4.2 which presents a soil study conducted at Mahendra's tea estate by a group of university academics.

Some of Mahendra's research partners include biologists, environmental scientists, accountants, soil and weed scientists, engineers and biodiversity specialists. This transdisciplinary approach helped him address the innovation process and

Sustainability work in plantation agriculture 57

PHOTO 4.2 A soil study at Mahendra's tea estate by a group of university academics

performance from different perspectives while making the results palatable to a wider audience from different backgrounds. These partnerships also facilitated his work in scientific and academic forums and conferences to create the needed industry awareness and recognition. He also published his work in reputable national and international scientific and business management journals such as the *Procedia Food Science*, the *Asian Journal of Sustainability and Social Responsibility* and the *Social Science Research Network Electronic Journal*, leaving little room for unfounded criticism.

Explaining his strategy, Mahendra said,

> I wanted to always first show solid credible results so that no one can really challenge them without a proper rationale. I therefore did my [innovative] experiments scientifically and presented them in scientific forums. My industry and academic partners helped me a lot to get my message across to the desired audience.

One of his research partners, a professor in Crop Science from an agricultural department of a leading university in Sri Lanka said,

> Mahendra always wanted to partner with us to improve the credibility of his innovations and to find some solutions to the issues he faced when carrying out his experiments. . . . I also saw his passion and determination to find

solutions to the sustainability challenges in his industry and community. As an academic and a scientist, I also learnt many things from his innovations. So, it was a win-win situation for both of us.

Second, in order to gain the acceptance of employees and the community for his innovations, especially for waste management and honeybee initiatives, Mahendra started an awareness program by conducting workshops and seminars on a volunteer basis. Convincing the plantation workers and plantation communities, who are generally less educated, to change the existing practices requires clear-and-yet-simple evidence-based instructional mechanisms. Mahendra, therefore, had to conduct these workshops and seminars in their mother tongue, Tamil or Sinhala, while following a demonstration-based approach rather than written rules and principles. Also, he first convinced the plantation communities of the immediate economic benefits of proper waste management such as how to use organic waste as an input for their livestock farming. As the financial benefits were appealing, the rest of the actions were accepted without much resistance.

Furthermore, he focused on children of school age as the change agents in these families to influence the parents to change the existing unsustainable waste management practices. In order to create a self-sustaining mechanism of waste management, he also liaised with the local government authorities, waste collectors and recyclers, community-based organisations and non-governmental entities. These novel, yet simple, approaches have become effective in prompting the necessary changes in the plantation communities to enhance their standard of living. A resident who participated in his waste management project explained how they benefitted:

> We had a huge problem in managing our day-to-day waste. This program showed us how we can utilize garbage [putrescible waste] to increase our income by using it as food for our farm animals. Thanks to this program, we can now sell other wastes [such as glass, cardboard and plastic] to the collectors who come and visit us every month.

A local government representative of the area appreciated Mahendra's waste management program by expressing the following comment:

> Waste management in this area was a great challenge for us. . . . But now after this program, we see very positive signs of improvement. I am thankful to Mr Mahendra for coming up with this community-centric program for waste management.

Third, although the innovative solutions such as integrated waste management techniques or soil enrichment techniques initially appeared promising, Mahendra was not in a hurry to take them to the external market or society. As with any innovation, there was obvious room for improvement and overcoming teething problems. If they were marketed hurriedly, these problems would be exposed and negative publicity created in the minds of stakeholders who would likely reject the innovative ideas in the first place. He therefore experimented with these novel methods always on a small scale for a considerable period to iron out any problems.

During this experimental period, Mahendra conducted many awareness campaigns that inspired the community to overcome the unsustainable problems they faced. Since he envisioned most of these sustainability challenges beforehand, by the time he had perfected his innovative ideas, society was looking for solutions to the problems they encountered. This created a viable pathway for him to obtain social acceptance and recognition for his time-tested innovative solutions.

Since Mahendra was deprived of his experimental plots in his tea estate, where he was a superintendent, he purchased his own private land for research and development. Then he partnered with national and international researchers to apply for financial grants for the development of the facilities while meeting the grant objectives. The Australian Department of Foreign Affairs and Trade–UNESCO grant for the development of woman tea holders is one such project. Although the private land block has not been fully developed yet, it has provided him an experimental piece of land to try his innovative ideas over time and without hindrance.

Moreover, Mahendra started conducting workshops and seminars to disseminate knowledge of his novel approaches such as *stripe-spreading of tea bushes* (SSTB) and *herbicide-free integrated weed management* (HFIWM) among the smallholder tea farmers who lacked technical know-how and capital. The healthy relationship he has with the Rainforest Alliance facilitated such workshops and seminars. Photo 4.3 shows Mahendra explaining his innovations to smallholder farmers in a tea estate.

PHOTO 4.3 Mahendra explaining his innovations to smallholder farmers

One of the smallholder tea farmers who attended his workshops on HFIWM stated the following:

> I really appreciate the advice provided by Mr. Mahendra. We had never attended a workshop of this nature before. His instructions were clear and very practical. This is really an eye-opener for us to understand the [innovative agricultural] practices to reduce chemical usage. It is good for us, tea land and the environment.

Another smallholder tea farmer who practised his innovative methods, such as HFIWM and SSTB, expressed how she benefitted:

> His [Mahendra's] advice has been really useful to improve my tea yield. Previously I got about 400 kgs of tea per acre. Now it is more than 500 kgs. Not only has this improved my family income but I was also able to reduce my input costs substantially. Also, I am happy that I am not damaging the environment now.

Another smallholder tea farmer who started practising Mahendra's innovative agricultural practices after attending a Rainforest Alliance workshop two years ago mentioned the improvements he and his villagers have made:

> We have completely stopped using herbicides for the past two years and reduced chemical fertilizers from 15,650 kg in 2013 to just 4,400 kg in 2016. This has benefited tea production and reduced our costs by 30 per cent. It has also been a strong incentive to start improving the quality of life in our village.

Lessons for future sustainability champions

Although the approach taken by Mahendra is not without setbacks and challenges, the path he followed provides highly useful lessons for aspiring sustainability champions. First, irrespective of the results or outcomes of the innovation, there is resistance to change from a variety of concerned stakeholders. It is therefore essential to find mechanisms to withstand or overcome these challenges through innovative approaches that are unique to one's industry, field of work or community.

Mahendra adopted several multifaceted strategies that include the following: maintaining continuous communication with stakeholders, creating awareness and educating direct beneficiaries of innovations, enhancing knowledge and skills in different fields, adopting scientific and standard procedures in innovation experimentation, establishing collaborative partnerships with key parties who support change, improving innovations before implementing them on a wide scale and exhibiting unwavering perseverance and passion for better results. Regardless of the specific actions followed, collaboration with external parties, such as academics or scientists in different fields of expertise, government institutions, not-for-profit organisations, community-based organisations and industry trade associations, is the key to success. These collaborative initiatives not only give the future sustainability champions credibility and acceptance but also become supportive pillars when they struggle with external forces. Furthermore, such collaborative efforts should involve multi- or transdisciplinary teams who share the same values. Since sustainability is a multidimensional construct, addressing its challenges requires multi- or transdisciplinary initiatives (Schaltegger, Beckmann, & Hansen 2013). This enables future sustainability champions to investigate and find solutions to sustainability challenges from multiple perspectives while addressing the concerns of a variety of stakeholders who will benefit from such innovations.

Another learning point that Mahendra's approach offers is the need to understand the key stakeholders who benefit or are affected by the innovations in order to build a long-lasting partnership. The use of the simple language of the community or stakeholders becomes a powerful tool in creating a desire for change and sustaining that change. Also, the proverb "actions speak louder than words" teaches that it is essential to show the results first to create a desire for the change towards more sustainable outcomes. In doing so, the sustainability champion is highlighting the significance of the economic gains for stakeholders rather than focusing on the environmental or social gains; this acts to convince the less educated stakeholders to come on board.

Finally, Mahendra's approach highlights the need for patience in introducing the change ideas or innovative solutions to society. Perfecting an innovative idea/experiment in a small group that you can rely on is a reassuring approach before spreading the ideas on a mass scale. It is also essential to evaluate the impacts of these innovations from a broader perspective, using a variety of sustainability indicators that encompass economic, environmental and social perspectives (Gunarathne & Peiris 2017). During this time, sustainability leaders would be able to create a demand for the change in society or the community for a more sustainable outcome through awareness building so that there will be ready acceptance and adoption of the innovative solutions offered. Developing personal stamina and persistence while improving the knowledge base in related fields is an absolute must for future sustainability champions to take their ideas to a wider audience while overcoming the challenges.

Mahendra's innovative approaches in the tea plantation sector in Sri Lanka have paved the way for the achievement of several SDGs. His innovative agricultural practices such as SSTB and HFIWM not only ensure responsible production patterns by minimising the use of natural resources and chemicals (SDG #12) but also improve the quality of water (SDG #6), economic growth and the standard of living of plantation communities (SDG #8) while protecting rivers, ecosystems and biodiversity (SDGs #14 and #15).

Furthermore, his community-centric waste management system and protection with the honey bee initiative have been very successful in providing a safe, resilient and sustainable environment for the community (SDG #11) while also promoting healthy lives and the well-being of the plantation workers (SDG #3). These initiatives have also contributed to ending hunger and achieving food security (SDG #2) while improving the income of the plantation communities to reduce poverty (SDG #1). This dauntless struggle of the sustainability champion offers invaluable lessons for aspiring sustainability champions around the world on how to strive for the simultaneous achievement of many SDGs amidst countless challenges.

References

Ali, R., Choudhry, Y. A., & Lister, D. W. 1997. *Sri Lanka's Tea Industry: Succeeding in the Global Market*. Washington, DC: The World Bank.

Berdegue, J. A., & Escobar, G. 2002. *Rural Diversity, Agricultural Innovation Policies and Poverty Reduction*. Agricultural Research & Extension Network, Network Paper No. 122.

Central Bank of Sri Lanka. (CBSL). 2016. *Annual Report 2016*. Colombo: CBSL.

Chang, K. 2015. *World Tea Production and Trade: Current and Future Development*. Rome: Food and Agriculture Organization of the United Nations.

Farming First. 2018. *The Story of Agriculture and the Sustainable Development Goals*. Accessed 14 June 2018. https://farmingfirst.org/sdg-toolkit#section_2

Forum for the Future. 2014. *The Future of Tea a Hero Crop for 2030*. UK: Tea 2030 Steering Group.

Geography. 2012. *Plantation Agriculture*. Accessed 4 July 2018. http://thestudyofearth.blogspot.com.au/2012/03/plantation-agriculture.html

Goldthorpe, C. C. 1988. "A definition and typology of plantation agriculture." *Singapore Journal of Tropical Geography*, 8(1): 26–43.

Gunarathne, A. D. N., & Peiris, H. M. P. 2017. "Assessing the impact of eco-innovations through sustainability indicators: The case of the commercial tea plantation industry in Sri Lanka." *Asian Journal of Sustainability and Social Responsibility*, 2(1): 41–58.

International Union for Conservation of Nature (ICUN). 2017. *Central Highlands of Sri Lanka 2017 Conservation Outlook Assessment*. Gland, Switzerland: ICUN.

Negny, S., Belaud, J., Robles, C., Reyes, R., & Ferrer, B. 2012. "Toward an eco-innovative method based on a better use of resources: Application to chemical process preliminary design." *Journal of Cleaner Production*, 32: 101–113.

Oxford Business Group. 2016. *Growth Prospects for Sri Lanka's Tea Industry*. Accessed 30 June 2018. www.oxfordbusinessgroup.com/news/growth-prospects-sri-lanka%E2%80%99s-tea-industry

Peiris, H. M. P., & Gunarathne, A. D. N. 2015. *Sustainable Weed Management in the Commercial Tea Industry: The Case of Hapugastenne Estate, Maskeliya*. 12th International Conference on Business Management (ICBM), University of Sri Jayewardenepura, Sri Lanka. Accessed 16 Feb. 2018. https://ssrn.com/abstract=2706978

Rainforest Alliance. 2016. *An Evangelist for Sustainable Agriculture*. Accessed 20 May 2018. www.rainforest-alliance.org/articles/an-evangelist-for-sustainable-agriculture

Schaltegger, S., Beckmann, M., & Hansen, E. G. 2013. "Transdisciplinarity in corporate sustainability: Mapping the field." *Business Strategy and the Environment*, 22(4): 219–229.

Sri Lanka Tea Board (SLTB). 2014. *History of Ceylon Tea-A Mature Industry*. Accessed 2 May 2018. www.pureceylontea.com/index.php/a-mature-industry

Sri Lanka Tea Board (SLTB). 2016. *Tea Market Update*, Volume 10(4). Colombo: SLTB.

United Nations Development Programme (UNDP). 2018. *Sustainable Development Goals*. Accessed 22 June 2018. www.undp.org/content/undp/en/home/sustainable-development-goals.html

United Nations Environment Program (UNEP). 2008. *Agriculture, Agro-Biodiversity and Climate Change*. Bonn: UNEP.

5
AMONG THE POOREST OF THE POOR

Tauhid's sustainability approach in Northern Bangladesh

Enrico Fontana

Abstract

The chapter examines the sustainability approach of Md. Tauhid Bin Abdus Salam (Tauhid) in northern Bangladesh. He is the founder of Classical Handmade Products BD (CHP), a firm operating as part of the global value chains (GVCs) in the international supply of rugs and baskets. Substantiated by face-to-face interviews in Bangladesh with Tauhid and secondary data (documents, online reports and press releases), this chapter contributes to the advancement of the sustainable development agenda, conveying useful lessons for management educators, scholars and practitioners. Tauhid's sustainability approach, based on his collaboration with NGOs and buyers for inclusiveness, engagement with rural communities and workers' empowerment, informs the practices of GVC firms that advance the United Nations Sustainable Development Goals (SDGs). This holds, more specifically, for poverty alleviation (SDG #1), gender equality (SDG #5), decent work and economic growth (SDG #8) and responsible consumption and production (SDG #12). This chapter also discusses the personal and organizational challenges potentially associated with work to advance the SDGs.

Introduction

> When we started the company, I encountered one lady. She was breaking stones with a hammer, in an open field. Her skin was red because she was working under the sun. And there were scars on her hands and feet because the stones hit her. I invited her to weave rugs for us. Through cases like hers, I became aware of the extreme poverty of that region. That made me even more determined to continue my work, to help create jobs for these ladies. I feel lucky that they are working for me. Thanks to their hard work, we have a big factory now [. . .] and this is their factory. This is what they have built with their own hands.
> – *Tauhid (Classical Handmade Products BD, owner)*

Although our human civilization faces overwhelming social and environmental challenges, these are especially critical in developing countries (Jamali & Karam 2016; Kolk, Rivera-Santos, & Rufin 2014). It is in these contexts that local firms, operating as part of global value chains (GVCs), create change and advance the United Nations Sustainable Development Goals (SDGs) (George et al. 2016). In GVCs, that is, systems of suppliers dispersed throughout the world (Lund-Thomsen & Lindgreen 2014), firms in developing countries play important roles in distinct ways. They, for instance, redistribute the value of their economic activities offering long-term employment (Yawar & Seuring 2017). They help to compensate for their countries' limited ability to provide essential public services, channeling resources and creating inclusive growth (Mair, Martí, & Ventresca 2012; Visser 2008). Analogously, they enact sustainability practices, offering a moral compass and empowering the marginalized communities (Muthuri, Chapple, & Moon 2009; Rasche, Morsing, & Moon 2017; Welford & Frost 2006).

Nevertheless, GVC firms' contribution to sustainable development, to date, remains surprisingly under-scrutinized (Banerjee & Jackson 2017; Fontana & Egels-Zandén 2018). This is exacerbated by the weak qualitative evidence at the micro-level of those women and men who, behind the scenes, reduce human deprivation, reduce disparity, foster social inclusion and, ultimately, improve human lives through their work in the GVC supply systems.

This chapter examines the case of Md. Tauhid Bin Abdus Salam (Tauhid). Originally from a middle-income family from southern Bangladesh, Tauhid studied garment design at the Bangladesh Garment Manufacturers and Exporters Association and the University of Fashion & Technology. After working as an employee for three-and-a-half years in Dhaka, Tauhid migrated with his family to New York in the United States. Nevertheless, he soon decided to return to Bangladesh, driven by his desire to support his fellow citizens and act against poverty. In 2008, he founded Classical Handmade Products BD (CHP), a manufacturing firm that operates in GVCs and supplies rugs and baskets for international sale from northern Bangladesh.

As one of the poorest rural regions on earth, northern Bangladesh suffers from famine, unemployment and child marriage problems (World Bank 2014). From an initial investment of 54 lakh taka (approximately US$64,000) and 90 employees in 2008, CHP has reached in 2017 an annual turnover of US$3.5 million and employs more than 2,000 individuals who are predominantly female workers. In 2017, Tauhid won the Exporter of the Year award by HSBC Bangladesh in the small and medium enterprise category due to his leadership in brightening the country's image and contributing to the nation's sustainable growth (*The Daily Star* 2017).

Tauhid's sustainability approach in GVCs and challenges draw inspiration and lessons for contributing to the advancement of the SDGs. This relates to the goals on poverty alleviation (SDG #1), gender equality (SDG #5), decent work and economic growth (SDG #8) and responsible consumption and production (SDG #12). By analyzing Tauhid's self-reflections, discursive accounts and personal narratives on his sustainability practices, gleaned through face-to-face interviews in Bangladesh and consolidated with secondary data (documents, online reports and press

66 Enrico Fontana

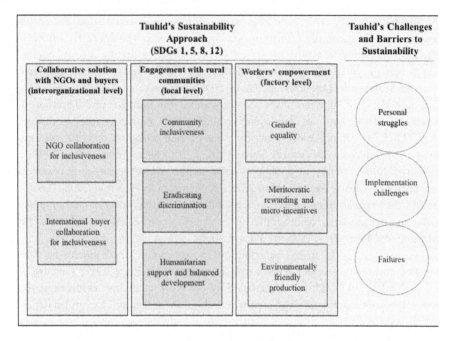

FIGURE 5.1 Tauhid's sustainability approach in GVCs

releases), this chapter delivers fresh learning materials for management educators, practitioners and scholars. It contributes to reframing and reformulating sustainable approaches of the GVCs to help achieve the SDGs.

The next section introduces Bangladesh as a pivotal context for the scrutiny of societal challenges in GVCs and the attainment of the SDGs. Tauhid's sustainability approach in GVCs (Figure 5.1) is illustrated with its three cornerstones: collaborative solutions with nongovernmental organizations (NGOs) and buyers; engagement with rural communities; and workers' empowerment. Before concluding, the chapter discusses the individual and organizational challenges Tauhid encountered to advance his sustainability agenda, as well as the societal challenges that arise in seeking to maintain business continuity.

The Bangladeshi context: a land of poverty, inequality and unsafe working conditions

As one of the least affluent countries of South Asia, a region where the share of inhabitants living with less than US$1.25 per day is the highest in the world (George et al. 2016), Bangladesh is a nation with some of the poorest of the poor. The UN Human Development Index highlights that 75.6 million Bangladeshis (49.5% of its total population) live under the multidimensional poverty bar, stressing the lack of income, inadequate schooling and limited access to potable water

(UNDP 2015). Most of its poverty is concentrated in rural areas, where the open scars of its decade-long war with Pakistan that ended in 1971 are still notable (Belal & Roberts 2010).

Numerous NGOs and civil society groups have long played an important role in the country, attempting to harness its rural communities' financial means, however, with limited results (Banerjee & Jackson 2017). The social void created by the weak government in enforcing laws and regulations (Mair, Martí, & Ventresca 2012) has contributed to a proliferation of religious extremism (BBC 2017) and the soaring power of an oligarchy of powerful families, which wield great influence on its economic and media sources (Rahim 2017).

Controversially, Bangladesh is also the second-largest manufacturing country in apparel and textile GVCs in terms of turnover, with US$28.1 billion worth of exports in 2017 (RMG Bangladesh 2017) and a labor force predominantly composed of female workers. Despite the pioneering role in apparel and textile GVCs, apparel workers receive the lowest salaries in the world, remaining vulnerable not only to rights abuses and violence but also to poor safety. The tragic 2012 Tazreen factory fire in Ashulia and the disastrous 2013 Rana Plaza collapse in Savar led to the death of more than 1,200 workers, spreading anger and concerns worldwide (Fontana & Egels-Zandén 2018; Labowitz & Baumann-Pauly 2015). As poverty and gender inequality, more specifically, can be ameliorated through employment opportunities (UN 2017c, 2017a), the strong industrial growth of Bangladesh paradoxically represents not only a source of human vulnerability but also a possible solution to improving employment conditions and life circumstances and potentially lifting workers out of poverty.

Tauhid's sustainability approach

As displayed by Figure 5.1 and presented in the following, Tauhid's sustainability approach is based on the collaborative solutions with NGOs and buyers for inclusiveness at the interorganizational level, the engagement with rural communities at the local level and workers' empowerment at the factory level.

Collaborative solutions with NGOs and buyers (interorganizational level)

Tauhid's sustainability approach has been facilitated by the establishment of long-term partnerships with (a) local NGOs and (b) buyers to create inclusiveness (SDGs #1 and #5). This has been possible by participating in poverty and women empowerment-focused initiatives, such as Social and Economic Transformation of the Ultra-poor (SETU). Organized by CARE Bangladesh, a local NGO, and supported by KiK Textilien und Non-Food GmbH (KiK), a buyer from Germany, SETU has worked with some 45,000 extremely poor households to lift them out of poverty (Rahman & Bari 2014).

(a) NGO collaborations for inclusiveness

NGOs in GVCs have a highly relevant role in ensuring the advancement of the sustainable development agenda (Lund-Thomsen & Nadvi 2010). Tauhid's regular interface with NGOs allows him to select the benefits needed by the workers and locate the most economically vulnerable individuals. Since the outset of CPH in 2008, Tauhid joined CARE Bangladesh's SETU to identify and provide these individuals compensation and training (Rahman & Bari 2014). Their collaboration helped the local women, with CARE Bangladesh "supporting CHP to employ them and to meet KiK's orders" (CARE Bangladesh 2014, 2). As acknowledged by Tauhid,

> CARE Bangladesh helped us find out extreme poor people who do not have their own land, who live or cultivate other people's land, who do not have enough food around the year or three meals a day. These are the extreme poor people or ultra-poor people. As [a] company, we do not know who are they. CARE Bangladesh helped us find them out.

CPH and CARE Bangladesh's collaboration is possible thanks to frequent meetings, steadily increasing wages and improving working conditions. As part of SETU, CHP also provides health counseling, promoting exercises and stretching to promote the workers' physical well-being (Rahman & Bari 2014). Kolpona Begum, 42, an ultra-poor female worker identified by CARE Bangladesh and employed as a mat operator at CHP through SETU, disclosed that her earnings can now support her family and the educational expenses of her two children (*The Daily Star* 2013). These projects were reported by CARE Bangladesh (2014, 6):

> Twenty-five women initially went through a six month training on rug-making aligned to KiK's European customer's specifications and were paid a monthly stipend. Three production units were set up with 25 women workers in each. By December 2008, CHP established five village rug units employing 12 poor women. Gradually increasing demand for rugs helped CHP expand and create more employment[. . . .] Though in a relatively small scale, the model has had a remarkable impact on women empowerment in one of the most poverty stricken and remote areas of Bangladesh.

(b) Buyer collaboration for inclusiveness

Most scholarly work on working conditions in GVCs has focused on buyers and local suppliers' cooperation (Fontana & Egels-Zandén 2018; Lund-Thomsen & Lindgreen 2014). Tauhid's partnership with KiK not only guaranteed orders in difficult economic times but also helped spawn various social projects, including SETU. As pinpointed by Tauhid,

> I have to acknowledge that KiK has been really, really helpful. They helped me initiate a social project [SETU], growing from 90 people to become what

we are now[. . . .] They told me, "whatever they make, they can sell to us" [. . .] And KiK is giving back part of the profit to the community, not to CHP, as their corporate social responsibility.

The collaborative work of CHP with KiK was acknowledged by Patrick Zahn, KiK's chairman of the executive board, during a speech for the official opening of a new school financed by KiK in Rangpur, northern Bangladesh (2018):

> Helping to strengthen the underprivileged areas was the main impetus for KiK's engagement in Rangpur. Our commitment dates back to 2008, when we revived a traditional carpet making technique. Cotton waste from the textiles factories are delivered to Rangpur and made into various kinds of rugs. This project particularly supports families from the region by creating secure jobs close to home. Especially women are given the opportunity to support their families through this work [. . .]. We are proud of our supplier, Mr. Md. Tauhid Bin Abdus Salam.

Engagement with rural communities (local level)

With the support of NGOs and buyers, Tauhid aims to advance SDGs #1, #5 and #8 by (a) facilitating community inclusiveness, (b) eradicating discrimination and (c) ensuring humanitarian support and balanced development at the local level.

(a) Community inclusiveness

Tauhid reaches out to those at the fringe of Bangladeshi society, decentralizing CHP units next to remote rural communities, particularly in the Nilphamari and Rangpur Districts. Establishing a firm next to remote rural communities fosters their social cohesion, mitigating the negative implications of migration on their well-being (Welford & Frost 2006). Obiron Nesa, 52, a female doormat operator, explained that finding employment at CPH prompted her to push for collective change in the community (*The Daily Star* 2013):

> I have not only lifted myself and my family out of extreme poverty. Now I lead 25 other poor women in the village working in the doormat factory, which is a perfect model for eradicating poverty not only at Balapukur village but also in the district.

(b) Eradicating discrimination

Human inclusion can be facilitated by providing any woman or man with access to the labor market. Tauhid's effort to curb human marginalization occurs by systematically contacting and recruiting physically impaired individuals, who are the most vulnerable to both poverty and unequal treatment (Trani & Loeb 2012). Likewise,

Tauhid seeks to create the inclusion of sex workers in these projects. In line with Tauhid's experience:

> Our male supervisors were very anxious. "Sir, what will people say?" I said, no, you are not supposed to know they were sex workers. We appointed a supervisor who had no idea about their background. And that was key to our success. If you let others know who they were, there will be prejudice. People will behave differently. There is nothing written in their face[s] that they were sex workers. Our society always tries to push them back[. . . .] I was never proud of recruiting sex workers. If there is a job opportunity, it can be given to any woman.

(c) Humanitarian support and balanced development

Tauhid offers a variety of services for the community that range from not only the provision of goods (e.g., meat, rice and oil), the distribution of complimentary blankets during winter, the installation of road lamps but also the donations to educational institutions. Analogously, Tauhid ensures that its economic development does not come at the cost of its people's well-being. This requires an appraisal of social as well as environmental impacts (UN 2017b). Tauhid achieved them by using environmentally friendly products to promote a hand-made and couture production. On the other hand, he limits the vertical expansion of its buildings and the traffic going in and out CHP units. As he revealed,

> If you go to the middle of a village and you see a five-story building, many noisy trucks that break down the road, you understand that this is a heavy burden for its people. Yes, the workers are earning and they will keep their mouth shut because of their salary. But think about the disturbance you are creating.

Workers' empowerment (factory level)

By empowering workers, Tauhid aims to better their resilience and advance issues addressed in SDGs 5, 8 and 12. As shown in Figure 5.1, he attains that at the factory level by ensuring (a) gender equality, (b) meritocratic rewards and micro-incentives and (c) environmentally friendly production.

(a) Gender equality

In Bangladesh, women, in general, are the greatest victims of poverty, confined by patriarchal relationships and other social norms (Mair, Martí, & Ventresca 2012). Tauhid touts economic empowerment in GVCs by hiring and educating those women who have never been employed. He allows them to develop economic autonomy and raise their image within their own families and community. The narratives of Beauty and Ojitan, in particular, exemplify the success stories of two female workers from CHP.

Beauty, 25, used to be a housewife. She raised her nine-year-old son and six-year-old daughter on her own while her husband worked as a driver. After joining CHP, Beauty works as a weaver in rug production. Her children spend time with Beauty's mother while Beauty is at work, and she now earns more than her husband (CARE Bangladesh 2018):

> Our arms and bodies used to hurt when we first started making rugs, but now we only feel pain when we stop making them. It has become a habit[. . . .] There is less quarrelling in the house [due to her job]. I have more input into making decisions, and we are able to eat three good meals per day[. . . .] I am also saving for my children's weddings and education.

Ojitan, 40, used to be an unemployed divorcee and single mother. She lived with her parents and her daughter. In 2012, she joined CHP in the weaving section. She is now supporting her whole family. Her daughter is now studying in class nine. She has helped her parents build a new house and bought cows. She is now a role model among her co-workers and the underprivileged women of her community (Classical Handmade Products BD, 2018):

> My life was really miserable. My husband left us. He spent a lot of money on alcohol and would scream at my daughter and me when he was drunk. We did not have enough to eat so I had to spend hours working as maidservant to earn 30–50 taka [approx. US$0.5] per day. Some days there was no work so we were hungry[. . . .] I am lucky to get a job at CHP. This helped me gain confidence and continue.

(b) Meritocratic rewards and micro-incentives

Tauhid created a rewards-based system to reward the best-performing workers by donating solar panels to them. Although this has been restricted to only a few workers in the past, Tauhid is planning to deliver over 400 additional solar panels. Similarly, Tauhid also guarantees decent working conditions through the provision of multiple micro-incentives. These range from creating a friendly work environment, distributing free sanitary napkins, ensuring medical support and providing assistance to workers in urgencies.

(c) Environmentally friendly production

Tauhid avoids workers' exposure to hazardous chemicals by allowing no harmful dyes and gases. In particular, he collaborates with Kik Textilien und Non-Food GmbH (2017, 30) to reuse the cotton remnants from other textile factories and engender various kinds of products. The large presence of garment factories operating in the

Bangladeshi GVCs helps the manufacturing of many low-cost rugs, often woven with traditional handlooms and waste cloth (CARE Bangladesh 2014, 5).

Tauhid's challenges and barriers to sustainability

As displayed in Figure 5.1, Tauhid's constraints are summarized in terms of personal struggles, implementation challenges and failures.

Personal struggles

Tauhid experienced complex social tensions with other manufacturers. After he founded CHP, other factory managers started to criticize him for his sustainability practices, accusing him of unfair competition. Tauhid's life has been repeatedly threatened, obliging him to review some of his social activities and community projects:

> I was life-threatened because I was doing more. That was a very bad experience. When I started making my factory in the village, the surrounding small competitors felt threatened. This is because all of our workers have different kinds of advantages, including maternity leave, early leave and facilities. This is more than in any other factory. So, they threatened me and also urged me to not expand and to not do more than what I was already doing. [. . .] They accused me [of destroying] their business. I can do more than others, but in a different way [. . .] I have to find innovative ways to give.

Implementation challenges

Tauhid's sustainability approach still faces numerous challenges in its implementation. First, the decision to locate CHP in remote areas creates significant logistical impediments. Suppliers located near the city of Dhaka enjoy multiple advantages not available in remote communities. This has implications for Tauhid's family life and personal well-being. Second, Tauhid's reliance on environmentally friendly production processes has been an antithesis to the demands of some buyers, who favor the use of artificial techniques and continuous production shifts. The latter, typical for some fast-fashion buyers, are said to provoke stress among the workers, who are often unable to adjust to the pace of work and master new techniques on time. Last, Tauhid's sustainability approach is confronted with the cultural reality of Bangladesh. As narrated by Tauhid, this detracts from the outcomes of his work, particularly on women's empowerment:

> We had a worker with a skin mark from the chest to the neck. One day she came to me and she was very happy to let me know that she was getting married. I was really happy too. But then, she told me that she could get married because she saved 60.000 taka [approx. US $710]. When I asked why, she

told me that she had to give a dowry, because of her mark. Although she felt empowered and had earned enough money for herself, I was shocked and sad that such a young lady had to pay to get married.

Failures

Despite the success of Tauhid's sustainability approach, not all of his plans reached completion. For instance, he commenced projects on housing and potable water but with little results. As Tauhid remarked, on the contrary, these and future projects can be fostered through additional collaboration with NGOs, buyers and his own workers:

> I failed sometimes. For instance, I started a small project in the area[. . . .] I was promised false things by some people, and I lost 3 million taka [approx. US $35,640] within four months. Then it was very difficult for me to stand up, but I took the right decision and maintained the production of baskets. After one year, we recovered the losses. We struggled a lot, but, in most of the cases, we were right. I have to say that we were very lucky. The buyers, the NGOs, the workers, they all welcomed us. As we are doing good things for the ultra poor people, everybody helped us. We feel like a family. It is like a community where I say, ok, we have a problem that we need to solve. And everybody is with me when I explain that.

Conclusion

By providing a holistic understanding of Tauhid's successes and challenges associated to advancing SDGs #1, #5, #8 and #12 in northern Bangladesh, this chapter offers valuable learning material. Five takeaways for business practitioners and management educators are elicited:

- *Successful sustainability work is achievable through concerted efforts.* Tauhid's collaboration for inclusiveness with CARE Bangladesh and KiK through SETU led to two fundamental outcomes. On one hand, it accelerated and enabled his contribution to the sustainable development agenda by obtaining constant support, widening employment opportunities and lifting hundreds of women out of extreme poverty. On the other hand, it helped Tauhid build loyalty with Kik as well as its workers, reinforcing its market capabilities. GVC practitioners should always consider the relevance of establishing interorganizational relations and long-term collaborative projects. This can lead to superior results both to contribute to the SDGs, but also to consolidate one's competitive position.
- *Sustainability work is harnessed by defined and long-term objectives.* Tauhid framed his sustainability approach while channeling his resources toward a circumscribed segment of the overall population (e.g., women and, more specifically, individuals in need) and with specific objectives for it (e.g., providing access to

the labor market while ensuring better working conditions). GVC practitioners should emphasize the significance of scope in advancing the SDGs. This implies the identification of clear beneficiaries and benefits, with the purpose of avoiding overly aspirational goals.

- *Sustainability work might require multilevel action.* Tauhid's attempt to reduce social challenges for his workers was facilitated by including the surrounding people and environment at the local level. GVC practitioners should be aware that working to advance the SDGs in GVCs might require extended action at different levels. Empowering workers might be difficult without an appropriate and holistic consideration of the impacts of their social context and the surrounding environment on their well-being.
- *The success of sustainability work hinges on personal dedication and time.* By locating CHP in northern Bangladesh, Tauhid boosted his chance to advance the sustainable development agenda. This, however, also came at great operational and personal cost for him. GVC practitioners should be reminded that accomplishing the SDGs in GVCs requires long-term passion and a strong moral drive. Although it is likely to turn into an extremely fulfilling experience, it seldom bears immediate rewards.
- *Sustainability work might require negotiations and overcoming uncertainties.* Tauhid's sustainability work led to additional negotiations with some buyers, as well as distancing him from the rest of the local business community. GVC practitioners should be aware that acting differently in GVCs might carry both business (e.g., business project delays) and personal (e.g., life threats from local actors) risks. The latter is likely to be the case in those developing countries where norms of reciprocity are particularly ingrained in everyday business life. Persistence after failure and self-determination might be necessary to contribute to the SDGs and change the status quo.

Acknowledgments

The author is particularly grateful to Tauhid and the different collaborators of Classical Handmade Products BD for sharing their experiences and perspectives with him. Part of this research was conducted while the author was a post-doctoral fellow at the Centre for Social and Sustainable Innovation (CSSI), Gustavson School of Business. CSSI receives funding from Newmont Goldcorp Inc.

References

Banerjee, S. B., & Jackson, L. 2017. "Microfinance and the business of poverty reduction: Critical perspectives from rural Bangladesh." *Human Relations*, 70(1): 63–91.

BBC. 2017. *Bangladesh Country Profile.* www.bbc.com/news/world-south-asia-12650940

Belal, A. R., & Roberts, R. W. 2010. "Stakeholders' perceptions of corporate social reporting in Bangladesh." *Journal of Business Ethics*, 97(2): 311–324.

CARE Bangladesh. 2014. *Rugs to Riches: Rural Women from Bangladesh Weaving the Way to Export Markets in Europe.* www.carebangladesh.org/publication/Publication_1496293.pdf

CARE Bangladesh, 2018. *CARE Bangladesh's SETU Project: Partnering with the Private Sector to Provide Employment Opportunities for the Ultra-Poor*. Unpublished manuscript. CARE Bangladesh.

Classical Handmade Products BD, 2018. *Workers' Stories*. Unpublished manuscript, Classical Handmade Products BD.

The Daily Star. 2013. Welcoming development. *The Daily Star* (July 17). www.thedailystar.net/news/welcoming-development

The Daily Star. 2017. HSBC honours export heroes. *The Daily Star* (Nov. 19).

Fontana, E., & Egels-Zandén, N. 2018. "Non sibi, sed omnibus: Influence of supplier collective behaviour on corporate social responsibility in the Bangladeshi apparel supply chain." *Journal of Business Ethics*. http://doi.org/10.1007/s10551-018-3828-z

George, G., Howard-Grenville, J. A., Joshi, A., & Tihanyi, L. 2016. "Understanding and tackling societal grand challenges through management research." *Academy of Management Journal*, 59(6): 1880–1895.

Jamali, D., & Karam, C. M. 2016. "Corporate social responsibility in developing countries as an emerging field of study." *International Journal of Management Reviews*. http://doi.org/10.1111/ijmr.12112

KiK Textilien und Non-Food GmbH. 2017. *Sustainabilty Report 2017: Working Together for Good Conditions*. www.kik-textilien.com/unternehmen/fileadmin/user_upload_de/Kategorien/Verantwortung/Nachhaltigkeitsbericht/Nachhaltigkeitsbericht_2017_englisch.pdf

KiK Textilien und Non-Food GmbH. 2018. *Patrick Zahn's Speech for the Opening of KiK UCEP School in Rangpur*. Unpublished manuscript, Classical Handmade Products BD.

Kolk, A., Rivera-Santos, M., & Rufín, C. 2014. "Reviewing a decade of research on the 'base/bottom of the pyramid' (BOP) concept." *Business & Society*, 53(3): 338–337.

Labowitz, S., & Baumann-Pauly, D. 2015. *Beyond the Tip of the Iceberg: Bangladesh's Forgotten Apparel Workers*. New York. http://people.stern.nyu.edu/twadhwa/bangladesh/downloads/beyond_the_tip_of_the_iceberg_report.pdf

Lund-Thomsen, P., & Lindgreen, A. 2014. "Corporate social responsibility in global value chains: Where are we now and where are we going?" *Journal of Business Ethics*, 123(1): 11–22.

Lund-Thomsen, P., & Nadvi, K. 2010. "Clusters, chains and compliance: Corporate social responsibility and governance in football manufacturing in South Asia." *Journal of Business Ethics*, 93(2): 201–222.

Mair, J., Martí, I., & Ventresca, M. J. 2012. "Building inclusive markets in rural Bangladesh: How intermediaries work institutional voids." *Academy of Management Journal*, 55(4): 819–850.

Muthuri, J. N., Chapple, W., & Moon, J. 2009. "An integrated approach to implementing community participation in corporate community involvement: Lessons from Magadi Soda Company in Kenya." *Journal of Business Ethics*, 85(2): 431–444.

Rahim, M. M. 2017. "Improving social responsibility in RMG industries through a new governance approach in laws." *Journal of Business Ethics*, 143(4): 807–826.

Rahman, M. M., & Bari, M. A. 2014. *The Role of the Private Sector in Building Resilience among the Extreme Poor: A Case Study of a Collaboration between SETU Project of CARE Bangladesh and CHP BD, a Private Company*. Shiree Working Paper No. 17. www.gov.uk/dfid-research-outputs/the-role-of-the-private-sector-in-building-resilience-among-the-extreme-poor-a-case-study-of-a-collaboration-between-setu-project-of-care-bangladesh-and-chp-bd-a-private-company-shiree-working-paper-no-17

Rasche, A., Morsing, M., & Moon, J. 2017. "Corporate social responsibility: Strategy, communication and governance." In A. Rasche, M. Morsing, & J. Moon, eds., *Corporate Social*

Responsibility: Strategy, Communication and Governance. Cambridge: Cambridge University Press.
RMG Bangladesh. 2017. Readymade garment industries going green. *RMG Bangladesh*. http://rmgbd.net/readymade-garment-industries-going-green/
Trani, J. F., & Loeb, M. 2012. "Poverty and disability: A vicious cycle? Evidence from Afghanistan and Zambia." *Journal of International Development*, 24(S1): S19–S52.
UNDP. 2015. *Human Development Report*. New York. http://hdr.undp.org/sites/default/files/2015_human_development_report.pdf
United Nations. 2017a. *Goal 1: End Poverty in All Its Forms Everywhere*. www.un.org/sustainabledevelopment/poverty/
United Nations. 2017b. *Goal 12: Ensure Sustainable Consumption and Production Patterns*. www.un.org/sustainabledevelopment/sustainable-consumption-production/
United Nations. 2017c. *Goal 8: Promote Inclusive and Sustainable Economic Growth, Employment and Decent Work for All*. www.un.org/sustainabledevelopment/economic-growth/
Visser, W. 2008. "Corporate social responsibility in developing countries." In A. Crane, A. McWilliams, D. Matten, J. Moon, & D. Siegels, eds. *Oxford Handbook of Corporate Social Responsibility*. Oxford: Oxford University Press: 473–479.
Welford, R., & Frost, S. 2006. "Corporate social responsibility in Asian supply chains." *Corporate Social Responsibility and Environmental Management*, 13(3): 166–116.
World Bank. 2014. *Bangladesh Poverty Maps 2010*. Retrieved from www.worldbank.org/en/news/press-release/2014/08/27/latest-bangladesh-poverty-maps-launched
Yawar, S. A., & Seuring, S. 2017. "Management of social issues in supply chains: A literature review exploring social issues, actions and performance outcomes." *Journal of Business Ethics*, 141(3): 621–643.

6

A GOOD CUP OF COFFEE FROM ECOCAFÉ HAITI

Timothy Ewest, Kacee A. Garne and Tom Durant

Abstract

This chapter presents a case study, which describes the origins and evolution of the social venture EcoCafé Haiti, founded by co-author Tom Durant. EcoCafé Haiti is a business built around the once well-established Haitian coffee industry while simultaneously addressing local environmental and social needs. Since its inception in 2006, EcoCafé Haiti has made more than 1,000 Haitian workers and their families food secure, provided benefits of employment to over 500 farmer families, restored over 300 acres of land and employed a workforce of over 25 people. EchoCafé Haiti has also provided help to the poorest of the poor in one of the most economically challenged countries in the Western Hemisphere. EcoCafé Haiti directly addresses 5 of the 17 Sustainable Development Goals (SDGs), demonstrating that even with severe social, economic and ecological challenges, implementation of the SDGs is possible.

Haiti, a country in despair

Haiti is home to nearly 9 million people, located on the western half of the island of Hispaniola, the second-largest island in the Caribbean after Cuba. Comprising 29,418 square miles, Haiti is roughly the same size as South Carolina (*The World Fact Book* 2016). Haiti shares Hispaniola with the Dominican Republic, but the two nations are vastly different. The Dominican Republic has a gross domestic product 10 times that of Haiti and corresponding significantly higher standards of living, for example, in health and education (Lundahl 2015). At one time, Haiti was the largest coffee producer in the world and had a proud and rich culture, with a spirited tradition of independence, and a vibrant economy (Coupeau 2008).

Today, political, economic and ecological problems have crippled this once-vibrant nation. Haiti is ranked as the lowest in the Western Hemisphere regarding access to potable water and clean sanitation (World Health Organization & UNICEF 2017; Gelting et al. 2013). Haiti also has experienced significant deforestation, with a 2016 study finding only 30 percent of Haiti's land area has tree cover, down from 60 percent coverage in 1923 (Tarter 2016). The lack of forestation has led to devastating soil erosion, with an estimated 15,000 acres of topsoil being washed away each year (Blaikie 2016). Moreover, Haiti is the poorest country in the Americas and one of the poorest countries in the world. Most Haitians live on less than US$2.41 a day (The World Bank 2017). Moreover, Haiti suffers from high childhood mortality rates, where approximately 25 percent of the children die before the age of five and many other children suffer from chronic malnutrition (Hoffman 2012). The average life expectancy in Haiti is only 53 years. The average adult has only 2.8 years of education, and when coupled with high inflation and inadequate public infrastructure, it results in the absence of economic opportunity for many, if not most, Haitians (Balsari et al. 2010).

Life in Haiti is further complicated by natural disasters. The country is subject to hurricanes, severe storms and flooding for over half of the year and severe drought for the other half. On January 12, 2010, at 16:53, the myriad issues faced by Haitians were made even worse by a 7.0-magnitude earthquake, causing catastrophic destruction. An estimated 300,000 Haitians were killed while at least 1million were left homeless (Pallardy 2015). All the aforementioned conditions make Haiti a dystopia for economic development and an unlikely venue for entrepreneurial investment.

This chapter presents a case study describing the origins of the social venture, EcoCafé Haiti, founded by Tom Durant, who built a business around coffee production, which also addresses local environmental and social needs. Since its inception in 2006, EcoCafé Haiti has made more than 1,000 Haitians food secure, provided benefits of employment to more than 500 farmer families, restored more than 300 acres of land and employed a workforce of more than 25 people. In doing so, it has helped the poorest of the poor in a country, which is arguably the most challenged in terms of several socioeconomic indicators in the Western hemisphere (Balsari et al. 2010; Durant 2014). EcoCafé Haiti directly addresses five of the 17 Sustainable Development Goals (SDGs), demonstrating that even with severe social, economic and ecological challenges, the advancement and implementation of the SDGs are possible. See Table 6.1.

Yet, the next steps for EcoCafé Haiti are unclear, and the sustainability of the business model is coming into question. Despite successful harvests, EcoCafé Haiti, initially supported through in-kind donations and grants, has struggled to reach a financial break-even point in a market crowded by fair-trade coffee. For EcoCafé Haiti's founder and chief executive officer, Tom Durant, with 38 years' executive experience, Ranquitte, Haiti was specifically chosen as a place to focus his social mission because of the region's overwhelming needs, but now the sustainability of operations has come into question (Durant 2015).

TABLE 6.1

SDG Goals Addressed by EcoCafé Haiti	
1 Poverty	End poverty in all its forms everywhere
2 Hunger	End hunger, achieve food security and improved nutrition and promote sustainable agriculture
6 Water	Ensure availability and sustainable management of water and sanitation for all
8 Economy	Promote sustained, inclusive and sustainable economic growth, full and productive employment and decent work for all
15 Ecosystem	Protect, restore and promote sustainable use of terrestrial ecosystems; sustainably manage forests; combat desertification; and halt and reverse land degradation and halt biodiversity loss

The story of Madame Edgar

The plight of Haitians can be seen in the vignette of Madame Edgar who lived in Ranquitte, a rural hillside in the northern region of Haiti (Durant 2014). Her husband died in 2000, and since then, Madame Edgar has struggled to grow enough food for herself and her son, Jameson. Like most Haitian mothers, she wanted her son to have a better life than she herself has experienced. Madame Edgar wanted Jameson to complete school, to be able to read, write and be in good health. She wanted Jameson not only to be a mature, healthy grown-up and to have the opportunity to work and make an income but also to be enriched by the dignity that comes with meaningful employment. Yet, she knew that in rural Haiti, the future for most residents was in subsistence farming with no other realistic opportunity. Subsistence farming is a very challenging way to live. Each year the rains come and small farming plots, hers included, are subject to flash flooding from the steep, sparsely wooded hills surrounding the farm quickly washing away soil and plants. Unfortunately, Madame Edgar's story is representative of countless other Haitians who are simply doing their best to survive but hoping for the type of work that will build a better future for themselves and the next generation. Yet, in a country ravaged by social, economic and environmental issues, most people like Madame Edgar are only left with their dreams.

EcoCafé Haiti, good coffee

The issues that Haitians like Nazillia have to face each day are well known to the global community, making Haiti the recipient of an estimated $4 billion in international aid from 1990 to 2003 (Alesina & Dollar 2000). Even larger amounts were pledged following the 2010 earthquake. Yet, ongoing international aid projects, such as that of the United States Agency for International Development, have met with frequent failure since they have not made a lasting change and, in turn, have further eroded trust and optimism among the Haitian people (Buss 2009). Alternatively, local community-based entrepreneurs have largely remained unsuccessful because of government interference and oligopolistic market structures, which restrict entry into markets (Lundahl 2009). The only limited success has been with entrepreneurial ventures in tourism (Séraphin 2013). The result is that most Haitians, as well as many in the global community, believe the economic conditions and corresponding substandard living are permanent problems.

Durant believed that true progress could not be made if outside parties continued to try to solve the community's issues by merely offering short-term, donation-based solutions, often viewed as handouts by the locals. Nor could local entrepreneurs be expected to change Haiti's situation of having a lack of economic infrastructure and inadequate start-up capital. A locally supported and focused effort was needed (Durant 2015). Therefore, Tom Durant envisioned the possibility of a new business model that viewed Haiti's economic, ecological and societal problems as interrelated, thus requiring a holistic social venture conjoined to a long-term environmental sustainability effort (Durant 2014). To accomplish this, the EcoCafé Haiti strategic business model incorporated a three-part vision with initiatives to improve the triple-bottom-line outcomes (people, planet and profit) for the community of Ranquitte. The model included long-term coffee plant cultivation, increased food sources, environmental restoration through forestation and an additional focus on improving the societal relationships within the community (Durant 2015).

Specifically, Durant's business model vision involves building a self-sufficient organization in Ranquitte that would cultivate, process and export Haitian coffee. The business would also be committed to cultivating land to provide food for the workers (e.g., corn, beans, peanuts, leguminous trees) and restore surrounding deforested land to prevent washouts. Each component of EcoCafé Haiti's business strategy directly addressed the needs of the community in Ranquitte (EcoCafé' Haiti 2016).

Therefore, in 2006, Durant formed EcoCafé Haiti, a for-profit corporation in Haiti, and forged a partnership with Christian Flights International (CFI), a US-based 501(c) (3) nonprofit organization. The director of CFI was excited about Durant's proposal, since CFI "had just abandoned [its] agricultural initiative for lack of funds" (Booram 2015, 140). Soon after, with the help of CFI, land was secured to house the coffee-production machinery. Investors were provided the schematic of the intended production process, based on geographic location and processing requirements. (See Figure 6.1.) An initial US$50,000 was attained in start-up funding (Durant 2014). Ranquitte, a city formerly known for its coffee production, was chosen to be a place of economic, social and environmental renewal. Beginning that year, EcoCafé Haiti facilitated reforestation and terracing of the mountains above and began construction of a coffee-processing plant.

The land used for planting was owned by Ranquitte citizens, and they would retain ownership as provided for in the cooperative business agreement. Many of these landowners were infirmed or widowed and thus unable to provide for themselves. For use of their land, landowners were given food and coffee crops, with an

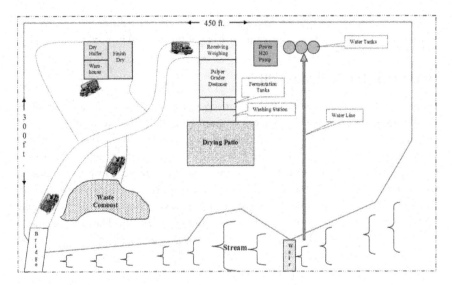

FIGURE 6.1 Layout of EchoCafe Operations Site

agreement that the landowners would return the land to a healthy state and leave reforested lands undisturbed. Landowners were also given a return on the sale of fair-trade coffee from their land. Local residents in Ranquitte who joined Durant's vision began planting coffee plants and trees around Madame Edgar's home and provided her and others quality agriculture seeds. Residents of Ranquitte who shared Madame Edgar's plight, like Nanotte, who were widows left alone to support a family, joined this cooperative business. As the business moved forward in the next few years, there were plentiful crops of corn and beans, with enough surplus to sell in the marketplace, and abundant coffee to sell (Durant 2014). By 2008, Eco Café Haiti employed 25 full-time workers who were paid "fair" wages to plant and cultivate the land with food crops, as well as *Arabica Typica* coffee plants. As the coffee crop matured, an additional 50 seasonal workers, who could harvest and process the coffee during the August–December harvest season, were employed at fair wage rates.

Today, EcoCafé Haiti has cultivated specialty coffee crops (more than 50,000 coffee plants) for export to the United States and Canada and has re-terraced and reforested more than 200 acres of land (Durant 2015). EcoCafé Haiti continued to employ approximately 25 individuals full-time and works with more than 500 farmers who are all now paid above "fair trade" prices for their *Arabica Typica* coffee (Durant 2014). Moreover, 1,000 Haitians within the Ranquitte community have been made food secure and are no longer dependent on handouts, food scraps and marginal subsistence crop harvests. Haitian farmer families have also benefited from coffee production, receiving a modest income that allows them to purchase food, medicine, education and housing. Finally, approximately 300 acres of land have been fully restored to a healthy state with trees and crops, thus eliminating the environmental effects of runoffs, silted streams, deforestation and soil erosion.

Next steps for EcoCafé Haiti

Despite ambitious yet reasonable expectations, a high-quality product and positive on-the-ground outcomes in coffee production (Durant 2014), Eco Café Haiti faces challenges to its long-term financial sustainability because of increasing market segmentation. Initially funded through grants and donations, the company hoped to be able to depend fully on coffee sales for ongoing funding. However, despite a record harvest, initial volumes of coffee sales have not reached the break-even point, largely due to the overestimation of coffee projected sales through exports (Durant 2014, 2015). Attempts to obtain additional funding to expand Haitian operations continue, but EcoCafé Haiti finds itself at a strategic crossroads in an increasingly crowded fair-trade coffee marketplace without a reliable external source of funding (Fridell 2007; Jaffee 2014; Trends in the Trade of Certified Coffees 2011).

Initially, the fair-trade coffee concept was a means to ensure that coffee farmers in third-world countries, such as Haiti, would be justly compensated as workers and assured working conditions and the preservation of property rights (Walton 2010). While fair trade as a concept can be seen tacitly in early history, the modern concept of fair trade emerged in the 1940s, with movements such as Ten Thousand Villages. Founded by Edna Ruth Byler, Ten Thousand Villages was based on Mennonite values of compassion, service, mutual aid and peacemaking. Byler led a group of people to fund a company, which endeavored to connect individual entrepreneurs with North American markets (Wolfer & del Pilar 2008). The group became more fully formed in the 1960s but did not focus on commodities such as coffee. The fair-trade coffee industry is generally believed to have begun in 1988 when numerous products were identified as having global market potential, including coffee, which soon after was offered globally (Haight 2011),

From 1990 to the present day, fair trade as a concept was embraced globally, and fair-trade coffee imports grew. In 1990, global imports of fair-trade coffee were at 74,131 pounds, and this number has steadily increased to 126,110 pounds. In the United States alone, fair-trade coffee imports in 1990 were 21,007 pounds and remained relatively stable through 2017, a year in which 29,491 pounds of imported fair-trade coffee were reported (International Coffee Organization 2018). While fair-trade coffee imports in the United States remained stable, global imports of fair-trade coffee have grown substantially. (See Table 6.2) Yet, the demand for fair-trade coffee has caused that market to become crowded; competition negatively affected sales, and the market became highly segmented. The fair-trade market is now driven by profit models, which seek to increase their scale of production as a means to produce the same fair-trade-certified coffee, at a greatly reduced cost (Mutandwa et al. 2009).

As global demand has increased for Fairtrade coffee, Raynolds (2009) suggests the market has segmented into three distinct categories. The first is producers, which

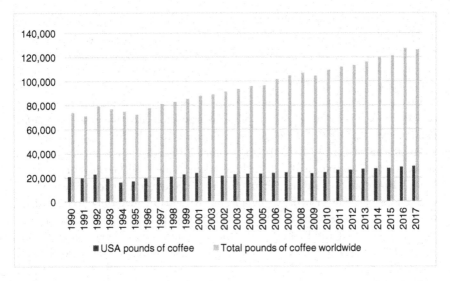

FIGURE 6.2 Imports of fair-trade coffee
Source: International Coffee Organization.

are "mission driven" who endeavor to produce Fairtrade coffee but adhere to a social mission. This is the business model adopted by EcoCafé Haiti. The second is "quality driven," where producers focus on developing excellent coffee and, correspondingly, demand a high price, honoring fair-trade agreements but forsaking additional social or environmental commitments. Finally, there are "market-driven" organizations, which pursue commercial/industrial conventions and compete on quantity and price. The market-driven competitive segment is responsible for both creating surplus in the market, as well as driving down fair-trade coffee prices. With such a diverse group of competitors, there is increasingly a wide range of goals, strategies and tactics regarding fair trade, as many of the new entrants who are market-driven do not share the same ideological motivation as the incumbent competitors (Jaffee 2014).

EcoCafé Haiti, a mission-driven organization that considers both profitability and social and environmental values that go beyond the aforementioned globally accepted fair-trade principles in its strategic decisions, is thus placed at a competitive disadvantage, since a larger missional scope can add to cost. Moreover, as a cooperative organization, strategic decision-making has involved disseminating decisions among all members, again creating additional challenges. Levi and Linton's (2003) research identifies EcoCafé Haiti's plight, noting that many small-scale fair-trade coffee organizations do increase the living standards for those who are employed or are part of the cooperative, but collectively, they are only able to sell about half of their crops at market price. However, these problems are well known in the fair-trade market. Research by De Pelsmacker, Driesen, and Rayp (2005) surveyed 808 Belgians, who were asked their willingness to pay for fair-trade products. Their research found that only 10 percent of the sample was willing to pay the price premium of a 27 percent mark-up, which is generally representative of fair-trade coffee prices.

One possible solution is recognizing how market segmentation is representative of a Fairtrade coffee company's inability to reposition itself regarding its market (Mutandwa et al. 2009). There are lessons learned from the Rwandan market that faced similar challenges. In 2008, for example, Rwanda predominantly exported coffee to the European market, namely, Sweden, Switzerland, Germany, France, the United Kingdom and Russia. From 2005 to 2008, the market for coffee experienced a 287 percent growth worldwide, but Rwandan coffee only accounted for 0.69 percent of these markets, making the Rwandan market a fitting representative for the conditions faced by EcoCafé in the fair-trade market. Thus, understanding the predicament of the Rwandan coffee market may provide insight into how to position EcoCafé.

To better understand how Rwandan coffee fared in the international market, Mutandwa et al. (2009) used the Boston Consulting Group (BCG) matrix to categorize markets where coffee was imported as a means to determine which markets would have the greatest market share and which was expected to experience the highest market growth. More specifically, the BCG matrix places markets into four categories based on their potential for market growth and market share.

The BCG matrix, initially developed in 1968, has experienced continuous use for the last 50 years because of its ability to help companies understand how their products are positioned within various markets. To accomplish this, organizational strategists are initially asked if their product has a high or low share of the market and correspondingly if their product is experiencing a high or low market growth rate. The evaluation of products by market share and market growth places the organizations in one of four quadrants: (1) "Question Marks," for products that experience high market growth but low market share; (2) "Stars," for products that experience high market share and high market growth; (3) "Dogs," for products that experience low market growth and low market share; and (4) "Cash Cows," for products that experience high market growth and low market share (Morrison & Wensley 1991). (See Table 6.3.)

The designated market position also has a corresponding strategic consideration. The BCG matrix suggests that Dog markets should divest or liquidate those markets; Cash Cow markets are ones where there should be further product development or diversification; Stars represent markets where strategic decisions should be committed to market penetration, product development or horizontal integration. Finally, Question Marks also involve product development and market penetration but, additionally, with a possible commitment to divestiture. When Mutandwa et al. positioned Rwandan coffee into segments, recommendations emerged regarding which countries could be divested in (reduced) and which countries should be

TABLE 6.3

Boston Consulting Group (BCG) Matrix Categories

BCG Category I	Market Share/Growth Position	Recommendation
Question Marks	Low market share and high market growth	The opportunities no one knows what to do with. These opportunities need serious thought as to whether increased investment is warranted.
Dogs	Low market share and low market growth	Market presence is weak, and it is difficult to make a profit.
Stars	High market share and high market growth	These represent fantastic opportunities.
Cash Cows	High market share and low market growth	The market is not growing and opportunities are limited.

Source: Stern and Deimler (2012).

TABLE 6.4 Imports of coffee by selected countries in thousand 60-kg bags

	May 2017	May 2018	% change
Total	11,049	11,317	2.4%
European Union	6 906	7 046	2.0%
Japan	671	714	6.4%
Norway	76	55	−27.2%
Russian Federation	462	480	4.0%
Switzerland	263	298	13.4%
Tunisia	28	40	42.8%
USA	2,643	2,683	1.5%

Source: International Coffee Organization.

scaled in production (increased). The result using the BCG matrix and identifying the proper market places was an increase in total sales for Rwandan coffee.

When this same methodology is applied to EcoCafé Haiti, which sells coffee primarily to the United States and secondarily to Canadian markets, other market considerations emerge. For example, when using the BCG matrix, fair-trade coffee imports from May 2017 to May 2018 show that some coffee import countries have negative growth and low market share (e.g., Norway), while others have high market share and high market growth (e.g., Switzerland and Japan). The United States has low market growth and high market share. The selected countries are determined by the International Coffee Organization and aligned with the matrix possibilities as a means to determine which markets present the best possibilities for EcoCafé Haiti and which markets should be divested (decreased). (See Table 6.4.)

TABLE 6.5 BCG Matrix for Fair Trade Coffee

	Growth – Share Matrix	
High Market Growth **Low**	**Question Marks** Have low market share and high market growth Country: • Tunisia	**Stars** Have high market share and high market growth. Countries: • Switzerland • Japan
	Dogs Have low market share and low market growth. Country: • Norway	**Cash Cows** Have high market share and low market growth. Countries: • European Union • USA • Russian Federation
	Low-----------------Market Share-----------------High	

When EcoCafé Haiti places its coffee within the various global markets, two markets have both high market growth and high market share and therefore should be scaled, exploited or expanded. In this light, serious consideration should be given to repositioning EcoCafé Haiti's coffee, divesting in the American market and expanding investment in Switzerland and Japan, along with a limited investment in Tunisia. (See Table 6.5.) Yet, even with the added insight of the BCG matrix, the certainty for EcoCafé in the future is still unclear and so, correspondingly, is the ability to sustain operations.

Conclusion

This chapter presents a case study describing the origins of the social venture, Eco-Café Haiti. It is a nonprofit cooperative founded by Tom Durant that built a business around the once historically established Haitian coffee and addresses the local environmental and social needs. Since its inception in 2006, EcoCafé Haiti has made more than a 1,000 Haitians food secure, provided benefits of employment to more than 500 farmer families, restored more than 300 acres of land, employed a workforce of more than 25 people and provided help to the poorest of the poor in a country arguably the most challenged in the Western Hemisphere (Balsari et al. 2010; Durant 2014). EcoCafé Haiti directly addressed 5 of the 17 SDGs (e.g., #1 Poverty, #2 Hunger, #6 Water, #8 Economy and #15 Ecosystems), thus demonstrating that even with severe social, economic and ecological challenges,

TABLE 6.6 SDG Goals Addressed by EcoCafé Haiti

SDG Goals		EcoCafé Haiti
1 **Poverty**	End poverty in all its forms everywhere.	Lifted 1000+ out of poverty
2 **Hunger**	End hunger, achieve food security and improved nutrition and promote sustainable agriculture.	1,000 Haitians food secure
6 **Water**	Ensure availability and sustainable management of water and sanitation for all.	Potable water
8 **Economy**	Promote sustained, inclusive and sustainable economic growth, full and productive employment and decent work for all.	Employment to more than 500 farmer families
15 **Ecosystem**	Protect, restore and promote sustainable use of terrestrial ecosystems, sustainably manage forests, combat desertification and halt and reverse land degradation and halt biodiversity loss.	Restored more than 300 acres of land

implementation of the SDGs is possible. (See Table 6.6.) Recently, however, it has experienced market growth and segmentation.

While uncertainty exists in the Fairtrade coffee market, the successful precedent set by the Rwandan coffee market represents a real need to reposition EcoCafé Haiti's fair-trade coffee exports into new markets, which potentially could provide better revenues. The ability of EcoCafé Haiti to meet the comprehensive and real day-to-day needs of Haitian stakeholders requires the development of a viable, sustainable business model if EcoCafé Haiti is to survive.

What is certain is that EcoCafé Haiti is not just helping "Haitians" but also changing the lives of individuals and their families such as Nanotte and Madame Edgar. Missional organizations, such as EcoCafé have made holistic and significant impacts. For EcoCafé the goals of reforestation, full-time employment, clean water, preservation of the ecology and movement of individuals out of poverty were a reality. The changes experienced by these individuals are due to the specific targeting of the SDG goals (see Table 6.6) and demonstrate the real-world impact organizations can have on creating a better world. However, the existence and impact of organizations that strategically take into account people, planet and profit are under the same uncertainties and challenges of market forces and financial sustainability as any other market-dependent organization. Therefore, the financial sustainability of EcoCafé Haiti, unfortunately, remains in question.

References

Alesina, A., & Dollar, D. 2000. "Who gives foreign aid to whom and why?" *Journal of Economic Growth*, 5(1): 33–63.

Balsari, S., Lemery, J., Williams, T. P., & Nelson, B. D. 2010. "Protecting the children of Haiti." *New England Journal of Medicine*, 362(9): e25.

Blaikie, P. 2016. *The Political Economy of Soil Erosion in Developing Countries*. New York, NY: Routledge.

Booram, B. 2015. *Starting Something New: Spiritual Direction for Your God-Given Dream*. Downers Grove, IL: Intervarsity Press.

Buss, T. F. 2009. *Haiti in The Balance: Why Foreign Aid Has Failed and What We Can Do About It*. Brookings Institution Press.

Coupeau, S. 2008. *The History of Haiti*. Greenwood Publishing Group.

De Pelsmacker, P., Driesen, L., & Rayp, G. 2005. "Do consumers care about ethics? Willingness to pay for fair-trade coffee." *Journal of Consumer Affairs*, 39(2): 363–385.

Durant, T. 2014. *Resourcing Proposal: EcoCafé Haiti, S.A.* Unpublished. Accessed 20 Oct. 2015.

Durant, T. 2015. *A Good Cup of Coffee for a Good Cause: Sustainable Enterprise Development for the Island Nation of Haiti*. Unpublished. Accessed 20 Oct. 2015.

EcoCafe' Haiti. 2016. Accessed 20 Jan. 2016. www.ecocafehaiti.com

Fridell, G. 2007. *Fairtrade Coffee: The Prospects and Pitfalls of Market-Driven Social Justice*, Vol. 28. University of Toronto Press.

Gelting, R., Bliss, K., Patrick, M., Lockhart, G., & Handzel, T. 2013. "Water, sanitation and Hygiene in Haiti: Past, present, and future." *The American Journal of Tropical Medicine and Hygiene*, 89(4): 665–670.

Haight, C. 2011. "The problem with fair trade coffee." *Stanford Social Innovation Review*, 3: 74–79.

Hoffman, D. M. 2012. "Saving children, saving Haiti? Child vulnerability and narratives of the nation." *Childhood*, 19(2): 155–168.

International Coffee Organization. 2018. *Historical Data on the Global Coffee Trade*. www.ico.org/new_historical.asp?section=Statistics

Jaffee, D. 2014. *Brewing Justice: Fair Trade Coffee, Sustainability, and Survival*. Berkeley: University of California Press.

Levi, M., & Linton, A. 2003. "Fair trade: A cup at a time?" *Politics & Society*, 31(3): 407–432.

Lundahl, M. 2009. "The failure of community-based entrepreneurship in Haiti." *International Journal of Innovation and Regional Development*, 2(1–2): 112–127.

Lundahl, M. 2015. *The Haitian Economy (Routledge Revivals): Man, Land and Markets*. New York, NY: Routledge.

Morrison, A., & Wensley, R. 1991. "Boxing up or boxed in? A short history of the Boston Consulting Group share/growth matrix." *Journal of Marketing Management*, 7(2): 105–129.

Mutandwa, E., Kanuma, N. T., Rusatira, E., Kwiringirimana, T., Mugenzi, P., Govere, I., & Foti, R. 2009. Analysis of coffee export marketing in Rwanda: Application of the Boston Consulting Group matrix. *African Journal of Business Management*, 3(5): 210–219.

Pallardy, R. (2015). "The Haiti earthquake of 2010." *Encyclopaedia Brittanica* (Oct. 26). Accessed 22 Jan. 2016. www.britannica.com/event/Haiti-earthquake-of-2010

Raynolds, L. T. 2009. "Mainstreaming fair trade coffee: From partnership to traceability." *World Development*, 37(6): 1083–1093.

Séraphin, H. 2013. *Entrepreneurship in Tourism as a Driver for Recovery and Sustainable Development of the Countryside in Haiti: The Guest Houses as a Strong Potential Option*. International Conference on Active Countryside Tourism, International Centre for Research in Events, Tourism and Hospitality (ICRETH), Leeds Metropolitan University. https://sites.google.com/site/activecountrysidetourism/conference-papers

Stern, C. W., & Deimler, M. S., eds. 2012. *The Boston Consulting Group on Strategy: Classic Concepts and New Perspectives*. Hoboken, NJ: John Wiley & Sons.

Tarter, A. 2016. "Haiti is covered with trees." *EnviroSociety*. www.envirosociety.org/2016/05/haiti-is-covered-with-trees

Trends in the Trade of Certified Coffees. 2011. "International trade centre." *Technical Paper*. Accessed 21 Jan. 2016. www.intracen.org/WorkArea/DownloadAsset.aspx?id=37613

Walton, A. 2010. "What is fair trade?" *Third World Quarterly*, 31(3): 431–447.

Wolfer, T. A., & del Pilar, K. 2008. "Ten Thousand Villages: Partnering with artisans to overcome poverty." *Social Work and Christianity*, 35(4): 449.

The World Bank. 2017. *The World Bank in Haiti*. www.worldbank.org/en/country/haiti/overview

The World Fact Book. 2016. Haiti: CIA. Accessed 20 Jan. 2016. www.cia.gov/library/publications/the-world-factbook/geos/ha.html

World Health Organization & UNICEF. 2017. *Progress on Drinking Water, Sanitation and Hygiene: 2017 Update and SDG Baselines*. United Nations.

PART III

Championing education and gender equality

7
M IS FOR MALALA

Laura Jackson Young

Abstract

In advanced economies around the world, children become accustomed to a similar routine. Primary school marks the beginning of a fulfilling journey as an active member of the educational system until the age of 18. It is difficult to fathom a situation in which one's access to education might be terminated abruptly. The Taliban assumed control of the Swat Valley in Pakistan in 2007 and prohibited girls from attending school. At 11 years old, Malala Yousafzai emerged as an activist fighting to ensure access to education for all girls, in particular in the Swat Valley. The Taliban attempted to silence her efforts, attacking her on the school bus at the age of 12. Malala survived and her perseverance only grew stronger as she healed. At the age of 15, she was recognized as one of *Time*'s "100 Most Influential People in the World." Later in 2014, Malala and Kailash Satyarthi won the Nobel Peace Prize for their efforts toward "the right of all children to education." Malala's story is one of courage and defiance, fueled by an ambitious child's love for learning. She advocates for gender equality in education and for ending poverty by allowing everyone to actively contribute toward their own economic advancement. These efforts make Malala a true champion working toward the United Nations Sustainable Development Goals, earning her a place among the most influential people in the modern day. Her inspirational story of becoming known simply as "Malala" marks only the beginning of her impact on the world.

End poverty. . . . .End hunger. . . . Ensure healthy lives. . . . Achieve gender equality. . . . The United Nations' inspiring list of Sustainable Development Goals (SDGs) continues. Imagine if a single initiative could serve as the catalyst for addressing each one of these goals and more. This is the vision of young activist Malala Yousafzai.

When asked in 2013 what the World Bank, and other international organizations, could be doing differently, Malala responded:

> I think that all these organizations must make education their top priority. If you educate a child, then you also help him how to protect himself from AIDS, how to protect himself from diseases. You tell him about clean water, you tell him about if you boil water, then it gets clean. So, I think education is the best solution to fight many other issues as well. Through education you can fight child labor. Through education you can fight child trafficking. Through education you can also fight poverty. So, all these problems are linked together. Poverty causes children not to go to school, but if you educate a child, in [the] future if he gets a job, then there will be no poverty. They would have opportunities in their lives. And, as well as, through education they will know about the world outside.
>
> *(Yousafzai 2013b)*

This may seem a simplistic and pragmatic narrative with regards to adversity faced by impoverished, neglected populations around the world. Yet it is just this modesty that may characterize the necessary response to such a formidable challenge. Malala faces this Herculean task, unencumbered by expectations, or doubt, that often plague the aspirations of seasoned professionals. She advocates for action with the innocent audacity of a child while simultaneously possessing a greater courage and ambition than those many years her senior.

Background on Malala's life

Malala spent her childhood in a world where female empowerment was not just arduous but also faced violent prohibition. Born in 1997 in Mingora, the largest city in the Swat Valley of Pakistan, to Ziauddin and Tok Pekai Yousafzai, Malala began her early years developing a love for learning in schools managed by her father. Ziauddin approached fatherhood more as a gardener working to cultivate an environment in which Malala could thrive rather than assume the role of oppressor, which had come to be expected in this part of the world. In Malala's own words, "[e]ducation had been a great gift for him. . . . He believed that schooling should be available for all, rich and poor, boys and girls" (Yousafzai & Lamb 2013).[1] It should come as no surprise that Malala would inherit this enthusiasm for knowledge and graciously shoulder the burden of ensuring access to education for all.

In 2007, when Malala reached the age of 10, the Taliban took control of the Swat Valley and banned girls from attending school. By the end of 2008, more than 400 schools had been destroyed. Unlike many of her peers, Malala had an insatiable appetite for learning and refused to be denied this one fundamental right to an education. Alongside her father, she actively engaged with politicians and news outlets to demand restoring the privilege of attending school for girls in the Swat Valley. Speaking on Pakistani television, Malala fervently questioned, "How dare the

Taliban take away my basic right to an education?" (Yousafzai & Lamb 2013).[2] This outspoken mission evolved in 2009 when Malala began to blog anonymously on the British Broadcasting Company website, under the pseudonym Gul akai, and share her insights on life under Taliban rule in the Swat Valley. Her first post, titled "I Am Afraid," would provide a marked premonition for how her perspective would come to evolve over the following years.

In the midst of the social and economic turmoil in the Swat Valley, Malala's voice shone through, and she was nominated in 2011 for the International Children's Peace Prize, awarded by children's rights foundation, KidsRights, for her efforts to gain access to education for all Pakistani girls. While she did not win the award that year, she gained even broader global recognition of her courageous undertaking. She would later win the award in 2013 (KidsRights Foundation n.d.) Also in 2011, the government of Pakistan awarded Malala the National Youth Peace Prize. When offered the opportunity to speak to the prime minister upon receiving the award, Malala uninhibitedly presented her demands for rebuilding schools and establishing a university for girls in the Swat Valley (Yousafzai & Lamb 2013). This fervent vow to spread awareness of the cause and remain committed to her primary mission would propel Malala to succeed when many others may have lost sight of the fundamental goals along the way (See Photo 7.1).

As the international recognition of her activism for girls' education gained momentum, Malala was shot by the Taliban on October 9, 2012. Despite efforts to silence her voice, this created an opportunity for her to come back even stronger, louder and more determined to fight for her cause.

PHOTO 7.1

Global recognition

The world watched with hopeful hearts as Malala survived the Taliban attack and emerged as one of the most powerful activists in not just her generation, but those before and those who would follow. In an interview on *CBS This Morning* in November of 2013, Malala provided a stark contrast from the girl who authored that first blog post, "I'm not scared of the Taliban at all. I might be afraid of ghosts and like dragons and those things, but I'm not afraid of the Taliban. . . . If you kill someone, it shows that you are afraid of that person. So, why shall I be afraid of someone who is afraid of me already?" (Yousafzai 2013a).

Her resilience prevailed and, from her new home in the United Kingdom, Malala continues to gain worldwide recognition for her efforts on behalf of young women. She is on the path to change the mindset of the people, and at the age of 15, she was listed as one of *Time*'s "100 Most Influential People in the World." In 2014, along with Kailash Satyarthi, Malala won the Nobel Peace Prize "for their struggle against the suppression of children and young people and for the right of all children to education."[3]

Malala was recognized, in part, for the efforts of the Malala Fund for Girls' Education, founded in 2013 in partnership with her father, Ziauddin. The fund works jointly with UNESCO and the government of Pakistan to advance educational opportunities for girls around the world. Upon receiving the award, Malala humbly expressed, "This award is not just for me. It is for those forgotten children who want education. It is for those frightened children who want peace. It is for those voiceless children who want change" (Yousafzai 2014). Malala does not forget. Malala will not be afraid. And Malala is the voice for these children.

Advocacy for the broader UN SDGs

Malala works with UNESCO and the government of Pakistan through the Malala Fund for Girls' Education. This fund allows girls the opportunity to advance their education, which creates countless opportunities for personal, community and economic growth. When speaking about the fund in her book, *I Am Malala*, she describes, "*My mission, our mission, demands that we act decisively to educate girls and empower them to change their lives and communities.*"[4] The fund's objectives focus on assisting girls and women in accessing the educational system, improving the quality of education and bolstering policies to maintain safe environments for learning (Malala Fund n.d.). As women progress toward greater scholastic achievement, they gain self-confidence and are better able to productively contribute to society.

The Principles for Responsible Management Education (PRME), a UN initiative founded in 2007, has created six guiding principles for institutions around the world to help realize the SDGs via responsible management education. The first principle (Purpose) emphasizes the task of developing "the capabilities of students to be future generators of sustainable value for business and society at large and to work for an inclusive and sustainable global economy" (PRME 2017). Inclusivity is a major component of Malala's efforts to allow all children access to the educational system. Equal opportunities for girls and boys to attend school will generate economic opportunities that vastly outweigh any potential costs of securing those institutions. In working to manage a changing landscape regarding societal values surrounding education and female empowerment, Malala has emerged as a unique and inspiring leader.

While it may seem that this is a story about education, about how this young girl has championed action toward achieving the UN's SDG #4 regarding "inclusive and equitable quality education," this is but one small component of something much larger. Access to education is tightly interwoven with ending poverty (SDG #1), achieving gender equality (SDG #5), promoting inclusive and sustainable economic growth (SDG #8), reducing inequality (SDG #10) and building peaceful, inclusive and accountable institutions (SDG #16). As Malala so aptly described in her response presented earlier regarding what international organizations need to be doing differently, making education a top priority effectively broadens the scope of developmental aid programs around the world. She easily recognized and communicated how "education is the best solution to fight many other issues as well" (Yousafzai 2013b).

A vast literature has developed on the link between economic growth and education, SDGs #8 and #4, respectively. One pioneer in this field is the recipient of the 1992 Nobel Prize in Economic Science, Gary S. Becker. Becker's research has studied how investing in human capital, via education and training, is comparable to business fixed investment in equipment (Becker 1994). It is the accumulation of this human and physical capital that provides the foundation for sustainable economic growth.

Reinforcing the importance of establishing opportunities for early education, Psacharopoulos (1981) describes how the returns to primary education outweigh those of other educational levels. Reaching children during the primary stages of brain development is essential to reap the greatest benefits. Additionally, multiple studies have drawn another parallel with physical capital in that returns to schooling seem to be higher for low- or middle-income developing countries (Psacharopoulos 1972, 1981, 1994; Psacharopoulos & Patrinos 2004). Economists often attribute diminishing marginal returns to capital. This characterizes the condition in which the gains from the further accumulation of capital are smaller when a country already enjoys a relatively abundant capital stock, reaping the rewards from productive business investment and well-trained and -equipped workers. Alternatively, countries that may be struggling with limited access to capital at the onset, can enjoy substantial gains and a much larger productivity boost should they be able to build up their capital stock overall. Thus, less developed countries with lower levels of human capital, perpetuated by reduced access to education, would benefit greatly from higher educational achievement. Providing further evidence of integration with SDG #5 and gender equality, Psacharopoulos and Patrinos (2004) also find that the empirically estimated returns to schooling may be higher for women than for men. Malala's modest intention can, and will, have an amplified impact on the standard of living for millions around the world.

Turning toward issues of inequality (SDG #10), Harmon, Oosterbeek and Walker (2003), among others, find significantly positive effects of education on an individual's career earnings. Kim and Sakamoto (2017) also study gender-specific financial returns to education and find that women have exhibited considerable progress in both educational attainment and improved labor market outcomes in recent years. Numerous UNESCO studies highlight the potential widespread benefits of enhanced educational opportunities (UNESCO 2014, 2016).[5] For example, economic stability is attainable as women become more educated and more able to actively participate in labor markets and contribute to economic growth. Investing an additional $1 in the educational system for girls, in particular, can result in $4 of earnings and health benefits for those in lower-middle-income countries and up to $10 in low-income countries (Education Commission 2016). Perhaps even more inspiring, increasing the average educational attainment by just one year can boost the growth potential of gross domestic product per capita from 2.0 percent to 2.5 percent (UNESCO 2014). In addition to quantitative gains in terms of income potential, greater access to education for girls can boost their confidence, help overcome gender discrimination, improve health outcomes, lower the occurrence of early births, encourage women to depart from situations of domestic violence and bolster support for democratic institutions (UNESCO 2014; Malala Fund 2015; Mocan & Cannonier 2012). Malala's movement may be but one of the most powerful catalysts for global economic and social transformation.

Successes of Malala's campaign

Malala has assumed responsibility for providing children, and young girls in particular, with the most powerful tools individuals can possess throughout their lives. She has already found her purpose and maintains a consistent and unwavering commitment, unwilling to accept anything less than complete success. At every opportunity, she is unafraid to remind others, especially those in power, of the importance of pursuing equal access to education around the globe. World Bank Group president Dr. Jim Yong Kim asked, "How do you get people behind you on this great movement for girls' education?" Without hesitation, Malala responded with an impressive confidence that would inspire even the greatest influencers of our time: "The first thing is I believe in the power of the voice of women. And then I believe that when we work together, that it's really easy for us to achieve our goal" (Yousafzai 2013b).

Through the Malala Fund, world leaders are held accountable for their actions, or inaction, and expected to fulfill their responsibilities in the realm of education and gender equality. The 2017 Malala Fund Education Progress Report reveals that "[e]arly indications suggest that, though 193 countries committed to the Sustainable Development Goals (SDGs), most leaders are failing to prioritize education, threatening the success of not only global education goals but also the wider sustainable development agenda" (Malala Fund 2017). Where progress has been made, even greater opportunities still exist.

Globally, we are seeing a resurgence of educational attainment among children, but girls are still denied access at a greater rate than boys, especially in impoverished nations (UNESCO 2016). This awareness has likely motivated Malala's growing web of cooperative efforts, now including a partnership with Tim Cook, chief executive officer of Apple, to increase grants to fund programs in Latin America and India to offer secondary education to thousands of girls. In parallel with governmental and international aid organizations, Apple can help expand the reach of the Malala Fund with improved technology and in-depth research on how best to implement policy changes (Apple 2018). The Malala Fund's joint initiatives with Apple and the UN exemplify the PRME Principles 4 (Research) and 5 (Partnership). As an emerging leader, Malala regularly interacts with powerful business leaders around the world to advance social responsibilities and promote valuable research into the economic stability of our current infrastructure.

Malala's sophisticated maturity is accompanied with a childlike wonder that keeps her grounded in this mission. In her book, *I Am Malala*, she remembers watching the *Wizard of Oz* while recovering in the hospital: "She (Dorothy) had to overcome a lot of obstacles to get where she was going, and I thought if you want to achieve a goal, there will be hurdles in your way, but you must continue" (Yousafzai and Lamb 2013).[6] Rather than succumb to the hatred and judgment that permeates her world view, Malala views this adversity as simply a hurdle she will undoubtedly overcome.

Challenges for Malala's initiatives

The notable success of Malala's efforts still comes with substantial obstacles that persist today. Religious extremists' and ultra-conservatives' opposition to girls in the education system continues to grow around the world. One story that has gained widespread recognition is the abduction of more than 270 schoolgirls by Boko Haram in Nigeria in 2014. Allowing these girls access to educational opportunities threatens the oppressive stronghold such extremist groups exert within their respective regions. In a case for management education, Ajao, Bozionelos and Quental (2017) discuss how issues of human rights, gender equality, governance and leadership are intertwined in the mismanagement of the Chibok tragedy and the role that multinational organizations can play in taking action to promote women's rights. Similar recommendations could be made to corporations operating near the Swat Valley. Among other things, Ajao, Bozionelos and Quental (2017) advocate for businesses to create job opportunities for youth in these areas and visibly promote local women's enterprises and opportunities to change gender stereotypes. Malala's efforts parallel this call to action and provide a strong case for decisive action, showcasing her leadership in propelling women and girls forward in both personal growth and economic advancement (See Photo 7.2).

Further violent acts have been documented in Afghanistan, where militant groups that oppose female education have committed attacks with acid or have

PHOTO 7.2

poisoned the water in the schools (Torgan 2016) and repeatedly in the Gilgit-Baltistan's Diamer district of Pakistan, where multiple girls-only schools were attacked or set on fire [Bacha 2018; United Nations General Assembly Security Council 2018]. In response to these acts of arson, Malala tweeted, "The extremists have shown what frightens them most – a girl with a book" (Yousafzai 2018). Having survived a personal attack and emerged as a strong leader, Malala continues to advocate for those without a voice and who continue to fall victim to these vicious attacks. She recognizes that the aggressors must acknowledge the power of getting an education, especially for girls who have been denied this access for generations.

A 2016 UNICEF study, "Beyond Chibok," found that around three in four child suicide bombers in Nigeria, Niger, Chad and Cameroon are girls. Furthermore, work in 2015 by the UN Organization Stabilization Mission in the Democratic Republic of the Congo found that many girls in the Congo were coaxed to join militant groups under false pretenses, having been promised the opportunity to get an education, to work or earn money. These vulnerable girls mistakenly agree to a life of extremist violence, coming from fragile and desperate conditions (MONUSCO 2015). The European Parliament's Committee on Women's Rights and Gender Equality is also working to promote its goals regarding "Radicalization and Extremism" with respect to women. These goals focus on exploring current and proposing new actions to prevent women and girls from radicalization in the first place and on identifying the role that women could play in preventing radicalization in their surrounding communities (De Leede et al. 2017). Early intervention via primary schooling could help diminish the misguided appeal of joining the terrorist cause to seek a new life in school or in the workforce.

A 2015 Brookings Report highlights further challenges that extend beyond extremist opposition, while they also discuss the manner through which school violence harms young girls. In addition to this, providing adequate protection for girls to attend school may be costly in some parts of the world. This explicit cost is accompanied by the opportunity costs related to forgone family care and housework that are often relegated to the women in families in these communities (King & Winthrop 2015). Alternatively, early marriage and teen pregnancy may prevent girls from attending school even if the opportunity were available. These social norms preclude much of the progressive work being done by the Malala Fund and others. Working to address the institutional expectations of women in societies in the developing world is, and must continue to be, at the forefront of initiatives to achieve equal access to education globally.

Following Malala's lead

The case of Malala's rise as a global icon in the campaign for equal access to education is a brilliant example in the study of leadership for managers and entrepreneurs of the future. David H. Maister, author of *True Professionalism*, introduces four criteria for leaders to successfully influence others and mobilize them to take action. These criteria address Motives, Values, Competence and Style (Maister 2006). An effective leader must communicate one's motives as being committed to the success of the group and ensure that his or her actions adhere to this mission. Malala maintains a consistent message and has exhibited remarkable resilience in her pursuit to realize the goal of gender equality for all potential students. Leaders must also lead by principle and share values with their organizational base. As demonstrated by her fervent insistence on maintaining perfect attendance at school as a child, or her pledge for the Malala Fund to work for a world where "every girl can learn and lead," Malala clearly upholds the values by which she has steadfastly lived her life (Malala Fund n.d.).

For others to follow, a leader must exhibit competence in progressing toward a shared goal, developing creative and constructive new ideas along the way. The work of the Malala Fund and its numerous partners showcases Malala's entrepreneurial spirit and aptitude for recognizing and seizing opportunities to expand her global efforts. Finally, a leader must exude a style that encourages growth and adaptation to help everyone strive to fulfill their goals. Despite repeated attempts to silence her, Malala has managed to stay resolute and devoted to her mission with honesty and integrity. She has emerged as a global leader, a champion of her purpose and a role model for both women and men.

Final reflections

Educators can be inspired by the simplicity and clarity of Malala's dream: education for all. Greater access to education, and the eventual achievement of SDG #4 of inclusive and equitable education, has the capacity to address so many of the world's issues. It is but one step in the direction of greater peace, improved health, a higher standard of living and quality of life, thus adding value to each and every individual. The economic potential for attaining SDG #8, in terms of global development and faster, sustainable growth is nearly unparalleled.

Women can be empowered by Malala's bravery. For girls around the world, working toward getting an education grants them the power of choice and rewards them with immeasurable opportunities, personally, socially and economically. When asked for words of advice for fathers with young daughters, Malala replied with wisdom from her own father, *"Do not cut their wings. And let them fly"* (Yousafzai 2013b). In 2018, Malala even returned to Pakistan for the first time since her attack to engage with government officials and young girls seeking fair and equitable schooling opportunities. Malala frequently engages with governments, educators and the media alike to foster dialog about the importance of global social responsibility, yet another guiding principle for promoting effective management education (PRME 2017).

Adopting this guidance for how we approach the structure of aid and development programs around the world could drastically improve outcomes, both in the immediate and in the long term. We should devote our time and resources to cultivating programs that allow individuals to discover the true extent of their talents and ideas. Rather than adhering to a rigid structure with inflexible expectations, we can allow for fluidity as we promote the growth of diverse ideas via a more amenable educational system. Malala has shown us the power of an alternative perspective. Having already constructed a resume that would impress even the fiercest critic, she has just begun to make her mark on the world. World leaders are still learning what it means to be *Malala*.

Notes

1 From *I Am Malala: The Girl Who Stood Up for Education and Was Shot by the Taliban* by Malala Yousafzai with Christina Lamb, copyright © 2013. Reprinted by permission of Little, Brown and Co., a subsidiary of Hachette Book Group, Inc.
2 From *I Am Malala: The Girl Who Stood Up for Education and Was Shot by the Taliban* by Malala Yousafzai with Christina Lamb, copyright © 2013. Reprinted by permission of Little, Brown and Co., a subsidiary of Hachette Book Group, Inc.
3 Mr. Satyarthi has worked closely with UNESCO and founded the Global Campaign for Education, the Global March Against Child Labor and Bachpan Bachao Andolan (Save Childhood Movement). His efforts have worked to end child slavery and preserve the rights of children to an education (Bokova 2014).
4 From *I Am Malala: The Girl Who Stood Up for Education and Was Shot by the Taliban* by Malala Yousafzai with Christina Lamb, copyright © 2013. Reprinted by permission of Little, Brown and Co., a subsidiary of Hachette Book Group, Inc.
5 See UNESCO (2014) for a comprehensive survey of the works related to the important linkages between education and sustainable development.
6 From *I Am Malala: The Girl Who Stood Up for Education and Was Shot by the Taliban* by Malala Yousafzai with Christina Lamb, copyright © 2013. Reprinted by permission of Little, Brown and Co., a subsidiary of Hachette Book Group, Inc.

References

Ajao, R., Bozionelos, N., & Quental, C. 2017. "Gender, poverty and leadership: The case of the Chibok girls." In T. K. T. A. P. M. F. Milenko Gudić, ed. *Beyond the Bottom Line: Integrating Sustainability into Business and Management Practices*. UK: Greenleaf Publishing: 131–141.
Apple. 2018. *Apple Teams with Malala Fund to Support Girls' Education*. s.l.: s.n.
Bacha, U. 2018. "12 schools burnt down overnight in Gilgit-Baltistan's Diamer district." *Dawn* (3 Aug.).
Becker, G. S. 1994. "Human capital revisited." In *Human Capital: A Theoretical and Empirical Analysis with Special Reference to Education*, 3rd ed. s.l.: The University of Chicago Press: 15–28.
Bokova, I. 2014. *Statement Made by the UNESCO Director-General, Ms Irina Bokova*. www.unesco.org/new/en/member-states/single-view/news/nobel_peace_prize_director_general_congratulates_malala_and/
De Leede, S., Haupfleisch, R., Katja, K., & Natter, M. 2017. *Radicalisation and Violent Extremism: Focus on Women: How Women become Radicalised, and How to Empower Them to Prevent Radicalisation*. s.l.: European Parliament's Committee on Women's Rights and Gender Equality.
Education Commission. 2016. *The Learning Generation: Investing in Education for a Changing World*. s.l.: s.n.
Harmon, C., Oosterbeek, H., & Walker, I. 2003. "The returns to education: Microeconomics." *Journal of Economic Surveys*, 17(2): 115–156.

KidsRights Foundation. n.d. *International Children's Peace Prize.* https://kidsrights.org/malala-yousafzai

Kim, C., & Sakamoto, A. 2017. "Women's progress for men's gain? Gender-specific changes in the return to education as measured by family standard of living, 1990 to 2009–2011." *Demography*, Oct., 54(5): 1743–1772.

King, E. M., & Winthrop, R. 2015. "Today's challenges for girls' education." *Global Economy and Development at Brookings Working Paper*, June, 90.

Maister, D. H. 2006. *Why Should I Follow You?* s.l.: s.n.

Malala Fund. 2015. *Beyond Basics, Making 12 Years of Education a Reality for Girls Globally.* s.l.: s.n.

Malala Fund. 2017. *Financing the Future: Education Progress Report.* s.l.: s.n.

Malala Fund. n.d. *About.* www.malala.org/

Mocan, N. H., & Cannonier, C. 2012. *Empowering Women Through Education: Evidence from Sierra Leone.* National Bureau of Economic Research Working Paper Series.

MONUSCO. 2015. *Invisible Survivors: Girls in Armed Groups in the Democratic Republic of Congo from 2009 to 2015.* s.l.: s.n.

PRME. 2017. *United Nations Principles of Responsible Management Education: The Six Principles.* Accessed 8 Aug. 2018. www.unprme.org/about-prme/the-six-principles.php

Psacharopoulos, G. 1972. "Rates of return to investment in education around the world." *Comparative Education Review*, 16(1): 54–67.

Psacharopoulos, G. 1981. "Returns to education: An updated international comparison." *Comparative Education*, Oct., 17: 321–341.

Psacharopoulos, G. 1994. "Returns to investment in education: A global update." *World Development*, 22(9): 1325–1343.

Psacharopoulos, G., & Patrinos, H. A. 2004. "Returns to investment in education: A further update." *Education Economics*, 12(2): 111–134.

Torgan, A. 2016. "Acid attacks, poison: What Afghan girls risk by going to school." *CNN* (17 Mar.).

UNESCO. 2014. *Sustainable Development Begins with Education: How Education Can Contribute to the Proposed Post-2015 Goals.* s.l.: s.n.

UNESCO. 2016. *Global Education Monitoring Report 2016: Education for People and Planet: Creating Sustainable Futures for All.* s.l.: s.n.

United Nations General Assembly Security Council. 2018. *Report of the Secretary-General on Children and Armed Conflict.* s.l.: s.n.

United Nations International Children's Emergency Fund (UNICEF). 2016. *Beyond Chibok.* s.l.: s.n.

Yousafzai, M. 2013a. *CBS This Morning* [Interview] (12 Nov.).

Yousafzai, M. 2013b. *"I Am Malala": A Conversation between Malala Yousafzai and World Bank Group President Jim Yong Kim* [Interview] (11 Oct.).

Yousafzai, M. 2014. *Nobel Lecture.* Oslo: The Nobel Foundation.

Yousafzai, M. 2018. *The Extremists Have Shown What Frightens Them Most: A Girl with a Book.* (3 Aug.): 10:20am. Tweet.

Yousafzai, M., & Lamb, C. 2013. *I Am Malala: The Girl Who Stood Up for Education and Was Shot by the Taliban.* New York, NY: Little, Brown, & Company.

8
ROLE OF PARTICIPATORY COMMUNITY EDUCATION IN IRELAND

Edgar Bellow

Abstract

This chapter presents the development of Longford Women's Link (LWL), an Irish center for women's empowerment, community engagement and education. Although Irish society is in transition, most recently referenced by the shift toward abortion rights at the very tail end of such ideological battles in Europe, there are extant imbalances in power and gender equity, which require a fundamental shift in the way that education is both presented to and utilized by women. The findings from LWL can extend to other global sites affected by gender imbalances in education at the adult level. Community education as praxis works especially well for female learners who have typically suffered from structural challenges and normative systems of hegemonic masculine education. The way in which community development is situated and its impact on structural norms in Ireland, under the leadership of Louise Lovett, who is the protagonist featured in this chapter, is connected to the Sustainable Development Goals and their broad application.

Introduction to the issue

Women have typically suffered from structural challenges and normative systems of hegemonic masculine education. Men have long had the privilege of controlling what we study and value in school: empirical assessments that are seen to be truths whether or not they are informed by a pro-male bias. Community education, on the other hand, is a flexible, emancipating process, which enables people to become more proactive in their own lives and to bring about change in their worlds no matter what their gender, sex or power level in the community (Adams 2016). The rise of new social justice inquiry in the latter half of the 20th century has therefore given credence to a different epistemological framework for education that challenged and deconstructed gendered relationships to knowledge and institutions. From a sociological perspective, women are often in a position in which the insistence on hierarchical rules of education serves to demonstrate power and ownership of information (Ellsworth 1989). This is because the typical power-based model of education privileges male knowledge, even if educators are female invisible power structures are upheld (Patterson et al. 2018). Women, however, may assert new types of knowledge and new value systems through community education by building social capital.

In this chapter, the establishment and ongoing development of Longford Women's Link (LWL), an Irish center for women's empowerment, community engagement and education, is presented. Although Irish society is in transition, most recently referenced by the shift toward abortion rights at the very tail end of such ideological battles in Europe, there are extant imbalances in power and gender equity, which require a fundamental shift in the way that education is both presented to, and utilized by, women. The findings from the LWL experience can extend to other global sites affected by gender imbalances in education at the adult level. Freire's (2000) pedagogy of praxis is a theory that suggests that people who are oppressed need to rise up and take an active role in engaging in change in the way that they are seen and heard in the larger community and society as a whole. This suggests that women cannot rely on government policies to reflect their interests without taking a revolutionary stance toward those governments. Women have to feel as if they have the right to demand equity and recognition. Community education as praxis works especially well for female learners who have typically suffered from structural challenges and normative systems of hegemonic masculine education (Ellsworth 1989). Revisions to traditional pedagogical structures must include methodologies focused on identifying and addressing key inequalities that prevent women from achieving their full economic potential and making possible an application of praxis that engages women in community development.

Case: community education at Longford Women's Link

The LWL framework

As AONTAS, the Irish National Adult Learning Organization, describes, in 1979 the Irish government revised its educational strategy based on long-term recommendations. Adult education organizers were tasked with the development of local responses to the provision of adult education. Although originally focused on literacy, the involvement of women in these efforts came early. The Catholic Church at this time, through community nuns, also supported the setting up of women's groups in disadvantaged communities as a response to high levels of unemployment and emigration, coupled with downgrades in public services (AONTAS 2017). At the same time, however, the Irish system has "proved remarkably resistant to transformation" (Connolly 2007, 116). Although policies have changed, embedded gender inequalities persist.

LWL is a women's center based in the rural Midlands town of Longford in County Longford, Ireland. Its vision engages women in the country in fulfilling their potential in a safe and equal society. Louise Lovett, the director of LWL, notes that LWL's services allow women to become more independent, support themselves and their children, connect with the community at large and gain an education that is both practical and interest-related. Its mandate is aimed at increasing the participation of women in Longford in the economic, social and cultural life of their community and engaging women directly in achieving their full economic and social potential. LWL's community education program offers training using what it calls the Women's Community Education model, which is woman-centered and based on women learning from, as well as with, other women (LWL 2017). It is meant to underline the achievement of equality for women across the affective, cultural, economic and political spheres of life and the transformation of the structures and systems of society that are essential for this vision to be fulfilled. The value of the contribution of each individual woman is centered on experiences that offer affirmation, recognition, dignity and leadership through learning.

The way in which community development is situated at LWL and its impact on structural norms in Ireland, under the leadership of Louise Lovett, who was interviewed for this chapter, is connected to the Sustainable Development Goals (SDGs) and their broad application to engendering change models in communities on a practical level. The SDG of gender equality (SDG #5) is tied intimately to education (SDG #4). This is because, in Ireland, there are also culturally bound social norms that differentiate the importance and power of women from that of men in this community. Gender roles are structurally bound up in both tradition and European constructs of gender, in which women are seen as socially secondary (John 2015). When women are isolated from power, Lovett states, they are subjected to gender role expectations that do not allow them to become either socially, physically, politically or economically in control of their own fates. As unpaid family workers, women are, therefore, both undervalued and invisible and subject to power dynamics that put their lives, and the lives of their children, at risk (Fleming et al. 2015; Namy et al. 2017). When gender roles such as protection or nurturing become aligned with actions, ideas or consequences that are repeated over time, then these become set in stone as normative values, Lovett states. Women's agency is therefore a key factor in ensuring that the SDGs are successfully applied in practice.

A focus on systemic participatory action at LWL relies heavily on a framework created, in part, by AONTAS. The focal point of AONTAS's structure is what the organization calls "the group." The group is both the supportive context for learning and the learning environment itself. Knowledge and experience are processes rather than outcomes of participation. In order for education to take place, therefore, the group must facilitate the development of relationships and trust, Lovett states. No matter what the subject area, this framework supports the development of ancillary skills such as social interaction, teamwork and communications, which are central to praxis. To this end, Lovett has shown herself to be a driving force for change, in that she always makes herself available to make a difference in the lives of others. Education is the cornerstone of her belief system: Lovett understands that in order for the community to move forward, people must have the opportunity to learn as much as possible. LWL supports this imperative through outreach and education focused on Women's Studies as a pathway to praxis.

LWL educational applications

Offering courses of study in history, literature, sociology, psychology, philosophy and politics, LWL develops access points to new understandings of feminism so that its members can develop new and more profound contexts for gender relations and of women's historical and contemporary experiences. By focusing an educational lens on power relationships, women can more concretely position personal experiences within the broader Irish normative structure. It is about recognizing the potential within every person that drives Lovett to reach her goal of bringing agency to the forefront of education. True agency is, for her, a moral undertaking and a response to human needs as they are expressed in human values.

Two LWL students were interviewed to understand the ways in which LWL has come to have an impact on their lives. Mary and Erin (both pseudonyms) have been a part of LWL's Gateway program training initiative for over a year. Mary is a 46-year-old mother of four children under the age of 12 who was widowed three years ago and who was unable to support herself. Erin is 53 and a homemaker who was caring for her elderly parents and disabled husband and needed support to move in a positive direction. Both women took part in a placement program that allowed them to gain skills for working outside of the home. Mary was able to get both financial and organizational support for her child care, and Erin was able to get residential care for her parents as well as home health support for her husband while she participated in the program. As LWL teacher Deandra Coll notes, this allowed both women the physical freedom that they needed to commit to their education. Mary explains that she was able to take on a two-thirds time job that still allowed her to be home when her children were finished school as a result of the program, and this did not affect her benefits but, rather, allowed the family to become more self-sufficient. Erin has been able to find full-time work as a result of this program and has shifted into higher gear over the last year, being awarded a promotion in a public care agency role that has built on her caregiving skills but allowed her to provide for her family financially. The group process, note both women participants, has allowed them to feel empowered to make changes that remain in place over the long term because of the social support it provides.

Economic programming also ensures that LWL extends women's personal freedoms and allows them increased agency, namely, their access to economic, social and educational resources from which they are able to choose and decide on their own and from which they can engage in social, political and economic activity in their local and national communities, as Lovett states. LWL's Gateway program provides training modules in employment-centered activities, combined with facilitated work experience. These include skills in job seeking, IT, customer relations, personal presentation and interviewing, as well as an understanding of rights in the workplace. With respect to community development, AONTAS, in its support of LWL, notes that LWL has become the primary campaigner for the rights of women in County Longford. As Coll explains, there is a positive impact on women understanding the role both that they have to play in their own futures and that of the community at large. Their education and the support of their agency therefore become paramount to their ability to make an impact on their local and national communities.

Analysis of the LWL community education framework

At AONTAS, community education has emerged as a response to nurturing the community and working against the hopelessness that can occur when development is stalled. As Zuber-Skerritt and Teare (2013) write, a key objective of community development is the empowerment of individuals at the local level to seek to have the needs of their communities met rather than passively accepting whatever is thrust on them by those with other interests. Participatory and educational development, conceptualized in the notion of praxis, is therefore meant to be a response to traditional growth and learning efforts that can lead to social justice. It takes into account cathexis, which is the division of labor, the structure of power and the structure of gendered social relations (Siemerling 2007), as well as action, research and decision-making processes at the grassroots level. As Kirst-Ashman and Hull, Jr. (2014) note, participatory development is meant to be a bottom-up approach, created to support poor and marginal social groups through their full participation in development efforts that directly affect their lives. This process enhances the sustainability of a development project in that the local community can build its own vested interest into the project's success, making possible rising incomes and increasing quality of life.

This is why the LWL framework seems to be so inherently effective in helping women reach their economic potential. Those without education generally have smaller businesses, more narrow streams of income, less cash flow altogether, lower literacy levels, fewer skills to be marketed and significantly more time constraints (Kabeer 2005). Agency in education can lead to specific outcomes, which extend outside the framework of praxis itself (Minkler & Wallerstein 2011). LWL overtly notes that the caring roles of women must be acknowledged as essential in holding the fabric of society together. Building connections between women through education will therefore lead to their sharing this education with their children, either directly or indirectly, which can have long-reaching effects on community health. Transformative learning is the process by which we transform our present mind-sets and ways of thinking (frames of reference) to make them more inclusive, reflective and open to change (Ellsworth 1989). This leads to empowerment and change for the typical LWL learner, based on the ability to question or critically reflect on ourselves and our society.

Successes at LWL

Over the last year, 162 women have partaken in LWL's Gateway courses, which is an increase of more than 10 times from its inaugural year more than 20 years ago. A majority (53 percent) has secured some form of employment as a direct result of the course. These jobs have included a range of employment outcomes, from self-employment to bridge to postsecondary education to working in local community roles in both the private and public sectors. LWL allows women the personal freedom to participate in economic programming by arranging access to child care services, currently serving 86 of the women in the program. This supplement makes it possible for women to attend training at the Link, or at an external venue.

Early on, notes Lovett, the graduates from their programs could be counted, on one hand; it is only in the last 10 years that the numbers have increased to what they are today. The reason that this is the case is predictive: Lovett and her team have not forced growth on the community but, rather, have expanded as the organization has found its place. The Gateway courses have been in place from the start, but LWL is now able to offer a broader support system for women that is not necessarily captured in their communication materials because it is so specific to the women who join them every year. As more women gain access to the workplace, the balance of power will shift, Lovett expects, which will change the way in which the community manages its own needs, and this, in turn, shapes the way that she and her team create programming mandates every year. As a whole, increased access to mechanisms, which create bridges to financial security, will help alleviate structural inequality in the long run, Lovett's aim is to help individuals prosper and thereby to help their families and increase the tax base through which government services provide education and training for the community. In addition, understanding that caring work, namely, the provision of caregiving and emotional work to her family and extended social circle, is central to a woman's life in this particular social context. What LWL is able to achieve, suggests LWL teacher Coll, is bridging the gap between self-belief and life choices and achievements so that women can create structured goals and objectives that integrate their lives inside and outside of the home with confidence.

What can be drawn from the LWL experience, and its links to the SDGs, is that community education needs to move toward creating the kinds of learning spaces and providing the kinds of content and learning opportunities that will enable groups of people facing oppression and discrimination to identify what would be really useful knowledge for them. In this way, they will understand their situation and take action to change it. This may be a time-consuming process, however, that requires skills such as openness, trust building, relationships, empathy and reflective practice, as Lovett explains. Although civil society provides an outlet for women's groups such as LWL to address such issues in the long term, swift changes in social structures can have a deleterious effect on the ability of women and communities to respond, as Lovett suggests.

Efforts to shift the status quo within the context of the SDGs, and of SDG #5 in particular, have been inordinately affected by a lack of attention to the stories and values of women, with, instead, a focus on empirical models for change (Razavi 2016). When women try to liberate themselves from this social structure, the literature suggests that they will face significant social, economic and personal repercussions. Men may deliberately hold women to more stringent traditional gender norms and thereby trigger women's emotional dysfunction when they try to achieve a goal outside of the home (Fleming et al. 2015). These social norms can also be reinforced by women themselves because they have been required to become complicit in their enforcement. Patriarchal norms are violently entrenched in women's lives (Fleming et al. 2015; Levanon & Grusky 2016). Women who are endemically poor are even more likely to face these challenges, but the reality is that this social structure is something that all women face even if they are extremely skilled, well educated and comparatively successful (Bennett-Alexander & Hartman 2015; Levanon & Grusky 2016).

To this end, Lovett suggests that listening needs to become the cornerstone of social work in community development education in both research and field application. For educators such as Lovett to have a definitive impact on the lives of their clients and on the community as a whole, they must be able to understand how and why individuals are affected by their own conceptualization of oppression and social inequity. Only by taking their own viewpoints of their social relationships and the structural context into consideration, which can only be accomplished through listening and believing their stories, may community education initiatives such as LWL be able to truly make a difference in helping those who are sometimes not able to help themselves. This is something that is not easily taught and understood, and yet, according to Lovett, it is something in which LWL excels.

Conclusion

Community educational praxis means looking beyond the individual and toward the community as a whole, whereby the needs of the many are idealized above the needs of the person. Community education, as exemplified by LWL, therefore has emerged as a response to nurturing the community, and working against the hopelessness that can occur when development is stalled. Nevertheless, it also has to be connected to shifting discourse towards the power of the learner over the power of the educator. From an educational perspective, the aim of praxis requires the opinions and values of learners. When students are disempowered through structural inequities because they live in rural areas, endemic poverty or traditional cultures, traditional education models may not be able to promote community development. Such situations make decision-making ineffective. Power dynamics are significant in considering viewpoints on access to resources. This is because even under the stress of having different economic powers, the oppressed are forced to work within social constructs, which situate them at the bottom of the social strata from very early on in their lives. The LWL example serves to show that we have long known that women have typically suffered more from structural challenges and normative systems of hegemonic masculine education in the past, which is difficult to unpack. But there is a need to shift the way in which we look at making substantive changes so that our methods reflect the need for equity.

The experiences of the LWL model suggest that those interested in fostering SDG #4 (Quality education), incorporate an experiential and learner-centered approach in their work. LWL teaches us is that this is best combined with a teacher or facilitator modeling praxis rather than rote learning. It can be concluded that the LWL model of community education as praxis can work especially well for female learners in transition. The aim is to be able to engage women at risk or in transition in a substantive rather than a superficial way. Addressing the issue of oppression provides some key learning for educators, in that it teaches the necessity of operating not only on a logical level when dealing with challenges linked to oppression but also on the level of intuition and intrinsic understanding of the human condition, something often missing within policy applications. Although the impact of the SDGs work on gender (SDG #5) has created a better situation for some women than that of the past, this mandate can be modified within each learning context. Challenging the cynics, as well, who state that things cannot change is often a losing battle, as Lovett explains. Oppressed individuals may not have the skills or social networks they need to create trusting relationships with others and therefore become part of the mainstream power structure. This is why Lovett approaches the work in the way that she does.

Women subjugated within their own lives, therefore, may very well be limited in their human rights and, specifically, in their access to information through education, as Lovett explains. Within unequal power systems, women are constructed to be undereducated because without knowledge of the world and of their rights, they are unable to fight against their oppressors over the long term. A great deal more empathy and collective will are necessary to ensure that women are provided with the support that they need to be recognized and for the barriers to women's economic freedom to be taken down. If, within the current social context, women are directly prevented from participating in public policy development, obtaining the education that they need or want or even deciding what they want to do as a career, then the argument goes beyond that of community development and toward equity and human rights.

The LWL experience, therefore, illustrates just how broad and endemic inequities are for women and why community education is such a profoundly needed aim for sustainable development. Its efforts are grounded in a holistic approach to knowing and believing in women. Women's experience of and participation in gender norms, whether grounded in religious, rights-based or political discourse may be a primary component of women coming to terms with their own legal and rights consciousness, which means that they themselves have to be a part of the conversation, as evidenced by the success of LWL. Grassroots programs such as LWL are able to be successful because it cut through the noise of structured, top-down educational frameworks that only serve to continue to build on the status quo. As noted earlier, this is because of the fact that listening needs to become the cornerstone of social work in community development education so that women are able to become full participants in, rather than subjects of, educational processes. In this way, women can begin to live lives that parallel those of men rather than lives that are constrained by power dynamics that continue to privilege others.

Bibliography

Adams, M. 2016. "Pedagogical foundations for social justice education." *Teaching for Diversity and Social Justice*, 27: 118–121.
AONTAS. 2017. *Organizational Website*. www.aontas.com
Barker, G. 2016. "Male violence or patriarchal violence? Global trends in men and violence." *Sexualidad, Salud y Sociedade (Rio de Janeiro)*, 22: 316–330.
Bennett-Alexander, D., & Hartman, L. P. 2015. *Employment Law for Business*, 8th ed. New York: McGraw Hill.
Connolly, B. 2007. "Beyond the third way: New challenges for critical adult and community education." B. Connolly, T. Fleming, D. McCormack, & A. Ryan, *Radical Learning for Liberation*, 2: 107–130.
Cornwall, A., & Rivas, A. M. 2015. "From 'gender equality and women's empowerment' to global justice': Reclaiming a transformative agenda for gender and development." *Third World Quarterly*, 36(2): 396–415.
Ellsworth, E. 1989. "Why doesn't this feel empowering? Working through the repressive myths of critical pedagogy." *Harvard Educational Review*, 59(3): 297–325.
Fleming, P. J., Gruskin, S., Rojo, F., & Dworkin, S. L. 2015. "Men's violence against women and men are inter-related: Recommendations for simultaneous intervention." *Social Science & Medicine*, (146): 249–256.
Freire, P. 2000. *Pedagogy of the Oppressed: 30th Anniversary Edition*. Bloomsbury Academic.
John, S. 2015. "Idle no more-indigenous activism and feminism." *Theory in Action*, 8(4): 38.
Kabeer, N. 2005. "Gender equality and women's empowerment: A critical analysis of the third millennium development goal 1." *Gender & Development*, 13(1): 13–24.
Kirst-Ashman, K. K., & Hull, G. H., Jr. 2014. *Brooks/Cole Empowerment Series: Generalist Practice with Organizations and Communities*. Cengage Learning.
Levanon, A., & Grusky, D. B. 2016. "The persistence of extreme gender segregation in the twenty-first century." *American Journal of Sociology*, 122(2): 573–619.
Longford Women's Link. 2017. *Organizational Website*. www.longfordwomenslink.org
Minkler, M., & Wallerstein, N., eds. 2011. *Community-Based Participatory Research for Health: From Process to Outcomes*. Hoboken, NJ: John Wiley & Sons.
Namy, S., Carlson, C., O'Hara, K., Nakuti, J., Bukuluki, P., Lwanyaaga, J., Namakula, S., Nanyunja, B., Wainberg, M. L., Nakera, D., & Michau, L. 2017. "Towards a feminist understanding of intersecting violence against women and children in the family." *Social Science & Medicine*, 184: 40–48.
Patterson, K. L., Ranahan, M., Silverman, R. M., & Nochajski, T. H. 2018. "Community development through participatory, engaged, and critical analysis." In *Community Development and Public Administration Theory: Promoting Democratic Principles to Improve Communities*. Routledge Research in Public Administration and Public Policy.

Razavi, S. 2016. "The 2030 Agenda: Challenges of implementation to attain gender equality and women's rights." *Gender & Development*, 24(1): 25–41.

Siemerling, W. 2007. "Ethics as re/cognition in the novels of Marie-Celie Agnant: Oral knowledge, cognitive change, and social justice." *University of Toronto Quarterly*, 76(3): 838–860.

Wong, Y. L. 2004. "Knowing through discomfort: A mindfulness-based critical social work pedagogy." *Critical Social Work*, 5(1).

Zuber-Skerritt, O., & Teare, R., eds. 2013. *Lifelong Action Learning for Community Development: Learning and Development for a Better World.* Springer Science & Business Media.

9
MEN AS GENDER ALLIES
Verizon's Craig Silliman and Walmart's Alan Bryan

Paola Cecchi-Dimeglio

Abstract

Gender (in)equality concerns both women and men and has a strong impact on their daily lives. Working toward gender equality means setting a long-term agenda that requires a change in attitudes and behaviors by both men and women. This chapter highlights how managers and organizations can enhance the participation of men in gender-parity initiatives.

Introduction

Women constitute 50.8 percent of the US population, yet many firms cannot close the gender gap, including that in leadership roles. Women compose 46.0 percent of the overall workforce and 59.0 percent of the college-educated, entry-level workforce but hold only 5.2 percent of chief executive officer positions and 20.2 percent of director seats at Fortune 500 corporations (McKinsey & Company 2015, 2017). Only 14.6 percent of executive officers are women, and only 8.1 percent are top earners (Catalyst 2018). In the United States, women are underrepresented at the mid- and senior levels and are less likely to advance (McKinsey & Company 2017).

The promotion gap is a root cause of this disparity. Women are 1.4 times more likely to receive critical subjective feedback (as opposed to positive or critical objective feedback; Cecchi-Dimeglio 2017). They often are criticized for the same attributes for which men are praised, and they receive vaguer feedback (Correll & Simard 2016). Differences in rewards between men and women are said to be 14 times larger than differences in their performance levels, further sustaining the promotion gap (Joshi et al. 2015).

At the current pace, it might take multiple generations before organizations reflect gender parity in upper management (LeanIn, McKinsey & Company 2016).

These trends are morally troubling and stand in contrast to the economic and other benefits that gender equality offers to society and organizations.

Gender parity can add US$28 trillion to the global economy. Firms with more female directors have greater returns and reduced corporate fraud (Post & Byron 2015). A workforce as diverse as its customers can better understand and anticipate customer needs, enable customized solutions and services, personalize advice and information, communicate and interact authentically, develop deeper connections and engage more meaningfully with customers (Noland et al. 2016).

Diverse teams consistently outperform homogeneous teams and produce stronger business outcomes (Cecchi-Dimeglio 2018; Rock, Halvorson, & Grey 2016, Apesteguia, Azmat & Iriberri 2012). Employees who are valued and included and who can "be themselves" are more engaged, motivated and productive (Dobbin, Kalev, & Kelly 2006). Co-workers who understand and respect differences collaborate more effectively and with less conflict (Ely & Thomas 2001).

Given these benefits, thoughtful leaders want to know how to accelerate this transformation and build a more diverse leadership. The impediment lies in the practice of using "women-only" approaches to close the gender gap. This approach disregards the untapped resource of men as gender allies.

This chapter employs the qualitative lenses of the empirical approach. Case studies of two men – Craig Silliman (General Counsel [GC] at Verizon Inc.), and Alan Bryan (Senior Associate GC at Walmart) – serve as springboards to understanding how men can contribute in closing the gender gap within their organization and beyond (Mills et al. 2010). These two men were selected because of their well-documented records, broad recognition in the areas of gender equality and diversity within their organizations and beyond and their accessibility, track records and personal commitment to actively pursuing diversity within their legal departments, organizations and beyond. To build these cases, semistructured interviews, phone calls, written questionnaires with open-ended questions and publicly available documents and speeches were used.

This chapter examines some of the male leaders' personal and professional motives for engaging in this cause and explores mechanisms that foster a larger participation by men in closing the gender gap. These findings also furnish insight into how male GCs can foster gender equality. The case studies and their findings supply lessons applicable beyond Verizon and Walmart. They offer practical contributions and implications for pursuing diversity in the legal profession and in organizations.

Literature review

The role of men as agents of change

Despite the fact that organizations work to improve gender parity, gender inequality remains omnipresent. Even among companies that have implemented programs to attract, develop and retain women and create an inclusive leadership, gaps in hiring, promotion and retention persist. The difficulty may reside in the underutilization of men as allies.

Change initiatives require the mobilization of the workforce (Lines & Selart 2013). Participation reduces employees' resistance. It enhances their commitment and improves the quality of enacted change (Lines 2004; Wanberg & Banas 2000). Mobilizing women and men to participate in these initiatives prevents marginalization of gender inequality as a "women's issue" (Joshi et al. 2015; Klaus 2016).

This approach is in line with the strategy developed by the Sustainable Development Goals (SDGs) set by the UN Development Programme. The SDGs are a collection of 17 global goals and are the blueprint to achieve a better and more sustainable future for all. Especially relevant to this chapter are the SDG #5 (Gender equality) aimed at leveling the playing field for women and SGD #16 (Peace, justice and strong institutions) focused on developing effective, accountable and transparent institutions for all.

The strategy of mobilizing women and men underlies movements such as Lean in Together and campaigns such as "HeForShe" launched by the United Nations (Wikipedia 2015, Grant 2014). Participation by men can be as important as that of women. Bringing men into diversity conversations is paramount to creating equality in business leadership (Prime & Moss-Racusin 2009).

Advocacy by majority-group members generates more positive attitudes than advocacy by minority group members (Czopp et al. 2006). Men are essential to advancing workplace leadership opportunities for women. Their participation and support can be critical for the success of such initiatives (Klaus 2016). Men have decision and implementation roles. Their participation is often crucial for the success of gender-parity programs.

When men remain outside, their ideas cannot be leveraged to improve gender parity. They become less likely to promote the implementation of those initiatives (Hideg, Michela, & Ferris 2011). Once engaged, men can illuminate and contextualize gender issues so that other men do not see gender equality as a zero-sum game that disadvantages them. Men's voices and efforts help men understand the benefits of gender equality, including improved health and higher marital satisfaction (Flood 2015)

The role of lawyers as agents of change

The influence of lawyers in new areas of business practice – including gender, diversity and leadership development – is inevitable. Lawyers can serve as mediators of the social order, helping to achieve the bargained-for (traded), principled (reasoned) and creative (problem-solved) arrangements that permit peaceful coexistence, social harmony and social justice.

In this role, lawyers need knowledge and skills beyond the legal framework. They must embrace opportunities to expand their influence beyond strict legal compliance and into new areas (Cecchi-Dimeglio & Kamminga 2014). For instance, in couching their responses, chief executives look to their GC to guide them in becoming active corporate citizens. While this is particularly true in the United States, multinationals in Europe, including Nestlé, Shell and BT, are also at the forefront of UN Global Compact obligations, seeking to support the rule of law in emerging markets as well as diversity and inclusion more broadly (SenGupta 2017). There is a noticeable trend that has been observed in recent years, where GCs and in-house corporate legal departments have increasingly used their power to influence diversity and leadership development, both within their own team and with their outside partners, such as suppliers and external law firms (Cecchi-Dimeglio 2015).

Why Craig Silliman at Verizon and Alan Bryant at Walmart?

Craig Silliman is Executive Vice President – Public Policy and GC, responsible for leading the public policy, legal, regulatory, government affairs and security groups at Verizon Wireless. Prior to that, Silliman served in a number of other senior management roles at Verizon, including as a senior vice president for public policy and government affairs and as a senior vice president and GC for Verizon's wireline consumer. Prior to joining Verizon in 1997, Silliman was an attorney in Washington, D.C., and taught international telecommunications regulation as an adjunct professor. Silliman has been the recipient of various awards. He received the 2018 "Employer of Choice Award," which honors outstanding law departments that are leading the charge in change and helping diverse attorneys break through the concrete ceiling from the Minority Corporate Counsel Association (MCCA). In addition, in 2017, he was given the "Leadership in the Promotion of Diversity" award from the Law and Education Empowerment Project. Silliman speaks out about gender and diversity issues, such as during his keynote address in 2017 at the Symposium on Design Equality in the legal profession held at Harvard Law School.

Verizon Wireless is a wireless communications company that connects people and businesses with some of the most advanced technology and services. It is the nation's largest wireless company and has more than 140,000 employees. Verizon serves 98.9 million retail connections and operates more than 1,900 retail locations in the United States. Globally, it offers voice and data services in more than 200 destinations. Women are 30.0 percent of Verizon Wireless senior leadership, 33.0 percent of its corporate directors, 43.0 percent of managers and executives and 50.0 percent of employees earning promotions to the manager level and above (*Working Mother* 2018).

Alan Bryan is currently Senior Associate GC for Legal Operations and Outside Counsel Management at Walmart Stores. Prior to managing the company's outside counsel, Bryan managed litigation for the nation's largest retailer in many of its approximately 5,000 Walmart stores and Sam's Clubs across the United States. Before joining Walmart in 2011, he was a partner with Arkansas's largest law firm. He has been the recipient of various awards including the 2016 "Lead by Example Award" from the National Association of Women Lawyers. This award recognizes a leading male attorney in a law firm, company, government agency or public interest entity who supports the advancement of women within his organization. Bryan is also an outspoken leader who speaks openly about his conviction and his engagement such as during the award night organized by Miss JD in 2017, where he was the recipient of The Incredible Men Initiative.

Walmart is an American multinational retail corporation that operates a chain of hypermarkets, discount department stores and grocery stores. It is the world's largest company by revenue – approximately US$486 billion according to the Fortune Global 500 list in 2017. It is the largest private employer in the world, with 2.3 million employees. At Walmart, women make up 31.0 percent of all corporate officers, 25.0 percent of the board of directors, 36.0 percent of managers and executives, 44.0 percent of promotions to the manager level and above and 49.0 percent of the top earners (*Working Mother* 2018).

Findings

A personal motivation informed by their own experience

For men to support gender initiatives within their organizations or beyond, they must accept that there is problematic gender bias in the workplace. This prerequisite led to an exploration of the factors that influence men's awareness of gender bias and their view of such inequality as an issue that warrants attention.

The findings reveal personal factors that motivate men's engagement. From their wives, daughters, mothers, sisters and friends, men hear about the barriers women face in the workplace (Farre 2011; Warner & Steel 1999). Understanding how these inequalities affect people in their lives represents an important motivating factor.

Verizon's Silliman recalled:

> My wife is my primary motivation. I saw how hard she had to work to balance everything when we began having children, and the choices she had to make. Ultimately, I think she is very happy with her choices, but I think her employers lost out on her experience when she dropped out of the corporate workforce and started her own business.

Bryan of Walmart mentioned:

> For me, personal motivation to be involved with gender diversity issues began with the women in my life, from my mother and grandmothers in the past to my wife and daughter today, along with many others in between. [. . .] living a belief of equality is simply how I was raised. I have a long-held egalitarian belief regarding people, no matter background or circumstance. I live this belief daily to the best of my ability.

Overall, both men recounted multiple reinforcing experiences as triggers for their evolving understanding and activism.

The persuasive rationales for diversity

Beyond personal motivation, the men in this study elaborated on the reasons why they champion diversity. Men must have a commitment to fairness – a personal conviction that bias is wrong and that equality is ideal and essential. Silliman notes: "Diversity isn't just some politically correct concept, a liberal agenda item, the right thing to do. Diversity is important because it strengthens our companies, our organizations, and our society."

These leaders also shared the arguments they use to persuade others internally and externally. Four types of reasons for diversity dominated their reasoning. The first three are "business-case" arguments: (1) to better reach diverse customer bases, (2) to fill talent needs and (3) to achieve greater diversity of thought and innovation. To explain the first argument, they noted that a global company needs to be diverse to appeal to its global customers and relate to its non-U.S.-based employees. Verizon's Silliman mentioned:

> We may believe that we are considering all aspects of an issue, but if everyone involved in the debate approaches the issue from the same perspective, we run the risk of thinking we have considered all options when in reality we are just operating in an echo chamber.
>
> It therefore is vital that our legal department and our outside counsel include individuals with diverse backgrounds, life experiences, and perspectives. Without that diversity, we can't produce the best and most complete legal guidance to our clients. Less gender diversity and inclusion therefore equals less diversity of thought, and that results in worse decision-making and business outcomes.

Bryan at Walmart noted:

> [D]iversity and inclusion are embedded in our culture, so we would practice it with or without having a strategic reason. But, there certainly are strategic benefits to a diverse workforce in my opinion. At Walmart, . . . our customers are of all different races, ethnicities, genders, orientations, situations, backgrounds, and beliefs. Walmart wants to serve a broad customer base.
>
> To do so, we seek diversity within our company and among our suppliers. . . . Beyond the sale of goods and services, without diverse perspectives we cannot remain relevant in a rapidly changing world. An inclusive workplace that supports the success of all its associates and reflects the diversity of our customers produces better results and is the foundation for business excellence.

The second business-case argument proposes that hiring women and other underrepresented minorities would help employers find talent for difficult-to-fill technical positions. A lack of talent puts companies in an undeniably compromising position. It slows them down when technical positions are not filled and innovation lags. To solve these problems, companies have to think of more creative ways to seek hard-to-find talent. For instance, companies need to think outside the box and not only look to universities as natural go-to talent pools for recruiting. Instead of focusing only on a specific college degree or past job experience, job descriptions should consider the candidate's skill set and willingness to learn. Firms should look for other ways to qualify individuals: If an applicant does not have a (specific) degree, can he or she take a short exam to test for the requisite skills? Is this candidate self-taught in a particular skill? Looking at the applicant pool more creatively can bring in more talent and include women and other underrepresented minorities.

The third business justification for investing in diversity is that diversity of thought associated with a diverse workforce leads to greater innovation which global companies rely on for competitive advantage.

The fourth reason for supporting diversity is the moral imperative to act fairly to all people. Silliman notes,

> Our purpose-driven culture gives everyone at Verizon a seat at the table to ideate and work together to solve the world's biggest challenges. Our company makes an important commitment to drastically improve the percentage of women and people of color in leadership roles and continue to support our diverse supplier community by awarding more subcontracting work to diverse businesses. . . . My goal as a GC is for the diversity of Verizon's legal and public policy team to mirror the diversity in the country as a whole.

Beyond the four reasons noted above, another argument used to combat gender bias points to the costs to women, men and organizations, with respect to leadership. Silliman and Bryant recognize that the core responsibility of leadership is managing and motivating people. Understanding the benefit of gender balance has become fundamental. Leaders with competency in managing gender issues have an advantage. Silliman states that

> a workforce that does not have men and women evenly represented is likely not to have all perspectives and personality types evenly represented . . . and results in worse decision-making and business outcomes. . . . The strength of an organization comes from bringing together a diverse set of ideas and approaches to find the best one for any given situation. This is leadership. And a diverse set of ideas comes from a team with a diverse set of experiences and backgrounds. So diversity isn't just a nice thing to have; it is essential for an organization's success.

Bryan adds:

> Beyond personal commitment, however, I believe that finding diverse opinions leads to greater success. Seeking to include perspectives beyond those

to which I personally relate, I have achieved greater success in my endeavors, both at Walmart and personally. Among other things, this practice guides my personal leadership philosophy.... As a practical matter, men must be part of this conversation. The case for men in leadership and influential positions to listen and act is clearly there. However, one does not necessarily need to lead a firm or legal department to make a difference. Leadership does not require title in this arena. Men at all levels of organizations and the profession can support this cause.

Changing the status quo by being outspoken and accountable

Men can play a special role, and contribute to, gender parity and diversity in organizations. In fact, if men hold most of the powerful positions in the corporate world, they can bring that power and authority to affect change. Research demonstrates that men, compared to women, are seen as more legitimate and credible when they confront sexist behavior and gender inequalities. This is, in part, because, as members of the out-group, they are seen as acting in the absence of self-interest (Drury 2013). Furthermore, having successful males as champions of diversity is an important milestone or threshold crossed as they often form the privileged inner circles of power that seek to perpetuate themselves. Research also finds that male allies allow others to challenge other discriminatory behavior and practices directed at minority groups (Swim & Thomas 2006).

Male supporters emphasize that talking to other men is critical for changing the status quo and see it as part of their leadership responsibility. They are driven by the cause – not ulterior motives, such as career advancement or public recognition. They truly believe the system is both unfair and capable of change. Some of their talk is private and some public; some raises awareness, and some encourages action. Silliman notes,

> Leveraging diversity to strengthen our society isn't just the responsibility of political leaders. We all must do our part in our individual roles through our everyday actions, large and small, to harness the potential of diversity to create more successful outcomes. I can't imagine being able to do the work we do without the incredible depth of talent, experience and intelligence of all of our legal team, male and female. So, it is hard to imagine a world in which half of this talent isn't available to us.

Bryan states,

> To continue making a difference, I always state that men must listen and observe, but importantly, they must also act. Men must make sure women receive fair credit for ideas and successes, they must not condone disparaging treatment through silence, laughter, or any other affirmation that overt bias is tolerable under any circumstance, and they must work against gender stereo-

types. They must react by educating themselves on the value of diversity and inclusion. They must foster honest dialogue. They must be mentors to and of women. They must hold themselves and others accountable for an inclusive workplace.

What gets measured gets done and fosters accountability. These male leaders referenced the importance of establishing metrics and measuring the progress of diversity efforts – from examining the gender and racial/ethnic composition of their workforce to establishing metrics to diversify internship programs, interviews, new hires, promotions and the composition of project teams as well as their supplier. Bryan explained that Walmart tracks the diversity of its partners on three levels: in the aggregate diversity of staff within the law firm, in the diversity of individual team members working on matters tied to Walmart and in the diversity of ownership in the company's legal partners. Gathering these data allow the Walmart legal team to see both where it can support diverse initiatives and where it needs to push its legal services suppliers to improve. "There are times when you may have diversity within a firm, and you may have diverse attorneys, but they're not advancing in the way they should. They're not getting the credit they should, and sometimes it requires a conversation," Bryan said.

Silliman underscores how metrics, accountability and measurement create ripples of change throughout organizations. He notes,

> Verizon is extremely supportive of diversity (and initiatives to improve diversity). Part of the calculation of annual bonuses for the entire company is based on meeting certain diversity metrics each year. . . . I think that one of the reasons we are having success in-house at Verizon is that our diversity numbers are very solid (about 40.0 percent of lawyers are women and almost 30.0 percent are people of color).

Lessons derived

Gender parity is an important challenge. Despite acknowledging that men's participation is essential to these initiatives, there has been little work in the academic literature on how to improve their participation. This research highlights how managers and organizations can enhance men's participation in gender-parity initiatives by affirming their sense of psychological standing on such initiatives. These case studies yield applicable lessons for enhancing that participation and is relevant for business and management overall.

First, men's family and personal stories tend to make them more aware of women's experiences in two key areas: (1) discrimination, harassment or more subtle biases in the workplace and (2) dilemmas related to work–life conflicts. Second, there are persuasive rationales for diversity that can be used with potential allies and advocates, including economic arguments. Third, encouraging men to change the status quo by being outspoken and creating accountable mechanisms has been proved effective.

Furthermore, SDG #5 and SDG #16 goals will be more quickly achieved if men support the strategy to advance workplace leadership opportunities for women in managerial positions and to ensure responsive, inclusive, participatory and representative decision-making at all levels in institutions.

The chapter provides applied perspectives as to how this information can be used to engage men as gender allies. It suggests creating organizational levers that trigger this engagement. Influencers within the organization can appeal to men using reasons and anecdotes that resonate. Work toward gender equality is a long-term agenda that requires a change in attitudes and behaviors by men and women. The benefits of broader equality – economic, social and legal – are a driving force behind these changes. Men and women change when they realize the opportunity and efficiency inherent in flexible gender roles.

Additional insights from the studies indicate that messages about gender and behavioral change are most effective when emphasizing the positive outcomes for men and their partners. It is important to have men talk to other men about gender issues. Identifying role models who have an influence on men and boys – peers, mothers, fathers, grandparents, community members and celebrities – is a good strategy for sending positive messages. Creating comfortable environments in which to engage men is important. Both men and women need their own spaces to discuss what can be intimate and difficult issues.

Bibliography

Apesteguia, J., Azmat, G., & Iriberri, N. 2012. "The impact of gender composition on team performance and decision making: Evidence from the field." *Management Science*, 58(1): 78–93.

Bertrand, M., & Duflo, E. 2016. *Field Experiments on Discrimination*. NBER Working Papers 22014, National Bureau of Economic Research, Inc.

Catalyst. 2018. *Women CEOs of the S&P 500*. New York: Catalyst. Accessed 1 June 2018. www.catalyst.org/knowledge/women-sp-500-companies

Cecchi-Dimeglio, P. 2015. "Legal education and gender equality." In P. M. Flynn, K. Haynes, & M. A. Kilgour, eds. *Integrating Gender Equality into Business and Management Education*, PRME Initiative. Sheffield, UK: Greenleaf Publishing.

Cecchi-Dimeglio, P. 2017. "How gender bias corrupts performance reviews, and what to do about it." *Harvard Business Review* [online]. Accessed 11 July 2018. https://hbr.org/2017/04/how-gender-bias-corrupts-performance-reviews-and-what-to-do-about-it

Cecchi-Dimeglio, P. 2018. "Making small changes to have big impact on gender diversity." *Forum Magazine*, Thomson Reuters, 19–23.

Cecchi-Dimeglio, P., & Kamminga, P. 2014. "The changes in legal infrastructure: Empirical analysis of the status and dynamics influencing the development of innovative practice." *Journal of the Legal Profession*, 38(2): 191–230.

Correll, S., & Simard, C. 2016. "Vague feedback is holding women back." *Harvard Business Review* [online]. Accessed 11 July 2018. https://hbr.org/2017/04/how-gender-bias-corrupts-performance-reviews-and-what-to-do-about-it

Czopp, A. M., & Monteith, M. J. 2003. "Confronting prejudice (literally): Reactions to confrontations of racial and gender bias." *Personality and Social Psychology Bulletin*, 29(4): 532–544.

Czopp, A. M., Monteith, M. J. and Mark, A. Y. 2006. "Standing Up for a Change: Reducing Bias Through Interpersonal Confrontation." *Journal of Personality and Social Psychology* 90(5): 784–803.

Dobbin, F., Kalev, A., & Kelly, E. 2006. "Best practices or best guesses? Assessing the efficacy of corporate affirmative action and diversity policies." *American Sociological Review*, 71(4): 589–617.

Drury, B. 2013. *Confronting for the Greater Good: Are Confrontations that Address the Broad Benefits of Prejudice Reduction Taken Seriously?* Doctoral Dissertation, Seattle, WA: University of Washington. Unpublished.

Ely, R., & Thomas, D. A. 2001. "Cultural diversity at work: The effects of diversity perspectives on work group processes and outcomes." *Administrative Science Quarterly*, 46(2): 229–273.

Farre, L. 2011. "The role of men in gender equality." *World Development Report 2012* [online]. https://pdfs.semanticscholar.org/92f5/d497cbf840f4244c35846cc76c5b71555848.pdf

Flood, M. 2015. "Men and gender equality." In M. G. Flood & R. Howson, eds. *Engaging Men in Building Gender Equality*. Newcastle upon Tyne: Cambridge Scholars Publishing: 1–31.

George, A. L., & Bennett, A. 2005. *Case Studies and Theory Development in the Social Science*. Cambridge: MIT Press.

Grant, A. M. 2014. "Why so many men don't stand up for their female colleagues." *Atlantic* (29 Apr.). www.theatlantic.com/ business/archive/2014/04/why-men-dont-stand-up-for-women-to-lead/361231/

Hideg, I., Michela, J. L., & Ferris, D. L. 2011. "Overcoming negative reactions of nonbeneficiaries to employment equity: The effect of participation in policy formulation." *Journal of Applied Psychology*, 96(2): 363–376.

Joshi, A., Neely, B., Emrich, C., Griffiths, D., & George, G. 2015. "Gender research in AMJ: An overview of five decades of empirical research and calls to action." *Academy of Management Journal*, 58(5): 1459–1475.

Kinsey & Company. 2017. "Women in the workplace." *McKinsey Quarterly*. Accessed 1 Sept. 2018. https://womenintheworkplace.com

Klaus, P. 2016. "Sisterhood is not enough: Why workplace equality needs men, too." *New York Times*. Accessed 1 June 2018. www.nytimes.com/2016/08/14/jobs/sisterhood-is-not-enough-why-workplace-equality-needs-men-too.html?_r_0

LeanIn, McKinsey & Company. 2016. *Women in the Workplace*. McKinsey & Company. Accessed 10 Mar. 2018. https://womenintheworkplace.com/Women_in_the_Workplace_2016.pdf

Lines, R. 2004. "Influence of participation in strategic change: Resistance, organizational commitment and change goal achievement." *Journal of Change Management*, 4(3): 193–215.

Lines, R., & Selart, M. 2013. "Participation and organizational commitment during change." In H. S. Leonard, R. Lewis, A. M. Freedman, & J. Passmore, eds. *The Wiley-Blackwell Handbook of the Psychology of Leadership, Change, and Organizational Development*. Oxford, UK: John Wiley & Sons: 289–311.

McKinsey & Company. 2015. "A CEO's guide to gender equality." *McKinsey Quarterly*. Accesssed 1 June 2018. www.mckinsey.com/insights/leading_in_the_21st_century/a_ceos_guide_to_gender_equality.

Mills, A. J., Durepos, G., & Wiebe, E. 2010. *Encyclopedia of Case Study Research*. London: Sage.

Noland, M., Moran, T., and Kotschwar, B.R. 2016. "Is Gender Diversity Profitable? Evidence from a Global Survey." *Working Paper Series* (WP 16-3), February. Washington, DC: Peterson Institute for International Economics.

Post, C., & Byron, K. 2015. "Women on boards and firm financial performance: A meta-analysis." *Academy of Management Journal*, 58(5): 1546–1571.

Prime, J., & Moss-Racusin, C. A. 2009. "Engaging men in gender initiatives: What change agents need to know." *Catalyst*. Accessed 1 June 2018. www.catalyst.org/system/files/Engaging_Men_In_Gender_Initiatives_What_Change_Agents_Need_To_Know.pdf

Rock, D., Halvorson, H. G., & Grey, J. 2016. "Diverse teams feel less comfortable and that's why they perform better." *Harvard Business Review*. Accessed 11 July 2018. https://hbr.org/2016/09/diverse-teams-feel-less-comfortable-and-thats-why-they-perform-better

SenGupta, R. 2017. "The multiple roles a modern in-house lawyer must play." *Financial Times* (20 June). Accessed 1 July 2018. www.ft.com/content/1a2adb76-503f-11e7-a1f2-db19572361bb

Swim, J. K., & Thomas, M. A. 2006. "Responding to everyday discrimination: A synthesis of research on goal-directed, self-regulatory coping behaviors." In S. Levin & C. Van Laar, eds. *Stigma and Group Inequality: Social Psychological Perspectives*. Abingdon: Taylor & Francis Group.

Wanberg, C. R., & Banas, J. T. 2000. "Predictors and outcomes of openness to changes in a reorganizing workplace." *Journal of Applied Psychology*, 85(1): 132–142.

Warner, R. L., & Steel, B. 1999. "Child rearing as a mechanism for social change: The relationship of child gender to parents' commitment to gender equity." *Gender and Society*, 13: 503–517.

Wikipedia, 2015. HeForShe. *Wikipedia, Free Encyclopedia*. [online]. Available at, https://en.wikipedia.org/wiki/HeForShe. [Accessed June 1, 2018].

Working Mother. (2018). *Best Companies*. Accessed 10 Sept. 2018. www.workingmother.com/best-companies-verizon

PART IV

Partnerships and programs that foster sustainable development

10

CHAMPIONS OF SUSTAINABLE DEVELOPMENT

The university for the common good and Grameen Caledonian College of Nursing in Bangladesh

Alec Wersun

Abstract

In January 2016, the United Nations launched its 2030 Agenda for Sustainable Development. Sustainable development is defined as "development that meets the needs of the present without compromising the ability of future generations to meet their own needs" (World Commission on Environment and Development 1987). The 2030 Agenda calls for countries to mobilize efforts to achieve 17 sustainable development goals (SDGs) to end all forms of poverty, fight inequalities and tackle climate change while leaving no one behind. The interrelated nature of the 17 SDGs recognizes that ending poverty must go hand in hand with strategies that build economic growth and it addresses a range of social needs including education, health, social protection and job opportunities. This case tells the story of how "Sustainability Champions" from Scotland and Bangladesh joined forces to establish the Grameen Caledonian College of Nursing (GCCN) as a social business "For the Common Good" and to contribute to the realization of this ambitious agenda. The case illustrates how the vision, unwavering belief and entrepreneurial spirit of these Champions, working in the spirit of SDG #17 (Partnerships for SDGs) have led to GCCN contributing to the achievement of SDG #1 (Poverty), SDG #3 (Health and well-being), SDG #4 (Quality education) and SDG #5 (Gender equality), as well as their predecessor, the Millennium Development Goals.

Introduction

In 2002, whilst working on AIDS prevention in India, Professor Pamela Gilles found a well-used, tattered copy of Professor Muhammad Yunus's moving and inspiring memoir, *Banker to the Poor*, in the office of a women's community development program in the Sonagachi District of Calcutta. This book outlines how the Grameen

Bank's model of microcredit lending to small groups of poor women helped them to create small microcredit enterprises, setting them free from loan sharks and crippling debt (Grameen Research, Inc.).

The origin of Grameen Bank can be traced back to 1976 when Professor Yunus, head of the Rural Economics Program at the University of Chittagong, launched an action research project to provide banking services targeted at the rural poor. The bank's model of microcredit lending was designed to reverse the vicious circle of 'low income, low saving & low investment', into a virtuous circle of 'low income, injection of credit, investment, more income, more savings, more investment, more income'. The cornerstone of the Grameen Bank's microcredit model and practices is the group lending methodology, which requires individuals to form a group of five and commit to financial training over five days in order to receive a loan. Group members provide mutual, morally binding group guarantees in lieu of the collateral required by conventional banks. In this sense, collective responsibility of the group serves as collateral on the loan.

The emphasis from the outset is to organizationally strengthen the Grameen clientele and build its capacity to plan and implement micro-level development decisions. The assumption is that if individual borrowers are given access to credit, they will be able to identify and engage in viable income-generating activities. Discipline, supervision and servicing characterize the operations of the Grameen Bank, which are carried out by "Bicycle bankers", staff based in branch units, close to their rural client base, who enjoy considerable delegated authority. The customary mode of transportation from branch to village for these bank workers is the bicycle. The rigorous selection of borrowers and their projects by these staff, the powerful peer pressure exerted on these individuals by the groups and the repayment scheme, based on meticulous bookkeeping and 50 weekly instalments, contribute to operational viability of this innovative rural banking system designed for the poor.

Four years later, in March 2006, Professor Gillies took up a post as vice-chancellor of Glasgow Caledonian University (GCU). She was excited by the potential of this new University in Scotland, which included on its coat of arms the words "For the Common Weal" (For the Common Good). She carried these words with her as she constructed plans for the University's future development. The chance reading of *Banker to the Poor* had left a deep impression on her and led to the university granting Nobel Laureate Professor Muhammad Yunus an honorary doctorate. This string of events and Yunus's 2008 visit to Glasgow marked the start of an extraordinary relationship, forged through a partnership to tackle serious health and inequality issues in both countries. Professor Gillies explains:

> Yunus laid a challenge at my door! How can we create a nursing college (nursing was a great strength of the University), using a social business model? Will you help us? I said to him "I will – if you will give me a gift in return! Will you work with the University to bring the Grameen Bank to Scotland"? And he agreed! This was a good "gift exchange"!
>
> *(Prof. Pamela Gillies)*

Less than 15 months later, on 1 March 2010, the Grameen Caledonian College of Nursing (GCCN) in Dhaka opened its doors to students. It was a partnership between Glasgow Caledonian University, Scotland, and the Grameen Health Care Trust in Bangladesh. By the end of the first five-year plan, GCCN had established itself as a sustainable social business with 500 students, contributing to achievement of the UN Millennium Development Goals (MDGs) and its successor, Sustainable Development Goals (SDGs), related to poverty alleviation (SDG #1), health and well-being (SDG #3) and gender equality (SDG #5). Led initially by GCU staff, GCCN is now governed solely by Bangladeshi nationals.

Through several multistakeholder partnerships, GCCN is accelerating national adoption of international standards for nursing-midwifery in a country facing severe challenges related to poverty, infant and maternal mortality and serious social inequalities. At the same time, it is alleviating a chronic shortage of nurse-midwives and transforming the lives of families and communities through the empowerment of disadvantaged young girls from rural areas of Bangladesh.

This chapter tells the story of a group of sustainability champions from Scotland and Bangladesh who, through their individual and institutional commitments and actions, forged a "partnership for the goals" (SDG #17). The case is compiled from documentary evidence (primarily internal GCU reports, website and published news, GCCN Annual Reports and Prospectuses) and face-to-face and online interviews with Professor Pamela Gillies and Professor Barbara Parfitt, the founding principal of GCCN. A special focus is placed on Professor Parfitt due to her pivotal role in implementing GCCN and her being at the centre of the program's struggles and successes.

GCCN and sustainable development

The 2030 Agenda for Sustainable Development, consisting of 17 SDGs and 169 targets, provides a global blueprint for dignity, peace and prosperity for people and the planet. This agenda learns from, and builds on, the successes and failures of the predecessor MDGs, an ambitious eight-goal agenda for the 2000–2015 period. Both sets of Goals were designed, among other things, to eliminate extreme poverty and hunger, promote gender equality and empower women, reduce child mortality and improve maternal health.

In July 2018, the United Nations reported that three years into the implementation of the 2030 Agenda, countries are translating this shared vision into national development plans and strategies but that much more needs to be done (UN 2018a, 3). For example, while the rate of extreme poverty has fallen rapidly and to just a third from its 1990 baseline, the latest global estimate suggests that 11 per cent of the world population, or 783 million people, lived below the extreme poverty threshold in 2013, leaving much work to be done to achieve SDG #1 – No poverty (UN 2018a, 4).

Similarly, while the maternal mortality ratio (associated with SDG #3, Health and well-being) has declined by 37 per cent since the dawn of the millennium, hundreds of thousands of women around the world died in 2015 due to complications during pregnancy or childbirth (UN 2018a, 5). These deaths are attributed, in large part, to a persistent lack of nurses and midwives, especially in developing countries.

This is associated with gender inequality that continues to hold women back and deprives them of basic rights and opportunities. The United Nations reported that empowering women (SDG #5) requires that structural issues, such as unfair social norms and attitudes, be addressed and that progressive legal frameworks that promote equality between women and men be developed (UN 2018a, 6).

GCCN in the Bangladeshi context

Bangladesh is the world's largest least-developed country (LDC) in terms of population and economic size, albeit on target to leave this category in 2024 (UN 2018b). It has a ratio of just one nurse per 8,000 people, or 25,000 nurses for a population of 160 million (Ministry of Health and Family Welfare 2011). Unusually, there are twice as many doctors (53,000)! Bangladesh has fewer nurses and midwives than Scotland, which had 41,705 qualified nurses in 2017 for a population of just 5 million (Nursing Times 2018). This shortage means that 90 per cent of women in Bangladesh's rural areas are delivering their babies without a skilled birth attendant. This may explain why Bangladesh has a high maternal mortality rate of 194 deaths per 1,000 (2010), compared to the United Kingdom of 4 per 1000. The need for developing highly skilled nurse midwives is critical.

GCCN 2009–2012: from idea to reality

The speed with which Professors Gillies and Yunus translated their vision into reality demonstrates both leadership and entrepreneurial drive, and they can be framed in the context of Timmons's model of the entrepreneurial process (1990). Timmons argues that the entrepreneurial process has three key elements: opportunity recognition, resources and team, which must fit together and be properly aligned with each other in order to make any (business) plan successful. Alignment of these factors in the case of this partnership is summarized in Table 10.1.

TABLE 10.1 Key factors contributing to the success of GCCN

Success Factor	Explanation
Opportunity recognition	Professor Yunus's knowledge of Bangladesh sustainability challenges and experience of launching multiple social business ventures with international partners identified a clear market opportunity, based on a social business model. This opportunity was embraced by Professor Gillies.
Resources	A 2 million USD$ start-up investment from Nike, secured by Professor Yunus and long-term investment in cash and in-kind from GCU combined with corporate donations for equipment, and a plethora of international volunteers enabled the partners to set this up as a social business.
Team	Staff drawn from both sides of the GCU–Grameen Healthcare Partnership social business venture brought together complementary knowledge, skills and networks to drive forward and resource the venture.

Source: Adapted from Timmons's *New Venture Creation* (1990).

Pamela Gillies (2018) reflected:

> Our Emeritus Nobel prize-winning Chancellor had the cache, the confidence and esteem of investors through his work on Grameen to encourage people to invest (money) in his vision of the future. . . . GCU had people with the knowledge and experience of delivering nurse-midwifery education of an international standard.

The team had its roots in two main networks, one of which revolved around the Grameen family of organizations, led by Professor Yunus and the others around GCU. Central to plans to operationalize the venture were GCU's Professor Barbara Parfitt and Grameen's Dr. Nazmul Huda. When asked why Professor Parfitt was approached to lead GCU's efforts in implementation, Professor Gillies answered:

> Barbara was a former Dean of Nursing in GCU – and she had been a missionary in her younger years. She had tremendous experience . . . of taking nursing and midwifery education into challenging situations in emerging nations (Central Asia, Africa), so she was ideally suited. . . . She had the skill-set, the energy and the determination to lead that for us.
>
> *(Professor Gillies)*

In turn, Professor Parfitt emphasized the critical importance played by Dr. Huda, who was appointed by Grameen to assist her in setting up the college:

> Working with Dr. Nazmul Huda was a great privilege. Much of the early success of the college was due to his hard work and his extraordinary ability to network with the right people at the right level. He took me all over Bangladesh and introduced me to many important contacts including the then Minister of Health and Director of Health Services.
>
> *(Professor Parfitt)*

Professor Gillies also emphasized the key role of several other stakeholders: Parfitt's successor as GCCN principal, Professor Frank Crossan; the first Bangladeshi principal of the College since 2016, Dr. Niru Nahar (appointed Vice Principal in 2011); Professor Alison Britton of GCU, who worked tirelessly to audit and improve the framework and procedures for quality assessment and enhancement; and the many academics and health care students who volunteered their time and expertise in pursuit of a noble venture. Table 10.2 captures the action steps taken to put in place the resources, plans and a team to move from venture idea to launch in just 15 months.

The uniqueness of GCCN

GCCN is unique in a number of ways. First, it has been set up as a social business (as opposed to a charity, or a for-profit venture), defined as a non-loss, non-dividend company dedicated entirely to achieve a social goal. A social business is designed so

TABLE 10.2 GCCN – from idea to reality

February 2009	Further discussion took place between Professors Pamela Gillies and Muhammad Yunus for development of a College of Nursing using a social business model, targeting young women from Grameen Bank families.
April 2009	GCU senior management, Dr. Valerie Webster and Dr. Frank Crossan, visited Dhaka to assess the situation and discuss the way forward.
May–August 2009	Professor Parfitt was approached in May 2009 to lead the project (she was finishing a project in Africa). She visited Bangladesh in August to scope out the work required.
November 2009	Professor Parfitt visited Dhaka and developed initial plans together with Dr. Huda, who was seconded from the Grameen family of organizations.
January–February 2010	Six core staff were recruited, students selected, accommodation identified, equipment and supplies purchased, hostels equipped, teaching and learning materials prepared and the application for approval submitted to the Bangladesh Nursing Council.
March 2010	First cohort of 38 students, daughters of Grameen Bank borrowers, entered GCCN to start their Diploma in Nursing Science and Midwifery (DNSM).
April 2010	The DNSM was approved by the Bangladesh Nursing Council.
June 2010	Agreements were signed with partner hospitals for students to access clinical placements.
October 2010	Students' first clinical placements took place in four partner hospitals, after which they participated in their first community visit spending one week in a community health centre in Parbatipur.
November 2010	The Computer Laboratory opens. First international volunteers arrive: Ms. Yumi Oshida from Japan; Professor Cam Donaldson, Ms. Kellie Gibson and Ms. Freya Brannan (UK); and Ms. Susana Marcos (Spain).
December 2010	The Students' Association was established with its first student chair, Ms. Setu Mondol.

Source: Grameen Caledonian College of Nursing, *Annual Report 2012: Milestones* (2012).

that the investor gets his or her investment money back over time but never receives a dividend beyond that amount (Forbes India 2010). Social businesses operate on a commercial basis inasmuch that they are set up to cover their costs and generate profits. However, unlike a for-profit organization, any profits are always reinvested, as social businesses do not seek to maximize profits for redistribution as dividends but rather to develop their operations and support their beneficiaries. For investors or lenders, the success of a social business is measured by its impact on the environment or on the lives of those who benefit from its actions, rather than financial returns on the investment.

Second, the partnership with the Grameen Bank network, which has more than 2,500 branches, covering more than 97 per cent of villages in Bangladesh, means that staff in Grameen branches promote the opportunities to study at GCCN to account holders. This channel enables young women to access loans otherwise unavailable to them elsewhere to continue their education. Coming from families of Grameen Bank borrowers, which, by definition, means that they are very poor, the future of these young women would normally involve no further education, early marriage and early pregnancy with a significant risk of maternal mortality.

> If I had not undertaken this course I would most certainly be married now, this is what we have to do if we live in the village.
> *(Satu, GCCN graduate)*

Third, GNCN challenges conventional thinking in Bangladesh that says that nurses are low-level workers and that young women from poor families cannot reach the same standards as those with more advantages:

> We have created a society that does not allow opportunities for people to take care of themselves. GCCN was set up to show not only can these young women achieve as much as their fellows but that they can go beyond that, and make a difference in their society and community and to the health of the Bangladeshi population.
> *(Muhammad Yunus, GCCN 2013 Annual Report, p. 1)*

Fourth, GCCN is unique within Bangladesh because of the successful transfer of internationally recognized academic curricula, pedagogy and administrative systems from GCU to GCCN; the quality of the nursing training; and the fact that all coursework and teaching is completed in English.

> The rationale for this is that these young women would have the skills and abilities to be leaders on behalf of women within health care in Bangladesh at an international level. Within four years, GCCN became recognized as the best nursing college in the country and the curriculum used by the Bangladesh Nursing Council has been developed as a result of the work being done at GCCN.
> *(Professor Barbara Parfitt, Founding Principal, GCCN)*

Challenges in establishing the GCCN

Challenges were encountered from the start. To establish the college in 2010 the Bangladesh Nursing Council required that GCCN admit the first cohort of students by the beginning of March or it would be necessary to wait another year. The team therefore had to move fast. Within six weeks, it had identified the Grameen building as a site for the college, renovated and refurbished it, purchased the necessary furniture and equipment, refurbished the hostel to take 40 students and prepared the curriculum. Some 350 students applied for a place, and this number was narrowed down to 120 on the basis of exam results. The remaining students were invited to a two-day selection event, made up of a combination of individual tests and team exercises, designed to assess general knowledge as well as interpersonal, leadership and communication skills, both in Bangla and in English. The selection process recruited 38 young women. Three further challenges emerged:

Challenge 1: The *bureaucracy of administrative systems* within Bangladesh. These extended to the Grameen organization where the total commitment to the project of Professor Yunus was not matched in the wider Grameen network. There were often difficult discussions when the college management committee challenged decisions or proposals made by Professor Parfitt and her team:

> The Grameen Bank was very slow at paying GCCN the student fees and often we were almost in [a] position of not being able to pay the monthly salaries and it required pressure from Professor Yunus for them to make the payment.
> *(Professor Barbara Parfitt)*

Challenge 2: *Appointing staff.* The challenges lie with both the administrative/finance side and the academic side, charged with setting up the standards for an international college. The administrative side responded to the support and development given to them, apart from the first finance-administration officer who ran away with the keys to the safe and the filing cabinets! Development of the administrative side progressed well with support from a volunteer administrator from GCU. Policies were developed for finance, administration, academic quality and student life to ensure the smooth running of the college.

The academic side presented more of a challenge. Professor Parfitt attributed this to a traditionally non-collegial culture and persistent infighting and jealousy among the staff. The academic challenge was exacerbated by difficulties retaining young, enthusiastic and ambitious nurse teachers.

> In the college we did not have the funds to provide salaries any higher than the government provided and we could not set up a pension fund due to our very tight budgets. This meant that as soon as a young nurse teacher saw a job going in the government sector she would apply and invariably get appointed. So the return on our investment in training and mentoring went to the government.
> *(Professor Parfitt)*

Challenge 3: A further difficulty was the *ongoing relationship* of Professor Yunus with the prime minister of Bangladesh, Sheikh Wasina Wajed. This relationship was very strained in 2011, and the government was reportedly doing everything it could to undermine him (Bunting 2011). The consequences of this were that any official approvals needed to advance the college's application for the Bachelor of Science or for similar approvals were delayed or not acted upon. A further example of this was the delay in processing Professor Parfitt's application for a work permit.

Things did improve as time went on, and by the time Professor Crossan succeeded her, the situation was much easier, although difficulties continued between Professor Yunus and the government.

Solutions and lessons learned

Professor Parfitt reported that balancing the demands of the culture and the need to encourage development amongst student and staff was a constant challenge – and represented a fine line between offending and challenging. It was very important for her to tread sensitively as she tried to introduce new ideas and practices while at the same time respecting the culture. For example, Professor Parfitt forbade the students to cover their heads whilst in the college but did allow them to do so when they travelled by the bus to the hospital. Their original uniform was styled after the GCU student nurses' uniforms, but the GCCN students requested a change, as they felt very exposed in such a different style of dress when in the clinical areas. GCCN then changed the uniform to the same one worn by all student nurses in the Bangladesh government sector.

Solution and lesson 1: dealing with the bureaucracy

From Professor Parfitt's perspective, communication in every respect was key in dealing with bureaucracy, be that an ability to speak to local people in their native language or ensuring that local communities were aware of what GCCN was trying to achieve:

> I wish I could have been more fluent in speaking Bangla. I took lessons regularly and my understanding was good but because I demanded that in the College everyone spoke English I did not get the opportunity to speak sufficiently. . . . An important lesson for me was the importance of networking and communication with all interested parties and stakeholders. Hence the blog that I wrote detailing the growth of the college, the production of the annual report and a regular newsletter.
>
> *(Professor Parfitt)*

Solution and lesson 2: recruiting, training, developing and retaining staff

The nature of GCCN's business meant that people and people management skills were of the utmost importance. Being aware of one's own strengths and weaknesses and having the confidence to adapt one's leadership and management styles to the local context made people management much easier.

> The most important lesson for me was to realize that I could make a difference if I used all the expertise I had available, and maximized the cultural styles of management to achieve results. I had to work towards a less

authoritarian style – a style of management that involved everyone. This was new to the staff, who were averse to taking decisions because normally there was a risk of getting it wrong and heavy penalties would follow if they did so.

(Professor Parfitt)

Solution and lesson 3: dealing with the government

Having a confidante who understood how things worked locally and "knew who is who" was instrumental in establishing and developing the relationships with people who could make things happen:

> Working with Dr. Nazmul Huda of Grameen was a great privilege. Much of the early success of the college was due to his hard work and his extraordinary ability to network with the right people at the right level. Sadly, his contract was terminated by Grameen, because he wanted to work part time with GCCN and continue with a WHO [World Health Organization] job with the Ministry.

(Professor Parfitt)

Solution and lesson 4: managing with limited resources

Professor Parfitt strongly believed that there were always people out there ready to contribute to a worthy cause! Attending and speaking at conferences and at the World Health Assembly helped with publicity of the college and enabled contact with donors. In addition to smaller donations of books, equipment and funds to buy the school bus, Professor Parfitt was able to fund staff to travel overseas for experience and to receive a donation of sophisticated manikins for use during clinical practice sessions. Having worked in developing countries over many years of her life, in circumstances where she had few or no resources, Professor Parfitt was used to "managing" with limited resources. While this experience proved to be an advantage in these circumstances, Professor Parfitt also felt it to be a disadvantage as her expectations of what she could ask for were probably too low.

Concluding remarks and implications for management education

The GCCN in Bangladesh is a testimony to what can be achieved when resources and a capable team are identified and mobilized to transform the vision of sustainable development into reality on a local level. GCCN is a shining example of the enactment of SDG #17 (Partnerships for the goals), which calls for a revitalized and enhanced global partnership that brings together governments, civil society, the private sector, the UN system and other actors and mobilizes all available resources.

Partnerships for the goals is critical because the 17 SDGs are *"indivisible"* (Atkisson 2017). In this case, SDG #17 served to catalyse and mutually reinforce SDG

#1 (No poverty), SDG #3 (Good health and well-being), SDG #4 (Quality education) and SDG #5 (Gender equality). GCCN contributes to SDG #3 by reducing child and maternal mortality rates by increasing the number of qualifying nurse-midwives year on year (SDG #4). Making financing for nursing education available to young women excluded from financial markets promotes gender equality (SDG #5). It also empowers these young women by enabling them to secure a sustainable livelihood for themselves and their families, thereby reducing poverty (SDG #1).

The critical role played by the partnerships is confirmed by Parfitt and Nahar (2016) who cite four key components for GCCN's development:

1   the start-up funding from Nike that enabled the partners to put in place all the necessary infrastructure and provided breathing space to establish the sustainable self-funding social business model;
2   a partnership with the Grameen Bank that provided educational loans to students, who otherwise had access neither to financing nor education;
3   long-term commitment and support from GCU to provide leadership and expertise in administration, nursing and midwifery and know-how to support and develop Bangladeshi staff; and
4   the successful establishment of an administrative and academic infrastructure that could be used as a "lighthouse" for all nursing-midwifery educational institutions in the country.

While these four factors can be thought of as building blocks put in place by institutional partners, the "glue" that held them together came from three sustainability champions who dared to believe, worked tirelessly to engage multiple partners, leveraged social capital in both personal and professional networks for the benefit of GCCN and adapted leadership styles to the Bangladeshi context. Professors Yunus, Gillies and Parfitt exemplify what Patzelt and Shepherd (2011, 632) term "sustainable entrepreneurship", the creation and exploitation of opportunities to create future goods and services that sustain the natural and/or communal environment and provide development gain for others.

Professor Muhammad Yunus enjoyed the confidence and esteem of investors through his work on Grameen to encourage people to invest in his vision of the future. Professor Gillies held an unwavering belief that GCU had people with the knowledge and experience of delivering nurse-midwifery education of an international standard, in a challenging environment. In addition to vision, Professor Gillies stressed the importance of long-term commitment to the success of the venture. This was underpinned by a belief that education unlocks the talent of young people and has the capacity to transform their lives and that of their families whilst providing huge benefits in terms of our social and economic well-being.

In addition, for sustainability champion Professor Parfitt, GCCN was a passion and labour of love. For her, setting up GCCN represented an opportunity to use all the personal and professional skills and expertise that she had acquired in both the United Kingdom and internationally: her networking, interpersonal and communication skills; her teaching, academic writing and research skills; and expertise in management, finance and administration. Professor Parfitt exemplifies the idea of values-based leadership and, along with Professors Yunus and Gillies, leaves a lasting legacy in Bangladesh.

Lessons learned from the case of GCCN should be of interest to faculty and students of several disciplines, ranging from business and management to international development, social sciences and the humanities. While the traditional focus of management educators is on commercial, for-profit firms, discussion of GCCN offers educators an opportunity to help students to challenge established conceptions of business and management. For example, the case highlights the tremendous potential of social business, as an alternative to traditional business models. The former prioritizes a positive impact on society and/or the environment over profit maximization and financial return on investment. Furthermore, social business is an innovative and dynamic concept, the growth of which is linked to new, and non-traditional financing methods and opens the door to new forms of inter-organizational collaboration. The GCCN case can therefore be used as a basis for class discussion on leadership, strategy, entrepreneurship, collaboration, cross-cultural management and the UN SDGs, in different organizational contexts.

References

Atkisson, A. 2017. *With the SDGs Everything Is Connected.* Published 17 May on Greenbiz. com. Accessed 18 Sept. 2018. www.greenbiz.com/article/sdgs-everything-connected

Bunting, M. 2011. "Muhammad Yunus banks on beating the enemies of microfinance." *The Guardian* (11 July). Accessed 13 Sept. 2018. www.theguardian.com/world/2011/jul/18/muhammad-yunus-microfinance-bangladesh

Forbes India. 2010. *Muhammad Yunus: Social Business, Online News Article by Forbes India Staff* (15 June). Accessed 31 July 2018. www.forbes.com/2010/06/15/forbes-india-muhammad-yunus-social-business-opinions-ideas-10-yunus.html#5b980de26522

Grameen Caledonian College of Nursing (GCCN). 2012. *Annual Report,* GCCN, Mirpur-2, Dhaka-1216, Bangladesh.

Grameen Caledonian College of Nursing (GCCN). 2013. *Annual Report,* GCCN, Mirpur-2, Dhaka-1216, Bangladesh.

Grameen Research Inc. *The Grameen Group Lending Model.* Accessed 2 Jan. 2019. http://grameenresearch.org/grameen-group-lending-model/

Ministry of Health and Family Welfare (MFWH) Source Book. 2011. *Human Resource Development.* Human Resource Development Unit, Ministry of Health and Family Welfare, Government of Bangladesh.

Nursing Times. 2018. "Rise in number of nurses and midwives in Scotland 'undermined' by increase in vacancies." *News Article* (6 Mar.). Accessed 6 Aug. 2018. www.nursingtimes.net/news/workforce/number-of-scottish-nurses-and-midwives-rise-but-so-do-vacancies/7023561.article

Parfitt, B., & Nahar, S. N. 2016. "Nursing education in Bangladesh: A social business model." *International Nursing Review,* 63: 285–291.

Patzelt, H., & Shepherd, D. A. 2011. "Recognizing opportunities for sustainable development." *Entrepreneurship Theory and Practice,* 35(4): 631–652.

Timmons, J. A. 1990. *New Venture Creation.* Homewood IL: Richard D. Irwin.

United Nations (UN). 2018a. *Sustainable Development Goals Report*. UN Publications, 300 East 42nd Street, New York, NY, 10017. Accessed 2 Aug. 2018. https://unstats.un.org/sdgs/files/report/2018/TheSustainableDevelopmentGoalsReport2018-EN.pdf

United Nations (UN). 2018b. *Leaving the LDC's Category: Booming Bangladesh Prepares to Graduate*. Department of Economic and Social Affairs, News, 13 Mar. Accessed 3 Aug. 2018. www.un.org/development/desa/en/news/policy/leaving-the-ldcs-category-booming-bangladesh-prepares-to-graduate.html

World Commission on Environment and Development. 1987. *Report of the World Commission on Environment and Development: Our Common Future*. Accessed 18 Sept. 2018. www.un-documents.net/our-common-future.pdf

11

PATHS TO EMPOWERMENT

A case study of local sustainability from rural Nicaragua

Michael B. Smith, Susan Kinne, and Grupo Fénix

Abstract

"Paths to Empowerment: A Case Study of Local Sustainability from Rural Nicaragua" presents the history of an ongoing collaboration among a village, a domestic nongovernmental organization (Grupo Fénix) and the people and programs of dozens of international partners. These partnerships have created a path out of poverty and dependency for many of the villagers. Just as importantly, not only have many people in the community become more materially secure as a result of these collaborations, but they have also become teachers themselves – teachers both to others in the community and to visitors. Indeed, the increased confidence and self-esteem of the community members as a result of these genuinely reciprocal collaborations (both reported in oral histories and visible in the social empowerment, especially of the women) is perhaps the best evidence that the changes in the community are enduring and sustainable.

Introduction

We are unlikely to finance poverty out of existence. Mainstream development project financing has had mixed results in long-term poverty reduction and remains wedded to a model of economic growth from neoclassical economics that is no longer tenable in an era of rapid climate change and awareness of limits (Rosa & Henning 2018; AtKisson 2012). Some scholars and activists even contend that it is too late for sustainable development (Meadows 2012). This chapter, however, argues that the innovative sustainable development model bearing fruit in Totogalpa, Nicaragua, has a high potential for adaptation across a range of technologies and environments in other parts of Latin America and in the global South. In harmony with the *buen vivir* movement in Latin America (Gudynas 2011; Hidalgo-Capitán &

Cubillo-Guevara 2017; Latouche 2018; Acosta 2017), where quality of life is enhanced in cohabitation with others and nature, the history of an ongoing collaboration among a village, a domestic nongovernmental organization (NGO; Grupo Fénix) and the people and programs of dozens of international partners is presented. This case study demonstrates that progress toward multiple Sustainable Development Goals (SDGs) can be achieved simultaneously, among them poverty alleviation (SDG #1), gender equality (SDG #5), clean water and sanitation (SDG #6), affordable and clean energy (SDG #7), and partnerships for the goals (SDG #17). Indeed, these partnerships have created a path out of poverty and dependency for many of the villagers. Not only have many people in the community become more materially secure as a result of these collaborations, but they have also become teachers themselves – teachers both to others in the community and to a global audience. Women, especially, have become empowered as social and political actors on both a local and regional scale. The increased confidence and self-esteem of the community members resulting from these genuinely reciprocal collaborations constitute perhaps the best evidence that the changes in the community are both enduring and sustainable.

Geographical, historical, and cultural context

In the northern highlands of Nicaragua, not far from the frontier with Honduras, lie Sabana Grande and Santo Domingo, both indigenous communities in the municipality of Totogalpa, Department of Madríz. The region is mountainous, with variable soil qualities and microclimates, but it lies squarely within the *zona seca* (dry zone) of the country, where average rainfall is less than 900 mm per year (Caracterización Municipal de Totogalpa 2017). Nicaragua itself has been deemed fourth most at risk from long-term climate change in the world (Kreft, Eckstein & Melchior 2017). Moreover, the impact of climate change in the region is already well documented (IPCC 2014) due to the dependence of its agricultural sector on seasonal rains that have become increasingly less predictable (Joint Global Change Research Institute 2009). Drought has become more frequent, as have destructively heavy downpours during the rainy season (Field et al. 2012). Regional food insecurity and the climate changes that seem certain to exacerbate it remain significant concerns for the municipal government (Caracterización Municipal de Totogalpa 2017; Bornemann, G., et al., 2012; FAO 2012). Although the region was once renowned for its *ocote* pine forests (Denevan 1961), deforestation has profoundly reduced tree cover of all types over the past century, a situation that is becoming a national crisis (MARENA 2015; Humboldt Center 2017). As one history of the Nicaraguan Segovias puts it, "[the extraction of *ocote*] forcefully altered favorable microclimates, and produced unprecedented erosion in the region" (CIERA-MIDIRA 1984, 226). The ruthlessly extractive practices of foreign timber companies (notably the Nicaraguan Longleaf Pine Company), clearance for agriculture, and the cutting of trees for fuel wood have all contributed to this transformation of the landscape, rendering the area even more vulnerable to climate change (Gourdji 2015).

According to a community history initiative undertaken in Sabana Grande in 2009, as recently as 1950, there were only about 60 people living in the community. Land was generally farmed in common (*ejidales*), an often-meager amount of water was drawn from a single spring, and the houses were constructed of grass with palm leaf roofs. Hunger was common, as was water scarcity. Only in the 1970s did families begin to construct dwellings from adobe and use tiles for roofing (Historia del Frayle 2009). The memories community members have of these times have contributed significantly to the transformation they have experienced because of the collaborations.

Collaborating for empowerment

There is no question that the members of the communities of Sabana Grande and Santo Domingo have been the principal agents of their communities' and their own personal transformations over the past 20 years. The seeds for the *mechanisms* of this transformation, however, were planted at the National Engineering University of Nicaragua in Managua (UNI). With Susan Kinne's (one of the co-authors of this chapter) guidance, a team of students interested in gaining hands-on experience in alternative energy technology founded Grupo Fénix in 1996. They took the name from the mythical phoenix bird, believing that their work would help in Nicaragua's rebirth from the ashes of years of conflict and privation. Within a year, Grupo Fénix and the UNI hosted the first of what became annual alternative energy fairs in Managua.

In 1998, the UNI formalized the students' renewable energy activities creating the Alternative Energy Sources Program (PFAE), and Susan Kinne became its director. Grupo Fénix became a nonprofit branch of PFAE. It was therefore well positioned to become the on-the-ground partner with the Falls Brook Centre of New Brunswick and the Canadian International Development Agency, for the New Energy Project in Nicaragua to provide support and employment for land mine victims. It was a chance for Grupo Fénix to live up to its name. This collaboration with the Falls Brook Centre allowed Grupo Fénix to expand its community partnerships into rural areas of Nicaragua, leading eventually to it being based in Totogalpa.

The initial project was focused on training land-mine victims to construct, install, and maintain solar panels in areas of northern Nicaragua without access to electricity from conventional sources. By 1999, the women in the community had begun to explore how solar energy might be used to improve their lives, especially through the construction and use of solar cookers. Empowerment was happening on two levels: For the first time, dozens of families had electrical power for illumination and radios, and in the social realm, individuals in the community were learning skills and becoming empowered to share knowledge with others in and beyond the community. Moreover, the PFAE initiated an innovative and paradigm shifting solution to continuing the project beyond the life span of the Falls Brook Centre grant. The knowledge gained by community members was converted into an income-generating service by offering international "hands-on" Renewable Energy Courses termed "Edutourism". Edutourism allowed the community to generate its own income for its postproject development and provided a mechanism for an ongoing increase in skills, knowledge, publicity, and, above all, empowerment of women.

Edutourism also included reciprocal learning experiences exemplified by the eight-year collaboration of Cornell University's Engineers for a Sustainable World (ESW), with the local women who build the solar cookers. In the first year, the women of Totogalpa taught the Cornell team to build solar cookers and discussed possible improvements. Back at Cornell in the United States, ESW students researched and tested prototypes based on the collaborations with the women in Nicaragua. In Year 2, both the local team and the Cornell team did presentations on what they had learned and together designed a new prototype with the improvements. Variations of this knowledge exchange continued for eight years continually strengthening the skills, knowledge, and confidence of the local team and introducing new groups of Cornell students to "hands-on" solar development.

No members of the community have experienced greater empowerment than the members of the cooperative the Solar Women of Totogalpa (Las Mujeres Solares de Totogalpa). Inspired by the possibilities of solar energy, a group of women in Sabana Grande began to coalesce around the development and use of solar cookers in 1999, eventually becoming a cooperative fully recognized by the Nicaraguan government in 2010. As others have documented (Botica Sevilla 2015; Farhar, Osnes, & Lowry 2015; Kruckenberg 2015), the community has acquired an international reputation due to the efforts of these women. In nearly 20 years of sustainable development initiatives, the Solar Women have seen their social and political capital amplified in ways that have benefited the entire community and that serve as an inspiration for others. Their efforts have led to recognition by numerous international agencies, including a 2008 United Nations SEED Award and a 2017 SEED-sponsored Hogan Lovells Community Solar Innovation Award. In a wonderfully organic way, the community of Sabana Grande has made considerable progress toward the SDGs of affordable and clean energy (SDG #7), partnerships developed around achieving goals (SDG #17), and women's equality (SDG #5) – not to mention ancillary benefits in the realms of clean water and sanitation (SDG #6) and quality education (SDG #4).

The empowerment of women has been the foundation of this progress. An extensive literature on women's empowerment in the global South frames the story of transformation in Sabana Grande. Work by Cornwall and Rivas (2015), Cornwall (2016), Chant (2016), Kabeer (2005), and Mosedale (2005) has helped to clarify the distinctions between gender equality and women's empowerment, as well as to anatomize the different dimensions of power (Charlier & Caubergs 2007). The assessment of the empowering effects of the projects are also laid out in the pioneering work of Sara Hlupekile Longwe (1998, 2002), who has looked particularly to the challenges of empowering rural women and laid out a useful taxonomy of progressive levels of women's empowerment and equality.

In general, this chapter follows Mosedale (2005) and Kabeer (2005) in defining women's empowerment as an ongoing (i.e., never completed) process through which women have been the agents of their own emancipation and growth. Collective action has been a powerful component. Moreover, the chapter argues that the initiatives in Sabana Grande have contributed to women's empowerment in a way that honors Cornwall and Rivas's (2015) call for collective transformation, not merely the enhancement of opportunities for individuals that has characterized so much conventional development.

The Pathways of Women's Empowerment Research Program Consortium now has more than a decade of research examining the efficacy of a wide range of interventions and initiatives that purport to empower women. As Cornwall (2016) notes, where women consistently and consciously reflect together on the changes in their own circumstances, the transformative outcomes of a project are amplified considerably. For more than 15 years, the Solar Women (and many of their relatives and friends who are not in the cooperative) have been reflecting on how involvement with Grupo Fénix has transformed their lives. Some of these testimonials, and projects that have transformed daily life in the community, are highlighted in the following.

Stories of empowerment

In 2017, Michael Smith (a chapter co-author) spent four months in Sabana Grande gathering evidence of these personal and communal transformations. He interviewed more than 30 community members (both female and male, ranging in age from 19 to 86), facilitated a community history workshop with the Solar Women, and collected details about the history of Grupo Fénix from the organization's informal archive.[1]

At the history workshop, members of the Solar Women responded in small groups to questions about how life had changed in Sabana Grande since the arrival of Grupo Fénix.[2] In describing their lives before 1998, a sense of *dis*empowerment is palpable – they felt themselves at the mercy of forces beyond their control, be they natural, political, social, or economic. They often used the word *timida* (timid and shy) to characterize both themselves and the community. They spoke of the relentless manual labor expected of women, from rising before dawn to fetch water from the single spring or to mill maize by hand, to cooking for hours a day in smoke-filled kitchens, to selling tomatoes by the side of the road, and to leaving the community for weeks at a time to harvest coffee. In summarizing how the workshop participants viewed the changes that had occurred over the intervening 20 years, Jennifer, the youngest member of the cooperative, said,

> We have moved forward with training. We now have solar electricity. Our lives have changed with the technical knowledge we have acquired through workshops about alternative energy, and through volunteers who have come to the community for exchanges about solar energy and agriculture.

PHOTO 11.1 History workshop with the Solar Women

As a result, she added, there is "greater confidence in ourselves" and "higher self-esteem" (Smith 2017).

In the workshop, women (and many of the men as well) consistently shared a profound understanding that their personal histories, their families' histories, and their community's history were characterized by courageous and tenacious resilience through troubling and tumultuous times. Being part of a collaboration that had led to such individual and community empowerment had permanently established a "before-and-after" dynamic in their perception of themselves and the community. The partnership was fundamental to the experience. Rumalda is an extraordinary example of a community member who has been transformed by her experiences collaborating with Grupo Fénix. A member of the Solar Women from the beginning, Rumalda often notes that before the arrival of Grupo Fénix in Sabana Grande, they did not recognize the power of collective action. "We were not very organized," she says, echoing a sentiment many others have expressed (Fedus 2017). "But once organized we became a cooperative and a sub-group within Grupo Fénix".

Reyna, who is in her late 40s and also a founding member of the Solar Women cooperative, described the grinding poverty of domestic labor and coffee harvesting in the years before the alternative energy projects in the community began, and of making *petates* (palm leaf bedrolls) to sell for pennies on the streets of Ocotal, the nearest city. Tears came to her eyes as she remembered. "So many big changes since", she said. "And the community has also experienced this change, not just the Solar Women . . . today the whole community . . . with solar systems, solar ovens, eco-stoves". Reyna noted how her energies can now be directed toward organizational and community development instead of mere survival, "working united to generate even more opportunities in the community" (Smith 2017).

Oscar, a young man who grew up in the community and now works for Grupo Fénix, has observed the transformations of the past 15 years and can see a difference in the general outlook of the residents. "I think that many people are very positive and they have that openness to learn new things", he said. The "ability to communicate with others, with people from outside is something that is very recognizable . . . and I think is something that is different from other communities" (Smith 2017).

Gemma Botica Sevilla (2015) undertook a participatory research study of the Solar Women that offers further evidence of the ways members of the cooperative and their families have become empowered through their participation in, and contributions to, the projects of Grupo Fénix. She explicitly oriented her investigation toward the empowerment of women as a central dimension of sustainable human development (using the UN's Human Development Indices as a frame of reference). Through interviews and focus groups with the women, Botica gathered a rich array of reflections about the changes the women had experienced in their lives since the arrival of Grupo Fénix. Using the taxonomy of empowerment developed by Rowlands (1995), Botica was able to show that the women had made gains in the power they had to control their own lives, in the power to collaborate with each other and with people from outside the community, and in their "power within" (self-esteem, self-awareness, and self-confidence).

Some examples of statements from each category that further illustrate the transformation of the community and the women who live there – especially in terms of increasing gender equality – follow.[3] Observations demonstrate how the relations of these women with the men in their lives have evolved, exemplify the feeling that they have more control over their own lives. One of the younger members of the cooperative commented on the changes she had observed in her household since her mother had begun working with Grupo Fénix:

> Since my mom works out of the house, my dad now cooks . . . before he had never done it. He sweeps, he makes coffee, [and] he washes dishes. He does everything, and he feels good about that. He serves as an example for others.

Years of collaborating in genuinely reciprocal ways with both fellow community members and visitors from elsewhere has been deeply valued not only in its own right but also for the ways that it generated self-confidence.

One woman, referring to the higher regard she was now accorded by virtue of having learned to build and maintain solar ovens (see Photo 11.3), said, "I'm very different now. Formerly I was not recognized as a technician and now, yes, I am known as such by society, and they respect me for my work". In addition, acknowledging the

PHOTO 11.2 Improved firewood stove

international reputation the women have garnered for their efforts, a member of the cooperative stated that it was

> incredible to have become something important in my life, the knowledge that I have today, that I have as a technician in renewable energy, even I can't believe it. We have achieved success at an international level, everyone can see what we have achieved in the field that a remote community is being talked about for something not yet known in Nicaragua.

In late 2017 came additional affirmation of the inspiring story that has unfolded in the community over the past decade. A production crew arrived in Sabana Grande to film a segment called "It Takes a Solar Village" for Al Gore's *24 Hours of Reality* (2017) program about climate change and climate change action. The segment featured women and men from the community sharing the story of the recent history of their community with a global webcast audience. The story they told was one about initially being an isolated community largely without electricity and trapped in poverty to becoming a place with both solar and gridded electricity where people now have a sense of agency about creating their own future and control over their own lives.

Toward resilience and *buen vivir* (good living)

As we have seen, the people of Sabana Grande and Santo Domingo have experienced more change in the material and organizational dimensions of their lives over the past 15 years than in the previous several decades combined. Almost without exception, the people interviewed for this project have characterized not just their standard of living but also their quality of life as having improved; they now view the future with optimism. Those improvements in material standards of living – better access to water, basic consumer goods, and electricity – account for some of that optimism. There are now 10 drilled well pumps in the community, although several are no longer used because the municipality has installed a piped water system for about 30 percent of the households. Every household now has access to some form of electrical power, often power from the grid that the national government has extended into the community but supplemented with solar power in more than a quarter of the houses.

More than 100 improved cooking stoves (see Photo 11.2) have been installed in the community, each of which reduces the amount of wood consumed through cooking by almost 70 percent. More significant than the conservation of wood (and therefore forest resources) are the health benefits to the women and children in these homes, whose exposure to smoke and particulate is reduced to a fraction of what it was with the open-hearth stoves. Finally, the overall activities of Grupo Fénix now generate significant income. For 2016, Edutourism and other income-generating activities brought in close to $66,000. This revenue is being returned to the community in the form of educational scholarships for youth, employment for nearly 20 people, small home improvement loans, and further investments in Solar Mountain, the epicenter of agro-ecological experimentation in the community.

PHOTO 11.3 Women with solar cooker frame they built

Paths to empowerment   **151**

The community members involved in the various sustainable development projects often espouse a commitment to more than material security. For example, one of the subgroups of Grupo Fénix, the PSAE has been working to restore a badly degraded landscape through reforestation, organic farming, and solar-powered irrigation systems. This is very much in the spirit of the "post-extractivist" philosophy of the *buen vivir* movement in Latin America (Hidalgo-Capitán & Cubillo-Guevara 2017; Acosta 2017), not to mention consistent with the SDG of more responsible consumption and production (SDG #12). Within the same ecological ambit are their efforts in the community to develop and deploy new dry latrine technology in order to protect the aquifers that provide drinking water but are vulnerable to contamination from waste in conventional pit latrines, modeling an approach to the SDG of clean water and sanitation (SDG #6). The nine of these latrines already constructed exemplify the efforts to meet basic human needs in ways that preserve the integrity of the ecosystem. As Hilario, one of the principal co-designers and builders, observed, not only do the dry latrines preserve the water system but "what we deposit there will [also] serve us as fertilizer for long-production plants" (Smith 2017), invoking the principle that in a natural system one organism's waste becomes another organism's food.

As these examples suggest, there is a sense in the community that a biocentric approach to development will both produce better living (including preserving community) and build resilience in the face of climate change impacts that are already being experienced. While "de-growth" is not the way community members would characterize development models there, they recognize that there is a "good life beyond growth" as conventionally defined by liberal economic theory (Rosa & Henning 2018).[4] In addition, they are ready, willing, and able to teach the rest of the world in their sustainable technology courses that have become one of their major sources of income.

Notes

1   Eric Fedus also conducted three interviews in 2017 that we have drawn on. The questions in the interviews asked both about general changes over time in the personal life of the interviewee and in the community and about changes in the way food, water, and energy were procured and used.
2   The five-hour workshop on October 20, 2017, was facilitated by co-author Michael Smith, Oscar Sánchez López (program assistant for Grupo Fénix), Yerill Tórrez (director of community development, Grupo Fénix), and Kristen Brennan.
3   All quotations can be found in Botica Sevilla (2015).
4   We write this cognizant of Ilan Kapoor's (2008) critique of participatory development: that there is a danger of projecting onto developing societies our own dreams, asking more of them than we do of ourselves, [perpetuating] the Third World as object and resource" (72). The years of collaborations that have taken the community to this point have been reciprocal, with local knowledge shaping innovation at every step of the way.

Bibliography

24 Hours of Reality. 2017. www.24hoursofreality.org/
Acosta, A. 2017. "Post-extractivism: From discourse to practice: Reflections for action." In G. Carbonnier, H. Campodónico, & S. Vázquez, eds. *Alternative Pathways to Sustainable*

Development: Lessons from Latin America. Leiden/Boston: Brill: 77–102. www.jstor.org/stable/10.1163/j.ctt1w76w3t.12

AtKisson, A., ed. 2012. *Life Beyond Growth: Alternatives and Complements to GDP-Measured Growth as a Framing for Social Progress*. Tokyo: Institute for Studies in Happiness, Economy, and Society.

Bornemann, G., Cuadra, O. N., Silva, C. N. and Solorzano, J. L., 2012. *Desafíos desde la seguridad alimentaria y nutricional en Nicaragua* (Food Security and Nutritional Challenges in Nicaragua), Oxfam. https://www.oxfamblogs.org/lac/wp-content/uploads/2013/05/Desafios-desde-la-seguridad-alimentaria-y-nutricional-en-Nicaragua.pdf

Botica Sevilla, G. 2015. *Mujeres rurales ante el reto del desarrollo sostenible. Análisis crítico de la experiencia de la Cooperativa Multisectorial "Mujeres Solares de Totogalpa" – COOMUSOT (Nicaragua)*. (Rural Women Confronting the Challenge of Sustainable Development: A Critical Analysis of the Experience of the Multisector Cooperative, "The Solar Women of Totogalpa": COOMUSOT (Nicaragua)]. M.A. Universitat Politécnica de Valencia.

Carbonnier, G., Campodónico, H., & Tezanos Vázquez, S. 2017. *Alternative Pathways to Sustainable Development: Lessons from Latin America*. Boston: Brill.

Chant, S., 2016. "Women, girls and world poverty: Empowerment, equality or essentialism?" *International Development Planning Review*, 38(1): 1–24.

Charlier, S., Caubergs, L., Malpas, N., & Kakiba, E. M. 2007. *The Women Empowerment Approach: A Methodological Guide*. Brussels: Commission on Women and Development.

CIERA-MIDINRA. 1984. *Nicaragua: y por eso defendemos la frontera – historia agrarian de las Segovias Occidentales*. (Nicaragua: And for This We Defend the Border: An Agrarian History of the Western Segovias). Managua: Centro de Investigaciones y Estudios de la Reforma Agraria.

Colocousis, C., Rebellon, C., Smith, N., & Sobolowski, S. 2015. "How long can we keep doing this? Sustainability as a strictly temporal concept." *Journal of Environmental Studies and Sciences*, 7(2): 274–287.

Cook, N. 1998. *Born to Die: Disease and New World Conquest, 1492–1650*. Cambridge: Cambridge University Press.

Cornwall, A. 2016. "Women's empowerment: What works?" *Journal of International Development*, 28: 342–359.

Cornwall, A, & Rivas, A., 2015. "From 'gender equality' and 'women's empowerment' to global justice: Reclaiming a transformative agenda for gender and development," *Third World Quarterly*, 36(2): 396–415.

Crosby, A. 1972. *The Columbian Exchange: Biological and Cultural Consequences of 1492*. Westport, CT: Greenwood.

Denevan, W. 1961. *The Upland Pine Forests of Nicaragua: A Study in Cultural Plant Geography*. Berkeley: University of California Press.

Ender, J., & Remig, M., eds. 2015. *Theories of Sustainable Development*. Abingdon: Routledge.

FAO. 2012. *Estudio de caracterización del Corredor Seco Centroamericano*. (A Descriptive Study of the Dry Zone of Central America]. New York: United Nations.

Farhar, B., Osnes, B., & Lowry, E. 2015. "Energy and gender." In A. Halff, B. Sovacool, & J. Rozhon, eds. *Energy Poverty*. Oxford: Oxford University Press: 152–179.

Fedus, E., & López, R. 2017. Interview.

Field, C., Barros, V., Stocker, T., Dahe, Q., Dokken, D., Ebi, K., Mastrandrea, M., Mach, K., Plattner, G., Allen, S., Tignor, M., & Midgley, P. 2012. *Managing the Risks of Extreme Events and Disasters to Advance Climate Change Adaptation*, 1st ed. New York: United Nations.

Gourdji, S., Craig, M., Shirley, R., & Ponce de Leon Barido, D. 2014. *Sustainable Development Opportunities at the Climate, Land, Energy, and Water Nexus in Nicaragua*. Center for Latin American Studies Working Paper. Berkeley: Regents of the University of

California. Accessed 15 June 2018. https://clas.berkeley.edu/sites/default/files/shared/docs/papers/ShirleyWorkingPaper%2002-18.pdf

Gourdji, S., Läderach, P., Valle, A., Martinez, C., & Lobell, D. 2015. "Historical climate trends, deforestation, and maize and bean yields in Nicaragua." *Agricultural and Forest Meteorology*, 22: 270–281.

Gudynas, E. 2011. "Buen Vivir: Today's Tomorrow," *Development* (54): 441–47.

Hidalgo-Capitán, A., & Cubillo-Guevara, A. 2017. "Deconstruction and genealogy of Latin American good living (Buen Vivir).: The (Triune) good living and its diverse intellectual wellsprings." In G. Carbonnier, H. Campodónico, & S. Vázquez, eds. *Alternative Pathways to Sustainable Development: Lessons from Latin America*. Leiden/Boston: Brill: 23–50. http://www.jstor.org/stable/10.1163/j.ctt1w76w3t.10

Hirshon, S., & Butler, J. 1983. *And Also Teach Them to Read*. Westport, CT: L. Hill.

Historia del Frayle, 2009. [Manuscript] Grupo Fénix Archives., Sabana Grande, Nicaragua.

Horton, L. 2007. *Grassroots Struggles for Sustainability in Central America*. Boulder: University Press of Colorado.

Humboldt Center. 2017. *En 10 años, Nicaragua podría acabar con sus bosques*. (In 10 Years, Nicaragua Could Cut Down Its Forests). Accessed 6 July 2018. https://humboldt.org.ni/en-10-anos-nicaragua-podria-acabar-con-sus-bosques/

Incer, B. J. 1985. *Toponimias Indígenas de Nicaragua*. (Indigenous Toponyms of Nicaragua). San José: Libro Libre.

Intergovernmental Panel on Climate Change (IPCC), 2014. *AR5 Climate Change 2014: Impacts, Adaptation, and Vulnerability*, pp. 1499–1545.

Joint Global Change Research Institute, 2009. *Mexico, the Caribbean, and Central America: The Impact of Climate Change to 2030*.

Kabeer, N. 1997. "Empoderamiento desde abajo: ¿Qué podemos aprender de las organizaciones de base?" (Empowerment from below: What can we learn from grassroots organizations?). In: M. León, ed. *Poder y empoderamiento de las mujeres*. (Power and Empowerment of Women). Sante Fe de Bogotá: TM Editores: 119–146.

Kabeer, N. 2005. "Gender equality and women's empowerment: A critical analysis of the Third Millennium Development Goal." *Gender and Development*, 13(2): 13–24.

Kapoor, I. 2008. *The Postcolonial Politics of Development*. London: Routledge.

Kreft, S., Eckstein, D., & Melchior, I. 2017. *Global Climate Risk Index 2017: Who Suffers Most from Extreme Weather Events?* Accessed 1 June 2018. www.germanwatch.org

Kruckenberg, L. 2015. "North-South partnerships for sustainable energy: Knowledge-power relations in development assistance for renewable energy." *Energy for Sustainable Development*, 29: 91–99.

Lade, S., Haider, L., Engström, G., & Schlüter, M. 2017. "Resilience offers escape from trapped thinking on poverty alleviation." *Science Advances*, 3(5): e1603043.

Latouche, S. 2018. "The path to degrowth for a sustainable society." In H. Lehmann, ed. *Factor X. Eco-Efficiency in Industry and Science*, Vol. 32. Cham: Springer.

Longwe, S. 1998. "Gender awareness: The missing element in the third world development project." In T. Wallace & C. March, eds. *Changing Perceptions: Writings on Gender and Development*. Oxford: Oxfam: 149–157.

Longwe, S. 2002. *Addressing Rural Gender Issues: A Framework for Leadership and Mobilisation*. Paper presented at the III World Congress for Rural Women, Madrid.

Ministerio del Ambiente y los Recursos Naturales (MARENA). 2015. *Apoyo a la preparación de la estrategia para la reducción de emisiones por deforestación y degradación forestal*. (Support for the Preparation of the Strategy for Reducing Emissions through Deforestation and Forest Degradation). Managua. Accessed 20 June 2018. http://enderedd.sinia.net.ni/Docs/Doc_PaqueteR/6.%20Estrategia_Comunicacion_ENDEREDD.pdf

McCormick, R. 2002. "Historia prehispánico de los Chorotega de Nicaragua." (Pre-Hispanic history of the Chorotegas of Nicaragua]." *Revista de historia*, 14.

Meadows, D. 2012. *It Is Too Late for Sustainable Development?* Symposium: Perspectives on Limits to Growth: Challenges to Building a Sustainable Planet, Washington, DC.

Mosedale, S. 2005. "Assessing women's empowerment: Towards a conceptual framework." *Journal of International Development*, 17(2): 243–257.

Municipio de Totogalpa. 2017. "Caracterización Municipal de Totogalpa." (Description of the Municipality of Totogalpa).

Pfister, F., & Baccini, P. 2005. "Resource potentials and limitations of a Nicaraguan agricultural region." *Environment, Development and Sustainability*, 7(3): 337–361.

Ponce de Leon Barido, D. et al. 2015. "Evidence and future scenarios of a low-carbon energy transition in Central America: A case study in Nicaragua." *Environmental Research Letters*, 10(10): 104002.

Ritchie, D. 2014. *Doing Oral History*, 3rd ed. New York: Oxford University Press.

Rosa, H., & Henning, C. 2018. *The Good Life beyond Growth: New Perspectives*. Abingdon: Routledge.

Rowlands, J. 1995. "Empowerment examined." *Development in Practice*, 5(2): 101–107.

Smith, M., & López, O. 2017. Oral History Interview.

Smith, M., & López, R. 2017. Oral History Interview.

Smith, M., & Martínez, H. 2017. Oral History Interview.

Smith, M., & Pérez, M. 2017. Oral History Interview.

Valenzuela, O. 2011. *Días de lluvia y sol*. (Days of Rain and Sunshine). Managua: La Prensa.

Van den Berg, M. 2010. "Household income strategies and natural disasters: Dynamic livelihoods in rural Nicaragua." *Ecological Economics*, 69(3): 592–602.

Vanhulst, J., & Zaccai, E. 2016. "Sustainability in Latin America: An analysis of the academic discursive field." *Environmental Development*, 20: 68–82.

12
POVERTY ERADICATION AND POLITICAL ENGAGEMENT

A case of sustainable entrepreneurship in China

Xuanwei Cao and Xiao Wang

Abstract

It has been widely believed that to create a sustainable world the power of business is indispensable. Facing grand challenges when following the old path of "business as usual", entrepreneurs are transforming their business practices for sustainable development in various ways. In this process of transformation, entrepreneurs also seek new paths to achieve sustained legitimacy and growth through simultaneously pursuing economic viability, social equity, and environmental stability. In spite of the rapid development of sustainable businesses in emerging economies, such as solar energy in China, there is still little understanding of what motivates entrepreneurs to pursue sustainable business in situations in which the relationship of private firms with the government is complex and paradoxical. This chapter addresses these issues and provides insights through an in-depth investigation into the case of the T Group, a company with unique dual businesses in aquatic feed and solar energy in China, which helps achieve several Sustainability Development Goals (SDGs), such as poverty alleviation (SDG #1), affordable and clean energy (SDG #7), and sustainable cities and communities (SDG #11). Hanyuan Liu, the founder and Chairman of the T Group, through his political engagement, demonstrated how entrepreneurs could positively transform their businesses towards sustainability while responding to and dealing with specific social problems.

Introduction

In the past four decades, entrepreneurship in every industrial sector in China has boomed in the context of the rapid transformation of the economy. In this process, however, entrepreneurs are confronted with a complex institutional environment implying both significant opportunities and attendant risks. For the sake of reducing uncertainties caused by these changes, such as industrial policy and regulations, on one hand, and seeking or even creating opportunities from solidifying legitimacy, on the other hand, many entrepreneurs try to maintain good relationships with the government. By responding to and engaging in government's initiative to solving certain social problems, such as poverty alleviation, which has been officially announced as a must-do task in China's Five-Year Plan period (2016–2020), some entrepreneurs could explore new opportunities and strengthen the legitimacy of their businesses.

However, in the process of engaging in government-initiated issues, entrepreneurs face great challenges in balancing different institutional logic, that is, the rules that shape the perception and behavior of actors in an organization's field. The institutional logic spectrum includes government logic, market logic, religious logic, and family logic (Thornton 2002). For example, under government logic, entrepreneurs' perception and strategic behaviors are dependent on national policies, so they often attach great importance to the implementation of relevant government policies. Under market logic, entrepreneurs would emphasize more market-oriented behaviors in pursuit of corporate profits. Therefore, it is interesting to observe how entrepreneurs in what is often an incomprehensive institutional context pursue their sustainable business and make balance and switch between different institutional logics.

A sustained path of business operation and competitive advantage would be impossible if business did not influence its surroundings and environment to achieve the coevolution of the "relational framework" between business and government institutions (Child, Rodrigues, & Tse 2012). This raises the issue of the ideology-critique of entrepreneur studies by Ogbor. He stated that more studies should be conducted "by questioning how and why particular ideational systems, institutions and belief systems produce and shape the pattern of entrepreneurship in contemporary society" (Ogbor 2000, 630). A recent study shows that entrepreneurs from publicly listed private firms in China had a notable increase in getting political appointments, that is, having closer political connections and more engagement with the political leaders and party officials between 1995 and 2012 (Li & Liang 2015).

The increasing pursuit of political appointment of private entrepreneurs in recent years has its ideological roots in Confucian values. In Confucianism, the ultimate purpose of life is that individuals extend themselves to serve the larger community and to pursue societal harmony. Thus, successful entrepreneurs with a cultural influence from Confucian values have a social orientation, including behaving compassionately to promoting social welfare, having concern for the public good, contributing to the greater commonwealth, and finding the ultimate way toward greatness. The pursuit of political appointment of those successful entrepreneurs could allow them to fulfill their ideological aspirations toward business and society, to give back to society and to promote public welfare while sustaining their businesses as well.

This chapter investigates a private-firm entrepreneur in western China who entered the solar photovoltaic (PV) cell business 10 years ago and achieved great success both economically and socially. This case illustrates how entrepreneurs can contribute to the achievement of Sustainability Development Goals (SDGs), such as those urgent issues such as poverty alleviation (SDG #1), affordable and clean energy (SDG #7), and sustainable cities and communities (SDG #11). The chapter illustrates how an entrepreneur's political engagement can help the transformation toward sustainable entrepreneurship by switching between different institutional logics and balancing "pro-self" (egoism) and "prosocial" (altruism) value creation.

Sustainable entrepreneurship

Entrepreneurship can help address societal issues such as sustainable development (Pacheco, Dean, & Payne 2010; York & Venkataraman 2010; Schaltegger & Wagner 2011; Pinkse & Groot 2015). Some scholars, however, remain skeptical claiming that "it remains an open question as to whether and, to what extent, entrepreneurs have the potential for creating sustainable economies" (Hall et al. 2010, 440). Others argue that entrepreneurship has an important role to play in the transformation toward a more sustainable future (Dean & McMullen 2007; Belz & Binder 2017). Entrepreneurs are expected to balance the triple bottom lines of economic, social, and ecological goals (Schaltegger & Wagner 2011) and thus simultaneously pursue economic viability, social equity, and environmental stability by altering or creating institutions (Pacheco, Dean, & Payne 2010).

Sustainable entrepreneurship is understood as "the recognition, development and exploitation of opportunities by individuals to bring into existence future goods and services with economic, social and ecological gains" (Belz & Binder 2017, 2). This definition acknowledges that some entrepreneurs, "unlike Schumpeterian entrepreneurs [may be] driven by a social instead of an economic motive" (Reinstaller 2005, 1366). Such entrepreneurs not only wish to capture economic value for themselves but also find new avenues towards social improvement and creating social value. Sustainable entrepreneurs address the sustainability of their business, as well as its ethical and long-term impact on society and on the natural environment, rather than blindly pursuing short-term business profit. They have the potential to contribute to environmental and social development through innovations aimed at the mass market and providing benefits to a larger society (Schaltegger & Wagner 2011).

Recent studies on entrepreneurs and sustainability reveal that sustainable entrepreneurs sometimes become politically active to overcome market barriers (Pacheco, Dean, & Payne 2010; Pinkse & Groot 2015). Prior studies on political strategy focused on how firms use their strategic political resources and capabilities to improve their profitability (McWilliams, Van Fleet, & Cory 2002) in Western contexts. To understand why entrepreneurs engage in sustainability-oriented business and how entrepreneurs secure both "pro-self" and "prosocial" interests, we need to develop broader insights beyond the provincial view on getting lucrative economic returns as indicated in Pacheco et al.'s study (2010).

Li and Liang's study (2015) illustrates the importance of cultural-dependent values that underline successful private-firm entrepreneurs' prosocial motives: with the mind of creating blended values, that is, both economic value and social value, the pursuit of political appointments is regarded as a means by those entrepreneurs to influence policymaking and contribute to the greater good. This greatly extends the literature on understanding corporate political activity in the non-Western context, despite extant studies narrowly regarded entrepreneurs in the context of institutional transition as morally insensitive monsters, just utilizing their political engagement to bypass institutions to gain more economic interests and triggering harmful results and risks (Lawton, McGuire, & Rajwani 2013; Mantere, Pajunen, & Lamberg 2009; Welter & Smallbone 2011). More recently, studies reveal that in an immature institutional environment of emerging economies, firms can adapt to institutional change and even develop considerable power to influence it (Dieleman & Boddewyn 2012). Managing political calculations during institutional transition, especially in emerging economies, is being recognized as an important capability of firms (Li, Peng, & Macaulay 2013).

In the process of institutional transition, more and more entrepreneurs have realized that their reliance on seeking speculative opportunities for maximum short-term profits in institutional voids could not sustain their business. The nuts and bolts of entrepreneurial opportunities in a transition economy context are the balance between exploiting business opportunities and creating social values and switching and balancing between different institutional logics, that is, market logic and government logic. Insightful entrepreneurs could explore opportunities to fill in the institutional void in a market-oriented way and seek political avenues and create more opportunities to make their businesses sustainable. On one hand, entrepreneurs, especially those with political engagement, are pulled to participate in institutional building to gain legitimacy for their business. On the other hand, they are pushed to respond quickly to institutional change by seizing market opportunities. Therefore, it is important for entrepreneurs to develop skills of ambidexterity to pursue both commercial and social values.

The lens of political engagement of entrepreneurs in a transition economy thus could help improve our understanding of how entrepreneurs could be "a significant conduit for a more sustainable society" through pursuing both "pro-self" and "prosocial" objectives with their market-political ambidexterity.

Sustainable entrepreneurship and poverty alleviation

In the past decade, the solar PV industry in China grew rapidly. Along with ups and downs within a short time, numerous entrepreneurs entered this field. Some of them had strong Confucian values and thus great concerns for the public good and the contribution to greater commonwealth through doing good business. They participated in establishing and improving important institutions for this industry, pursued political appointments to fulfill their values towards business and society, and sustained their businesses to help societal development and to promote public welfare. Thus, the solar PV industry is a suitable research subject in terms of the behaviors and activities of entrepreneurs and their impact on sustainable development.

In October 2014, the National Energy Administration (NEA) and the State Council Leading Group Office of Poverty Alleviation and Development (CPAD) collectively issued a guiding policy to launch a poverty alleviation program through the installation of solar PV panels in poor households. The program was designed to run for a period of six years starting from 2014/2015. In 2015, the PV Poverty Alleviation Project was approved by the State Council as one of the 10 targeted poverty alleviation projects.

Through installing rooftop or micro solar energy systems in the poorest villages and counties across China, this program aimed to help the local residents generate electric power for their own use and to make money by selling surplus electric power back to the grid. The scheme was designed to help 2 million households generate more than 3,000 RMB yuan each as extra income every year. In January 2016, the NEA issued another policy on promoting renewable energy development to support poverty alleviation. Through the first six months of 2018, at least 48 policies were released by either the central or local governments in China to further promote the PV approach to poverty alleviation.

In fact, the PV poverty alleviation model was invented and applied by those entrepreneurs in the solar PV industry who deeply understood the importance of maintaining ambidexterity in balancing their economic growth and social value creation. When the first solar PV poverty alleviation model was created and recognized by the government, it was soon adopted and replicated by many other entrepreneurs in this field, such as the PV-plus-vegetable-greenhouse model, PV-plus-sheep-pen model, and others. The practice has been developed into an effective policy tool in China which integrates the social goals of climate change response, low-carbon development, and poverty alleviation to promote sustainable development of inland rural regions. According to a rough estimation, these PV poverty alleviation projects could help reduce the nationwide emission of carbon dioxide between 8.4 to 42.0 million tons per year (NEA 2016). That creates huge ecological and environmental benefits.

With the strong support of government policy and innovative exploitation of entrepreneurial opportunities, companies in the solar PV industry in China could make great contributions to the implementation and achievements of SDGs in many areas, such as in poverty alleviation (SDG #1), affordable and clean energy (SDG #7), and sustainable cities and communities (SDG #11).

The case study: the solar PV business of the T Group

Generally, the focus on the solar PV industry stems from three aspects. First, the solar PV industry has been one of the most dynamic industrial branches in recent decades in China. Second, in the rapid development and fluctuation of the solar PV industry, entrepreneurs in this field witnessed intensive interactions with policy makers (central and local government). Third, the solar panels and solar energy in China are mainly installed and developed in the western inland regions where there were still more than 16 million people living in poverty in 2017. Thus, the solar PV industry is a good example to demonstrate how political engagement by entrepreneurs for business opportunity creation can help mitigate and eradicate poverty in western China.

Established in 1984, the Tongwei Group Co. Ltd. (T Group) was already, in 2006, a leading private enterprise of feed and aquatic products in Sichuan Province (western China). In 2007, with large-scale investments, the T Group entered the solar PV industry, initially producing polyvinyl chloride (PVC), the raw material for producing polycrystalline silicon. In February 2007, the T Group acquired a chemical factory producing PVC. From then on, the T Group marched into the solar energy industry, with the dual core businesses. In the visions of Hanyuan Liu, the founder and the board chairman, the T Group is a company devoted to providing green energy for society, with aquatic feed to satisfy the demand for food safety and with solar energy to satisfy the demand for energy safety and conservation.

Under Liu's strategic leadership and with his strong commitment to the PV cell industry, the T Group quickly became one of the largest PV producers and operators of PV power stations in China. With its own developed techniques and more than 100 technical patents on producing polycrystalline silicon, the T Group gained a dominant position in the Chinese market. It is one of the largest PV system solution providers with a self-developed comprehensive industrial chain.

As an exemplary entrepreneur at the early time of China's Reform and Opening-Up policy, starting from his career in 1984 at a local county, Liu has been receiving honors, awards, and high appreciation from governments on different levels as well as other organizations and social entities. During the T Group's successful growth and development, Liu also realized his political aspirations.

Since 1994, Liu has been actively engaging in political activities as a member of the China National Democratic Construction Association (CNDCA), which is one of the eight democratic parties in the Chinese political system. In 1998, Liu was elected as a member of the Central Standing Committee of CNDCA as well as a member of the Standing Committee of the Chinese People Political Consultative Conference (CPPCC), a political appointment of successful entrepreneurs in China. In 2018, Liu was selected as the representative in China's National People's Congress. All these high-rank political appointments could be regarded as the government's official recognition of Liu's great contributions, both economically and socially, to the country. For Liu himself, all those political appointments are very valuable intangible social capitals for his business. With those political appointments, he could build up more political connections and broaden visions as well as access to valuable information, which could, in turn, benefit his business. Apart from this, these political appointments are also a pursuit from the heart of Liu who believes entrepreneurs should have the responsibility to actively engage in institution building to contribute to the common good for more people. The main political appointments of Liu are illustrated in Table 12.1.

The T Group is the pioneer in exploring the PV poverty alleviation model in China. It donated funds for the construction of an independent distributed PV power station in a poor western region in 2007. In July 2007, Liu promised in the

TABLE 12.1 Mr. Liu's political appointments

Year	Political Appointment
1994	Member of China Democratic National Construction Association (CDNCA)
1998	• Member of the Standing Committee of Sichuan CPPCC (Committee of the Chinese People Political Consultative Conference) Committee • Member of the CPPCC National Committee • Member of the Entrepreneurs Committee of CDNCA
2002	Standing member of the Central Committee of CDNCA
2008	Member of Standing Committee of the CPPCC National Committee
2018	Representative in China's National People's Congress

CNDCA to initiate a philanthropy project called "Si Yuan Sunshine Plan" to donate 50 million RMB yuan to construct PV power stations in poor western regions in the following 10 years. He walked his talk. The T Group grew from the first 8-kWp (kilowatt peak, the peak power generated with the maximum illumination intensity) small PV power station to help provide local people with light and heat, to develop its first unique 1.5-MWp (megawatt peak) "aquatic fishing plus PV" poverty alleviation model to help improve income of fisheries and provide clean energy. Over time, it is continuously transforming its business as a sustainable enterprise. It is simultaneously creating environmental value, social value, and economic value (until 2017, Chinese average electric power consumption was 4,000 kWh).

At present, the T Group is constructing one of the largest PV (100-MWp) poverty alleviation projects in China. Located in western Inner Mongolia, it is estimated that it will produce 130 million kWp per year and help increase income at least 3,000 RMB Yuan for each of the 4,133 poor households over the expected project life of 20 years. Apart from this, the project could also help save the consumption of 45,000 tons of standard coal and reduce carbon dioxide emissions by 113,000 tons per year (out of 12 billion tons per year).

In 2014, the "aquatic fishing plus PV" model was highly complimented by NEA as an important development of PV power model. In the same year, this model also received recognition and support from CPAD. With Liu's further elaborations on the benefits of this model on poverty alleviation, National Reform and Development Commission (NRDC) released another policy to support the adoption of the "aquatic fishing plus solar PV" model as an effective policy tool to eradicate poverty.

The main activities of Liu's solar PV business are illustrated in Table 12.2, as are numerous awards presented to Liu and to the T Group.

Far-sighted entrepreneurs seek to balance their business success and positive societal impacts to ensure the sustained legitimacy and the support of government. In the T Group's development, Liu cautiously explored and exploited the business opportunities in the solar PV industry. Along with his political appointments, Liu also was able to submit policy proposals and suggestions to CPPCC and other central government bodies, and thus get feedback and confirmation on whether

TABLE 12.2 The T Group's activities and awards in the development of solar PV business

Year	Main Activities in Developing the Solar PV Business
2007	• Invested in a chemical factory to produce PVC with a production capacity of 5,000 tons per year. PVC is the material for producing polycrystalline silicon. This marks the milestone of the T Group making the decision to enter into the solar PV industry.
	• Donated 50 million RMB to construct 6 PV power stations in remote western rural areas with a total installed capacity of 1.355 MWp
2009	• Member of New Energy Chamber of Commerce under the umbrella of All China Federation of Industry and Commerce
	• Awarded "Responsible Leadership" of the 1st China Corporate Social Responsibility Summit
2011	• Made investment expansion in Chengdu
	• Increased investment for polycrystalline silicon production base in Jianwei County of the Sichuan Province, with 46.2 billion RMB
	• Standing deputy director of New Energy Chamber of Commerce (Liu)
	• Awarded "Global New Energy Business Leadership"
2012	• Approved by Sichuan Provincial Government to set up the demonstration project of 30-MW solar PV grid connection in Yanyuan County with a total installed capacity of 100 MW
	• Submitted proposals to government bodies to renew industrial policy to support the development of the PV Solar industry
	• Constructed the 1MWp philanthropic project in Fukang County, Xinjiang
	• Recognized as "the No.1 Figure in Solar PV Industry" by National Energy Administration (Liu)
	• Awarded "The Most Civil Responsible Chinese Entrepreneur" (Liu)
	• Awarded "2012 the Most Social Responsible Chinese Entrepreneur" (Liu)
2013	• Acquired the original PV producer LDK and expanded further investment of PV business in producing PV slice
	• Invented the unique business model of "PV+ aquatic fishing"
	• Awarded "2013 Caijing Figure with Impact" (Liu)
	• Awarded "Global New Energy Figure of the Year" (Liu)
2014	• Decided to extend the industrial chain to the construction and operation of decentralized PV power station
	• Ranked as one of the largest PV slide producers in China
	• The unique "PV+ aquatic fishing" model received government support and was recognized as one of the 10 poverty alleviation projects
	• Awarded "Global New Energy Business Leader" (Liu)
2017	• Invested two 10-GW polycrystalline silicon cell plants in Chengdu and Hefei
	• Invested in a 100-MWp poverty-alleviation solar PV power station in Inner Mongolia.
	• Awarded "2017 Global New Energy Top 500 Robust Growth Enterprise"
	• Awarded "China Si Yuan Philanthropy Award," the highest government philanthropy award

Year	Main Activities in Developing the Solar PV Business
2018	• Successful construction of highly purified polycrystalline silicon plant with annual productivity of 50,000 tons in Inner Mongolia • Awarded "National Excellent Entrepreneur" (Liu) • Selected as one of the "Hundred Distinguished Private-Firm Entrepreneurs in the Four Decades of Reform and Opening-Up" (Liu)

his judgment on investing in the new energy field was a correct strategic decision. The following two statements from an external government official and an internal senior manager of the T Group show the active political engagement and produced influence of Liu.

> This proposal [Suggestions to Accelerating Poverty Eradication through Developing Solar PV Industry] has critical points on poverty eradication through solar PV. The proposal, with its great successful practices by the T Group, gives us many feasible and valuable suggestions. NEA will push to implement the suggested actions to promote the model of poverty eradication with solar PV.
>
> *(A senior official in the NEA)*

> Liu keeps active political engagement due to his responsibility as Standing Member of the Central Committee of CNDCA, Member of Standing Committee of the CPPCC National Committee, as well as the recent appointment of Representative of China People's Congress. Many of his political suggestions and proposals stemmed from his considerations for the public interests and the entire solar PV industry. As an influential opinion leader – from a major company in solar PV industry, Liu is expected to bring in voices of other companies in this industry to policy makers. He believes that without a healthy industrial environment there would be no growth for the T Group. This helps to develop a long-term commitment of our company to solar PV business development and social and environmental value creation.
>
> *(A senior manager of the T Group)*

Externally, it is Liu's political capital and his civic engagement efforts that drove him to invest in the solar PV business at an opportune time. However, the internal motivations of Liu that pushed his firm for the development of the solar energy industry should not be ignored. With his deep-rooted belief of making meaningful business and creating greater value to society as well as the emotional and cultural embeddedness in the local region and institution system, Liu was able to find a good balance between pursuing his business interests as an entrepreneur and seeking to address public and societal issues as a public figure with his political appointment.

The T Group started this new business through financing public demonstration projects of PV power stations in the western rural areas of China and received good response and attention from broad stakeholders. For the development of those philanthropic demonstration projects, the T Group also was actively involved in institutional work, such as advising to build PV power stations to help eradicate poverty in those regions. In turn, the recognition and support from the government created more opportunities for the T Group. Namely, the market opportunities for the development of sustainable business are closely linked to its strategic philanthropic activities in constructing solar PV power stations. Those strategic philanthropic activities, in turn, further improved the legitimacy of the T Group and paved the way for exploiting market opportunities.

With this ambidextrous capability, the T Group realized a dialectical synthesis of creating values in the three dimensions of sustainability, as noted earlier. And in the policy context of leveraging all possible resources to eradicate poverty completely by 2020 in China, the model and practices initiated by the T Group were scaled up and replicated by many other solar PV companies. Entrepreneurs in this field thus are inspired to develop their business models in a way of "doing well by doing good."

Conclusion

This chapter illustrates a unique, exemplary Chinese company advancing the SDGs, especially on the eradication of poverty (SDG #1) in western inland regions of China. The company also shows the great power of private entrepreneurs on contributing to the achievements of SDGs through balancing different institutional logics. Through partnerships (SDG #17), private entrepreneurs in transition economies could actually play active roles in contributing to promoting some other SDGs, such as developing affordable and clean energy (SDG #7) and making human settlements more safe, resilient, and sustainable (SDG #11).

This case is not a lone-hero story about Chinese private-firm entrepreneurs. It shows vibrant entrepreneurial ambidextrous capabilities in the context of institutional transitions, where entrepreneurs can play very active roles in addressing indigenous social and environmental issues by developing sustainable entrepreneurship.

The institutional environment in a transition economy of rapidly industrializing China was able to induce entrepreneurs to pursue both the benefits of social and political legitimacy and more business opportunities through active political engagement and corporate social programs responsive to critical state targets. The T Group has developed rapidly into the second-largest PV solar energy company in China, with a comprehensive industrial chain from up-stream raw materials production to PV cells production to the building and operation of PV solar stations. The proactive strategic alignment with poverty alleviation paved the way for the legitimacy of the T Group's expansion in the PV solar business, which further greatly promoted the development of the whole PV solar energy industry in China.

To achieve the ambitious target of poverty eradication by 2020 in China, businesses and entrepreneurs are entwined in this important institutional arrangement, that is, to leverage all possible resources nationwide. In this process, entrepreneurs are facing challenges of complex and still evolving institutions. At the same time, they have opportunities to realize the transformation of their businesses by creating social value through engaging in institutional work favoring sustainable development.

The PV model of poverty eradication in China might provide valuable experience for other economies in transition. When influential business leaders explore business opportunities in an inclusive approach, that is, to create business opportunities through identifying and responding to certain specific societal challenges, they could take advantage of their interactions with national-level policy makers in more meaningful and positive ways.

Thus, entrepreneurs seeking long-term values could proactively create an environment of formal and informal norms that promotes a harmonization in aligning business strategy and state expected social responsibilities. The chapter might encourage scholars in other transition economies to investigate the connections between indigenous entrepreneurs' political engagement and their active contribution to push the achievement of SDGs in their specific institutional context.

References

Belz, F. M., & Binder, J. K. 2017. "Sustainable entrepreneurship: A convergent process model." *Business Strategy and the Environment*, 26(1): 1–17.
Child, J., Rodrigues, S. B., & Tse, K. K. T. 2012. "The dynamics of influence in corporate co-evolution." *Journal of Management Studies*, 49(7): 1246–1273.
Dean, T., McMullen, J. 2007. "Toward a theory of sustainable entrepreneurship: reducing environmental degradation through entrepreneurial action." *Journal of Business Venturing*, 22 (1), 50–76.
Dieleman, D., & Boddewyn, J. J. 2012. "Using organization structure to buffer political ties in emerging markets: A case study." *Organization Studies*, 33(1): 71–95.
Hall, Jeremy K., Daneke, Gregory A., Lenox, Michael J. 2010. "Sustainable development and entrepreneurship: Past contributions and future directions." *Journal of Business Venturing*, 25 (5): 439–448.
Lawton, T., McGuire, S., & Rajwani, T. 2013. "Corporate political activity: A literature review and research agenda." *International Journal of Management Reviews*, 15(1): 86–105.
Li, X. H., & Liang, X. Y. 2015. "A confucian social model of political appointments among Chinese private-firm entrepreneurs." *Academy of Management Journal*, 58(2): 592–617.
Li, Y., Peng, M. W., & Macaulay, C. D. 2013. "Market-political ambidexterity during institutional transitions." *Strategic Organization*, 11(2): 205–213.
Mantere, S., Pajunen, K., & Lamberg, J. A. 2009. "Vices and virtues of corporate political activity: The challenge of international business." *Business & Society*, 48(1): 105–132.
McWilliams, A., Van Fleet, D. D., & Cory, K. 2002. "Raising rivals' costs through political strategy: An extension of the resource-based theory." *Journal of Management Studies*, 39(5): 707–723.
National Energy Administration. PV Poverty Alleviation became new path for increasing farmers' incomes. http://www.nea.gov.cn/2016-11/28/c_135864449.htm

Ogbor, J. O. 2000. "Mythicizing and reification in entrepreneurial discourse: Ideology-critique of entrepreneurial studies." *Journal of Management Studies*, 37(5): 605–636.

Pacheco, D. F., Dean, T. J., & Payne, D. S. 2010. "Escaping the green prison: Entrepreneurship and the creation of opportunities for sustainable development." *Journal of Business Venturing*, 25(5): 464–480.

Pinkse, J., & Groot, K. 2015. "Sustainable entrepreneurship and corporate political activity: Overcoming market barriers in the clean energy sector." *Entrepreneurship Theory and Practice*, 39(3): 633–654.

Reinstaller, A. 2005. "Policy entrepreneurship in the co-evolution of institutions, preferences, and technology: Comparing the diffusion of totally chlorine free pulp bleaching technologies in the US and Sweden." *Research Policy*, 34(9): 1366–1384.

Schaltegger, S., & Wagner, M. 2011. "Sustainable entrepreneurship and sustainability innovation: Categories and interactions." *Business Strategy and Environment*, 20(4): 222–237.

Thornton, P. H. 2002. "The rise of the corporation in a craft industry: Conflict and conformity in institutional logics." *Academy of Management Journal*, 45(1): 81–101.

Welter, F., & Smallbone, D. 2011. "Institutional perspectives on entrepreneurial behavior in challenging environments." *Journal of Small Business*, 49(1): 107–125.

York, J. G., & Venkataraman, S. 2010. "The entrepreneur-environment nexus: Uncertainty, innovation, and allocation." *Journal of Business Venturing*, 25(5): 449–463.

13

GLOBAL CHAMPIONS OF SUSTAINABLE DEVELOPMENT

Uaná Refugees Program: an opportunity to start over

Norman de Paula Arruda Filho

Abstract

What does a business school have to do with refugees? That's a simple question with a straight answer: Everything. As a signatory of the United Nations Global Compact since 2004 and pioneer of the Principles for Responsible Management Education, Higher Institute of Administration and Economics Brazilian Business School mobilizes students by promoting values and responsible practices that generate social, corporate and economic development for society. In its mission to train globally responsible leaders, the institution has adopted the UN 2030 Agenda for Sustainable Development and started promoting a series of actions towards disseminating information on the Sustainable Development Goals (SDGs), among its stakeholders. Due to the refugee crisis that emerged in 2016, ISAE identified an opportunity to engage with society and act in favor of this specific group it created the Uaná Refugees Program. *Uaná* means "firefly" in Tupi-Guarani, the language spoken by Indian tribes that inhabited the Brazilian coast in Brazil in 1500, as a tribute to those beings that glow to illuminate the way they pass through. The Uaná Refugees Program is a volunteer training initiative promoted by the business school's students, alumni, teachers and staff, focused on providing refugees and migrants the tools that could contribute to their entry into the Brazilian labor market. Evidence of the results and impacts are shown via participants' feedback and in the continuity of the project.

Introduction

What does a business school have to do with refugees? That is a simple question with a straight answer: everything. Nowadays, globalization presumes collaboration. For a business school that promotes sustainable management education, it is expected to transcend the primary mission of executive training to include contributions to global development.

Due to the 2016 refugee crisis, the Brazilian business school, Higher Institute of Administration and Economics (ISAE) decided to engage with this specific group by creating the Uaná Refugees Program. This is a volunteer training initiative focused on providing refugees and migrants tools that can contribute to their entry and integration into the Brazilian labor market.

As a UN Global Compact and Principles for Responsible Management Education (PRME) signatory and member of the PRME Champions Leadership Group since 2013, the ISAE school acts as a mobilizer and partnership-creating agent in advocating for and/or implementing a rather unique legal framework for receiving and integrating refugees into Brazil's economic, social and cultural environment.

This chapter presents a summary of the world refugee crisis, especially its effects in Brazil, which has inspired a project developed by ISAE. The main purpose of sharing this experience is to reinforce the importance of the involvement of several actors to achieve a better world in line with the Sustainable Development Goals (SDGs).

The chapter is structured as follows: initially, a brief survey highlights the main data on refugees in Brazil and in the world. The literature presents studies that address the psychological implications faced by the target audience and the importance of work to these people's lives. This sets the stage for a case study of the Uaná Volunteer Program. The conclusion summarizes the main points of the chapter and the lessons learned from the program.

The configuration of the crisis

In the last decade, the problem of refugees has become a global crisis. According to the UN, refugees are people who have left their country of origin due to war conflicts and natural disasters or because of fears of persecution on the grounds of race, religion, nationality or political opinion. As such, they cannot, or do not want to, receive the protection of that country or return to it (UN 1951).

In 2017, the UN High Commissioner for Refugees (UNHCR) report revealed that more than 68.5 million people worldwide have left their places of origin because of conflict, persecution or grave human rights violations. This is a new record over the past five years. Refugee applicants for asylum in countries around the world totaled 3.1 million individuals. Internally displaced persons – people who are displaced within their own country – represent 40 million of the total. Figure 13.1 presents the refuge data in the world in the last ten years. (UNHCR 2018a)

The report also states that the number of refugees in 2017 was higher than the population of Australia. At the same time, the population of stateless people – who have no formal ties to any country – is estimated at 10 million people.

The UN Convention Relating to the Status of Refugees, which was formally adopted on July 28, 1951, defines who can be considered a refugee, clarifying rights and duties between refugees and the host countries. The document states that the request for refuge is a right guaranteed to foreigners. To be activated, the request for refuge must be made in the territory chosen as destination (Almeida 2000).

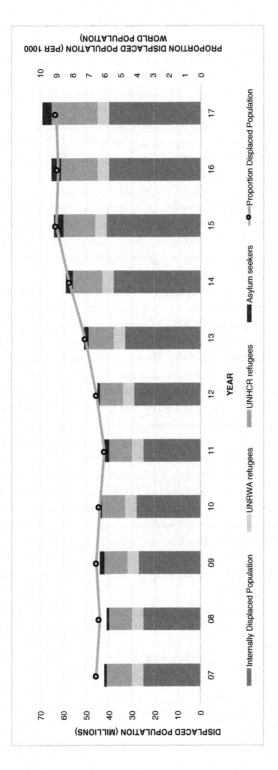

FIGURE 13.1 Global Displacement Trends and Proportion Displaced (2007–2017)

Source: Global Trends Report: Forced Displacement in 2017 (UNHCR 2018b).

In Brazil, this right is also guaranteed by Law 9.474 / 97 – Refugee Statute, the first law of the Brazilian legal system to implement a Treaty of International Human Rights Law (Brasil 1997). It is considered a true milestone in the trajectory of Brazil's commitment to refugee issues (Jubilut & Godoy 2017).

According to data released by Conare (National Committee for Refugees in Brazil) in the "Refuge in Numbers" report, by the end of 2017, Brazil recognized more than 10,145 refugees. These individuals are of various nationalities, mainly from Syria, Lebanon, Colombia, Congo, Iraq, Liberia, Nigeria, Morocco and Sierra Leone (Conare 2018). Even so, during the same period, Brazil registered about 85,000 applications for refuge (UNHCR 2018).

The great movement of refugees to Brazil began in the mid-2010s after a 7.0-magnitude earthquake hit Haiti. In addition to the numerous fatalities recorded, the disaster caused mass destruction in the capital Port-au-Prince, leaving one million people homeless. In 2012, due to the civil war in Syria and conflicts in Africa, requests for refuge in Brazil increased by 3,000 percent (Junior & Marroni 2017).

In the last seven years, Brazil has received 126,000 applications for recognition of refugee status (Conare 2018). In view of this reality, the New Migration Law (Law No. 13,445) was enacted in 2017 guaranteeing migrants the same rights to life, liberty, property and equality granted to Brazilians (Brasil 2017). In addition, this law establishes the Temporary Visa for Humanitarian Reception[1] and allows immigrants to occupy public positions and get employed. For the president of the National Committee for Refugees, Gustavo Marroni, the initiative serves as an example for the world because it is a law that has additional guarantees for the refugee by reducing the cases of statelessness, promoting integration into the workforce and facilitating Brazilian citizenship naturalization (Junior & Marroni 2017). Table 13.1 presents some statistics on refugees in Brazil in 2017.

The federal police in Brazil keep a record of states with most of the requests for refuge; these are Roraima, São Paulo and Amazonas. By May 2018, the state of Paraná has about 8 percent of refugees with active registration and has already accumulated 766 applications for recognition of refugee status (UNHCR 2018).

Forced to leave their countries of origin, many refugees find numerous social and economic difficulties in establishing themselves in a new territory. They need to count on the support of entities and projects aimed at their reintegration into the

TABLE 13.1 Refugees in Brazil, end of 2017

Refugees	10,264
Of whom assisted by UNHCR	4,427
Asylum-seekers (pending cases)	85,746
Stateless people	294
Others of concern to UNHCR	52,341
Total population of concern	148,645

country and local community. Many families have reached vulnerable conditions, requiring shelter, food and health care, which are being provided by the government in Brazil, the UNHCR and their partner organizations.

The psychological conditions of people undergoing compulsory migration also need to be considered in the reception process. According to Martins-Borges (2013),

> [t]hese unplanned and often unwanted departures are frequently filled with psychological distress directly linked to the trauma to which they were subjected in the pre-migratory and migratory period (various forms of violence, torture, witnesses and victims of massacres, death of relatives and friends, etc.).

This suffering can be exacerbated by other difficulties such as a lack of command of the language, cultural differences with the recipient country of refuge, bureaucracies for the legalization of the refugee situation and a lack of documentation on the knowledge and skills acquired. These last two factors are the main impediments to the insertion of the refugees into the local labor market, which can affect their economic well-being in the new country.

In the psychology of refugee resettlement, work represents a series of psychosocial attributes, such as the sense of belonging, time organization, social identity and survival. Thus, work becomes central to the constitution of the person, performing a specific psychological (mediating) function (Jahoda 1982). For Meyerson, the subject "only becomes a moral agent through acts regulated and ordered by work." As a consequence, when the subject "feels happy and free in his [or her] work, he [or she] has the feeling of being, of being more himself [herself]" (Meyerson 1987 apud Bendassolli and Gondim 2014).

From these convictions, acting to provide the means by which people can be integrated into the labor market drives improvement in their quality of life and contributes to other economic and social benefits.

In this sense, the project described in this chapter is an example of an initiative that aims to provide the means for refugees and migrants to resume their lives in a new place, seeking a more just and dignified existence.

ISAE as an agent of change

The ISAE Brazilian Business School was established in 1996 in the city of Curitiba, in southern Brazil. It promotes responsible management education through open courses (short, medium and long term), as well as undergraduate, postgraduate, master's degree and in-company courses.

The "b school" mobilizes students to perform responsible practices that generate social, corporate and economic development promoting values, principles and visions toward sustainable global management. Since becoming a member of the UN Global Compact in 2004, ISAE has worked to integrate academia and the corporate sector to contribute to the construction of a more inclusive and sustainable global economy.

In 2006 the school participated in the global task force that designed the UN PRME. With representatives from 60 educational institutions around the world, PRME established six principles for higher education institutions: Purpose, Values, Method, Research, Partnership and Dialogue (Haertle et al. 2017).

In support of these initiatives, ISAE's president took on the roles of board member of the Global Compact (2012–2015), head of PRME Chapter Brazil (2014–2017), head of PRME LAC Chapter (2017–2018) and counselor at the PRME Advisory Committee (2015).

The principles underlying the Global Compact and PRME were integrated into ISAE's mission and values (Arruda Filho 2017). After participating in the launch event of the SDGs in 2015 at the United Nations' invitation, ISAE began a series of actions to disseminate and adopt the SDGs in the management and educational approach of the business school. The main activities of ISAE were the following:

- The theme becoming the main focus of lectures and seminars given by ISAE's President in various business segments in the national and international arena, in big events and congresses in China, Colombia, Argentina, the United States, Finland, Slovenia and the United Kingdom
- The organization of events that mobilized government representatives, UN representatives, members of the private sector and educational institutions to discuss and outline strategies for implementing the Agenda 2030 locally and nationally
- A campaign internally that was carried out to disseminate the 17 SDGs, encouraging the mobilization of ISAE's stakeholders. In addition to strong visual communication, training was provided for employees, teachers, students and suppliers.
- Revision of ISAE's Sustainability Report to identify and document the actions performed in line with the SDGs. In 2017, ISAE's SIP (Sharing the Information on Progress) Report received formal PRME recognition for creativity in reporting on the SDGs.
- All courses offered by ISAE start with a special class about sustainable management and the UN SDGs so that all students can have access to more detailed information about the implementation of the agenda in business.
- Reformulation of the teaching methodology of the Sustainability in Organizations discipline in ISAE's Professional Master in Governance and Sustainability so that students recognize and understand the SDGs and promote their implementation within their companies' strategy.

For all these commitments, ISAE has always sought to transcend its role as a business school and act to contribute directly to society in projects not restricted to its students but also involving different members of the local community. Thus, the refugee crisis represented an opportunity to translate the principles ISAE advocates into practice and to act as an agent of social change.

As a way of inspiring other leaders, this chapter presents the development and implementation of the Uaná Refugees Program, as well as the main challenges encountered along the way.

The Uaná Refugees Program

During the UN Private Sector Forum, following the UN General Assembly Summit on Refugees and Migrants in September 2016 in New York City, the UN Secretary-General Ban Ki-moon directed attention to the refugee issue:

> Enterprises should allow equal employment opportunities for refugees and migrants. Companies should invest in education initiatives for displaced youth. Help us by raising their voices and taking action to defend those most vulnerable.

At that point, ISAE was already finishing the first cycle of training of the Uaná Refugees Program. The starting point for this project was a volunteer-driven social services project of an ISAE's corporate course in a dental health company. The action involved more than 50 volunteers, supporters, sponsors and employees from different companies in a social action to improve the oral health of immigrants in Curitiba.

Following this experience, ISAE created a volunteer network focusing on the development of skills that could help refugees in their inclusion in the local labor market.

Since 2002, ISAE has had an internal volunteer program where students, alumni, teachers and staff are invited to provide management consultancy services for local nongovernmental organizations and small and micro-enterprises (Arruda Filho 2015). Thus, the Uaná Refugees Program was conceived as a project within the overarching Uaná Volunteer Program.

The objectives of the project are to promote orientation and training of the refugees for the labor market, contributing to their autonomy, quality of life, exercise of their citizenship rights and responsibilities and their personal and professional development.

The first step was to seek partners to help identify and contact migrants and refugees who were interested in courses that could improve their vocational skills. For that, ISAE signed three partnership agreements with a school specialized in the professional relocation of foreigners in the Brazilian labor market (Linyon), the Institute for Refugee Reintegration (ADUS) and a local nonprofit institution (Unilehu), which promotes diversity through the inclusion of people and groups that are socially vulnerable. These entities were responsible for referring refugees and migrants to ISAE.

To put the project into practice, ISAE mobilized its key stakeholders and planned the modules that would be part of the training. The program was divided into eight-hour modules, which address five relevant issues to migrants and refugee empowerment through social and economic inclusion:

- **Personal development:** As an initial module provides basic knowledge on issues such as resilience, leadership, teamwork, empowerment, initiative and proactivity
- **Professional development:** Presents characteristics of the Brazilian labor market, information about the use of social networks and the importance of forming a network of contacts
- **Entrepreneurship:** Addresses the characteristics of an entrepreneur, teaches step-by-step how to make a business plan and explores some business modeling techniques
- **Leadership:** Seeks to develop the characteristics of a leader, the definition of purpose and the resolution of problems – all within a vision of sustainable development
- **Brazilian Labor Market:** Teaches participants how to develop efficient resumes and business cards, plus tips on how to behave in a job interview and foster good working relationships with coworkers. It also addresses in a more specific way the rights and obligations of citizens and residents under Brazilian law.

Still in partnership with Unilehu and ADUS, in 2017 a basic computer course was offered to a group of 43 refugees. The course lasted an average of four months and aimed to familiarize them with technological resources, teaching the participants how to use the computer for day-to-day tasks as well as for professional activities.

In 2016 and 2017, ISAE received refugees and migrants from countries such as Angola, Congo, Dominican Republic, Guinea Bissau, Haiti, Sudan and Syria. Many of these individuals already had a degree from their home country.

After the training, some refugees were able to be remarketed, while others were awarded scholarships at ISAE's Management Processes graduation.

One of the Angolan participants affirmed that, for him, the Uaná program was very interesting as it helps complement academic teaching: "We learn how to work in groups and how to make a difference in society. This course will help me gain many other opportunities for my professional career" (A. C., Angolan refugee, graduate in Logistics).

Likewise, a volunteer teacher pointed out the social role of the program as work is one of the pillars of life: "To give technical information, behavioral information, and guidance about how to prepare for an interview [. . .] so they understand what opportunities they can achieve is essential." She also notes that most Brazilian ancestors were immigrants and once needed help to settle in their new homeland, too.

Since it helps create opportunities for minorities, the Uaná Refugee Program is well aligned with the UN Agenda 2030. In particular, it reinforces the interdependence and interconnection of the SDGs, especially concerning SDG #1 (No poverty), SDG #2 (Zero hunger), SDG #8 (Decent work and economic growth), SDG #10 (Reduced inequality) and SDG #17 (Partnerships for the goals).

In addition to the Uaná Program, the ISAE has participated in the Refugee Women Empowerment Program – a partnership among the UN, the UNHCR and the Global Compact in Brazil. This program offers remote coaching and mentoring for a period of three months to empower a group of refugee women from São Paulo through professional orientation and access to work and networking opportunities.

Challenges, lessons learned and implications

Despite the close cooperation between the institutions involved in the Uaná Refugee Program, identifying stakeholders and keeping them in the project was a real challenge. As there are no records of where the refugees are allocated residence, it is not easy to locate and get in touch with them. Thus, it was necessary to turn to other support entities for help. The school also has to deal with many dropouts during the training period, because the participants often do not have the financial means to attend classes regularly due to the expenses of transportation. The language sometimes is also a difficulty. Other initiatives across the city aim to teach Portuguese to these new citizens. The cultural differences had to be overcome in the classroom, always respecting everyone's opinions and customs.

The main lesson learned in this project is that the help cannot be limited to activities within the classroom, it must go beyond it. Seeking solutions through training and mobilizing other actors in society to help will enable the refugee participants to continue their studies and, above all, facilitate their inclusion and integration into the local labor market. The humanitarian work does not end when students leave class.

Adapting to a new culture, a new language and new forms of development are difficult tasks even in normal situations. Living through all this change with the weight of forced migration, for a refugee, requires much more determination and resilience.

Refugees already face several political and religious problems that have taken on global proportions. Thus, companies, educational institutions and the government have a moral commitment to creating solutions to improve the living conditions of this group.

Finding solutions to the refugee issue is contributing to their dignified living conditions. More than articulating partnerships, designing projects and planning, knowing how to convert these into viable outcomes is what really brings positive results to society.

In this scenario, the Uaná Refugees Program meets a social demand to include and integrate different cultures, encouraging participants to exercise their skills and share knowledge, thus contributing to strengthening the local economy and generating income for participants.

Working with migrants and refugees promotes a movement for social transformation, professional development and the building of new leaders. Through the teaching of entrepreneurship and innovation tools, the program focuses on the professional development of migrants and refugees and their integration into the local labor market, as well as new opportunities to restart their lives.

The activities of the Uaná Refugee Program present an example of mobilization towards the focus of the 2030 Agenda for Sustainable Development Goals, which ensures that "no one will be left behind." Implementation of this project did not require considerable expense due to a strong mobilization of partners and volunteers. Thus, here is a high potential for replicability in other contexts. This is critical as the world needs to join hands in meeting the challenges of the largest refugee crisis since the Second World War.

Note

1 Humanitarian reception is a temporary visa for those who need to leave their countries of origin but are not considered as refugees, as well as for unaccompanied minors and foreigners who enter the national territory for health care.

Reference list

Almeida, G. A. 2000. "A Lei n. 9.474/97 e a definição ampliada de refugiado: breves considerações." (The Law 9.47/97 and the expanded definition of refugee: Brief considerations). *Revista de Faculdade de Direito*, 95: 373–383.

Arruda Filho, N. de P. 2015. "Perspectivação: A new educational framework to include sustainability in responsible management education." *Transformative Approaches to Sustainable Development at Universities: Working Across Disciplines*. DOI: 10.1007/978-3-319-08837-2_18

Arruda Filho, N. de P. 2017. "The Agenda 2030 for responsible management education: An applied methodology." *The International Journal of Management Education*, 15(2): 183–191.

Bendassolli, P. F., & Gondim, S. M. G. 2014. "Significados, sentidos e função psicológica do trabalho: Discutindo essa tríade conceitual e seus desafios metodológicos." (Meaning, sense and psychological function of work: Discussing this conceptual triad and its methodological challenges). *Avances en psicología latino-americana*, 32(1): 131–147.

Brasil. 1997. Decreto n. 9.474, de 22 de Julho de 1997. Estatuto dos Refugiados. (Decree 9.474, July 22nd 1997. Status of Refugees). Accessed 6 July 2018. www.planalto.gov.br/ccivil_03/leis/l9474.htm

Brasil. 2017. Decreto n. 13.445, de 24 de maio de 2017. Lei de Migração. (Decree 13.445, May 24th 2017. Law of Migration). Accessed 6 July 2018. www.planalto.gov.br/ccivil_03/_Ato20152018/2017/Lei/L13445.htm

Comitê Nacional para os Refugiados (CONARE). 2018. *Ministério da Justiça e Segurança Pública Governo Federal. Refúgio em números*. 3ª ed. (Ministry of Justice and Public Security Federal Government: Refugees in Numbers), 3rd ed. Accessed 6 July 2018. www.justica.gov.br/news/de-10-1-mil-refugiados-apenas-5-1-mil-continuam-no-brasil/refugio-em-numeros_1104.pdf/view

Heartle, J., Parkes, C., Murray, A., & Hayes, R. 2017. "PRME: Building a global movement on responsible management education." *The International Journal of Management Education*, 15(2 Part B): 66–72.

Jahoda, M. 1982. Employment and Unemployment: A Social-Psychological Analysis. Cambridge, MA: *University of Cambridge Press*.

Jubilut, L. L., & de Godoy, G. G. 2017. Refúgio no Brasil: Comentários à Lei 9.474/97 (Refugees in Brazil: Commentary to Law 9.474/97). Quartier Latin/ACNUR. ISBN 85-7674-812-6

Junior, V., & Marroni, G. 2017. *GloboNews Especial: Os refugiados no Brasil*. (GloboNews Special: Refugees in Brazil). Accessed 25 June 2018. www.youtube.com/watch?v=5mVpBJZGZ7I&t=271s

Martins-Borges, L. 2013. "Migração involuntária como fator de risco à saúde mental." (Involuntary migration as a mental health risk). *Remhu-Revista Interdisciplinar da Mobilidade Humana*, 21(40): 151–162.

Meyerson, I. 1987. "Le travail, fonction psychologique" in I. Meyerson. *Écrits 1920–1983: Pour Une Psychologie Historique*, (pp. 252–263). Paris: PUF.

United Nations (UN). 1951. *Convenção das Nações Unidas sobre o Estatuto dos Refugiados* (United Nations Convention of the Status of Refugees). Accessed 10 May 2018. www.acnur.org/fileadmin/Documentos/portugues/BDL/Convencao_relativa_ao_Estatuto_dos_Refugiados.pdf

United Nations High Commissioner for Refugees (UNHCR). 2018a. *Dados sobre refúgio no Brasil* (Data on Refuge in Brazil). Accessed 10 May 2018. www.acnur.org/portugues/dados-sobre-refugio/dados-sobre-refugio-no-brasil/

United Nations High Commissioner for Refugees (UNHCR). 2018b. *Global Trends of Forced Displacement in 2017*. Accessed 8 June 2018. www.unhcr.org/5b27be547

CONCLUDING REMARKS

Patricia M. Flynn, Tay Keong Tan and Milenko Gudić

The United Nations Sustainable Development Goals (SDGs) are wide-ranging and very ambitious – some would argue unattainable, especially by the year 2030, the target date for achievement of the goals. The scope and characteristics of the issues involved will vary widely by region, with those in developing countries, in particular, facing relatively complex challenges in seeking to make substantive progress toward these goals.

The chapters in this book demonstrate that progress is indeed possible even when circumstances appear dire. Case studies from more than a dozen countries across five continents (i.e., Asia, Africa, Europe, North America and South America) are included. While the details of specific cases differ widely, this volume shows an essential key to success is an individual or an organization, which we call a "Global Champion," that willingly and courageously takes on these challenges. This book celebrates these Global Champions and thanks them for their persistent and often painstaking actions on behalf of many people in need and of the planet itself. Their experiences also provide valuable lessons for others worldwide seeking to implement the SDGs.

The SDGs and their interlinkages

Each of the 17 SDGs is addressed in at least one chapter; many appear in numerous chapters. For example, SDG #1 (No poverty), SDG #2 (Zero hunger), SDG #3 (Good health and well-being), SDG #5 (Gender equality), SDG#6 (Clean water and sanitation), SDG #8 (Decent work and economic growth) and SDG #17 (Partnerships) are each discussed in at least five chapters. Moreover, the chapters often demonstrate how the SDGs are interrelated, for instance, with partnerships helping to reduce poverty, which, in turn, help promote good health and well-being and bring about opportunities for decent work and economic growth.

In Gunarathne's analysis of the tea industry in Sri Lanka (Chapter 4), for example, agriculture is shown to be a main contributor to reducing poverty (SDG #1) and ending hunger (SDG #2) while improving health and well-being (SDG #3) and providing decent work and economic growth (SDG #8). In addition, the responsible production practices used in the tea industry minimized the use of natural resources (SDG #12) while improving the quality of water (SDG #6) and protecting rivers (SDG #14), natural ecosystems and biodiversity (SDG #15). The waste management system implemented generated a safe, resilient and sustainable environment for the community (SDG #11).

The innovative sustainable development model described by Smith and Kline (in Chapter 11) demonstrates how Grupo Fénix in Nicaragua also made progress toward several SDGs simultaneously. Training land mine victims to make, install and maintain solar panels in areas lacking conventional sources of electricity benefited not only those individuals but also many others with whom they shared their knowledge and expertise. Progress was made in terms of reduced poverty (SDG #1) and hunger (SDG #2), decent work and economic growth (SDG #8) and partnerships (SDG #17).

Nwagwu (Chapter 2) explains how three diverse Nigerian companies, one each in financial services, agriculture and waste recycling, tackled poverty, inequality and climate change. Poverty (SDG #1), in particular, was viewed as a critical challenge that needed to be addressed before other SDG targets were viable. Poverty was not viewed as a condition to be accepted or as one that should be allowed to interfere with progress toward sustainable development. Instead, the global champions at the three companies developed locally appropriate business models to reduce poverty. The results proved beneficial to food security (SDG #2); sustainable agriculture, including expanded youth employment (SDG #12); reduced inequality (SDG #10); financial inclusion, including that for women (SDG #5); improved sanitation (SDG #6); greater sensitivity to climate change (SDG #13); environmentally friendly recycling (SDG #15); increased income of farmers (SDG #8); and improved health and well-being of rural dwellers (SDG #3). Partnerships (SDG #17) with organizations, such as local businesses, governments and nongovernmental organizations (NGOs), were also essential to the positive outcomes.

Local orientation and market-based solutions

Throughout the book, *Global Champions* highlights the importance of having sustainability programs and activities customized to the specific region and implemented by individuals from those communities. This is true even if initial funding is coming from national or foreign governments or international foundations. Kellogg's discussion of water and sanitation (Chapter 3), for example, emphasizes these features based on research at the Center for Science and Environment in India that recommends having control of projects in the hands of the local population, especially in rural areas. Global champion Peter Morgan's work on improved sanitation and water technologies in Zimbabwe is also cited as demonstrating the importance of local involvement. His commitment to sharing the results of his firsthand experience with different economic and social contexts has been influential in many countries. He emphasizes the importance of keeping in mind that circumstances and cultures in the developed world often differ from those in developing or emerging countries. The best technical solutions found to resolve problems in some countries might not be effective if local users and other stakeholders do not accept, or actively oppose, those options.

Another example of a global champion working with the local population to address its own issues is Vélez-Zapata, Cortés and Rosenbloom's discussion (Chapter 1) of what it means to be a Latin Family. In this case, Andrés Felipe Gómez Salazar, founder and chief executive officer of Grupo Familia in Colombia, transformed the company into one committed to sustainability. He succeeded by taking a long-term view, developing a corporate culture committed to sustainable development, employing community members many of whom had been living in poverty and providing social investments as well as quality products to individuals at the bottom of the pyramid (BoP). The results include a decline in poverty (SDG #1), reductions in hunger (SDG #3), improved education (SDG #4), less gender inequality (SDG #5), decent work and economic growth (SDG #8) and attainment of environmental and industrial goals (SDG #9).

Fontana's case (Chapter 5) on Classical Handmade Products in Bangladesh also highlights the critical role of engagement of the people in rural communities. Md. Tauhid Bin Abdus Salam ("Tauhid") focused on individuals in need, including those physically impaired and those "at the fringe of Bangladesh society." He educated these people; provided them jobs with rewards, such as free solar panels, for the best performers; and protected them from exposure to hazardous chemicals by avoiding use of harmful dyes and gases. Tauhid persisted in the face of significant and, at times, life-threatening pushback from individuals, including other employers who accused him of unfair competition.

Cases throughout the book show that once local individuals had become part of the solution in addressing sustainability development issues, they often then assisted others in becoming empowered and achieving results they never thought possible. Had they just been given handouts, the outcomes would have been short term and generally restricted to the initial recipients.

Education and training

Education and training are found to be essential for establishing viable, long-term sustainable development outcomes. For example, in Chapter 7, Young's discussion of Malala Yousafzai's pioneering work and influence on providing access to education for girls demonstrates its value for advancing other SDGs as well. The case shows, for instance, how quality education (SDG #4) for girls, leads to reduced gender inequality (SDG #5) and inequality more generally (SDG #10), while also promoting decent work and economic growth (SDG #8) and building strong, responsible institutions (SDG #16).

Bellow (Chapter 8) demonstrates the critical role of adult community education on women's empowerment and community engagement. The chapter highlights Louise Lovett's leadership of the Longford Women's Link (LWL) in Ireland, which provides courses in a variety of academic fields, as well as employment-related training, including job-seeking and interviewing skills. These tools helped the women become more independent, provide for themselves and their families and actively participate in the multifaceted civic life of their community.

Arruda Filno's (Chapter 13) analysis of the Uaná Refugees Program at the Higher Institute of Administration and Economics (ISEA) Brazilian Business School targets a different local population. This program trains migrants and refugees so that they can successfully enter Brazilian labor markets. By law, migrants in Brazil are guaranteed the same rights to life, liberty, property and equality granted to Brazilians. Language issues and cultural differences, however, have often made this difficult. The Uaná Refugees Program offers education and training and entrepreneurial and innovative tools both inside and outside the classroom.

Wersun's chapter (10) on the Grameen Caledonian College of Nursing (GCCN) in Bangladesh is also shown to foster sustainable livelihoods and empowerment. The product of three faculty members from Scotland and Bangladesh, the GCCN also collaborated with a local bank that offered loans so that these students could continue their education and prepare for a career in nursing.

Gender equality

Almost every chapter in the book addresses gender, as females are often a significant segment of the needy populations in the geographic areas involved. Reducing gender inequality (SDG #5) is a key factor in successful sustainable development. As highlighted in Section III of the book, three chapters focus specifically on girls or women with respect to sustainability development activities. Two of these chapters (those by Young and by Bellow) are highlighted in the prior discussion on education. The third, by Cecchi-Dimeglio (Chapter 9) addresses the critical role men can play in helping to level the playing field for women in the workplace. The commitment and actions taken by the legal counsels at Walmart and Verizon in the United States are powerful examples of how male executives and leaders can empower female employees and help focus attention more generally on the value of diversity of thought, perspectives and innovation in organizations.

Other gender-related examples include the EcoCafé Haiti (Chapter 6), where many of the individuals given jobs were not only female but were often women who had never been previously employed. Classical Handmade Products in Bangladesh (Chapter 5) involves a predominantly female workforce that became active in the social, economic and environmental development of the region. The GCCN in Bangladesh (Chapter 10) had primarily female students in its nursing program. And in Nicaragua, Smith and Kline (Chapter 11) explain how the provision of technical knowledge on alternative energy sources opened up employment options that transformed the lives of "Solar Women" and their families. As Reyna, one of the founding members of the Solar Women Cooperative noted, she could now direct her time and energy toward organizational and community development instead of "mere survival." The chapter shows how some of the individuals who benefited from technical training, in turn, became teachers themselves, thus helping to foster longer-term benefits of the sustainable development activities.

Partnerships

Partnerships are highlighted as essential components of effective sustainable development activities. Cao and Wang's discussion of social entrepreneurship in China (Chapter 12), for example, illustrates how Hanyuan Liu utilized his connections with NGOs, government agencies and politicians and local businesses to create innovative products and solutions that disrupted the status quo. Working with the National Energy Administration, Liu's company, T Group, launched a program involving the installation of photovoltaic panels in poor neighborhoods. This resulted in local residents being able to generate electric power for their own use (SDG #7); live in safer, healthier and more sustainable environments (SDG #11); and generate income by selling surplus power back to the grid (SDG #1).

The study on the tea industry in Sri Lanka (Chapter 4) emphasizes the critical role partnerships can play when some stakeholders are opposed to innovative sustainable development activities. Mahendra Peiris utilized collaborative partnerships with key supporters of change, including academics, scientists and activists from not-for-profit and community-based organizations, to help make the case for creative solutions. He effectively worked with national and international researchers to study and publish findings on various aspects of sustainable development programs that helped to educate and win over naysayers.

Motivation of global champions

Global Champions of Sustainable Development highlights the fact that one person or one organization can make a major difference in bringing about change and creating a better world. The book provides insights into the rationale, and reasons why, these global champions became involved and often persisted in the face of difficult circumstances or pushback from other people.

The Global Champions focus on both the people and the planet. They are determined to assist individuals in improving their employability and their integration into the community; at the same time, they are intent on reducing environmental problems in the area. Market-based strategies are recommended for fighting poverty and empowering the poor to become active players in economic, social and environmental progress over the long term. Cao and Wang (Chapter 12) highlight Confucian values underlying the success of social entrepreneurs who are committed to promoting social welfare and to serving the larger community. Interactions between business and social purposes are also highlighted as some of the poorest individuals in Sri Lanka (Chapter 4) and Bangladesh (Chapters 5) became workers in the tea and the basket and rug industries. Social ventures and the goal of reducing poverty also drove Tom Durant to create EcoCafé Haiti (Chapter 6). And in India and in Zimbabwe (Chapter 3), the desire to address the specific needs and cultures of local people resulted in Global Champions ensuring access to waste treatment facilities and clean water.

The role of family is highlighted in several of the stories of global champions. Malala (Chapter 7), for example, became an activist at the age of 11, when the Taliban prohibited girls from attending school in Pakistan. She had inherited her father's enthusiasm for learning and knowledge and refused to be denied access to education. Her father supported her incredibly courageous path to help girls worldwide gain access to education. In Colombia, the family values that Andrés Gómez (Chapter 1) gained in his childhood highly resonated with the company values of the Grupo Familia. These helped transform the company into a sustainable development powerhouse, engaging marginalized BoP individuals, respecting BoP consumers and empowering impoverished communities. In the United States, the male legal counsels who were strong allies of their female colleagues (Chapter 9) were very much influenced by their families, for example, their wives, daughters, mothers and sisters. Global Champion Tauhid (Chapter 5) actually migrated with his family to the United States; however, he soon returned to Bangladesh to fight against poverty and assist his fellow citizens.

Some of the global champions came from or subsequently joined the world of academia, extending their outreach and educational focus to individuals much in need. For example, Grupo Fénix (Chapter 11) was established by coauthor Susan Kinne and her students at the National Engineering University in Nicaragua, while Michael Smith was a Fulbright Scholar in Nicaragua as part of a collaboration with the Grupo Fénix and the National Engineering University. The LWL in Ireland (Chapter 8) provided community education that proved instrumental in bringing women into viable positions in the workplace. Faculty in Scotland and in Bangladesh joined forces and created the GCCN that enables women to secure a sustainable livelihood for themselves and their families. And global champions at the ISAE Brazilian School of Business provided educational offerings specifically designed to help integrate migrants and refugees into the Brazilian economy. Tom Durant, the founder of EcoCafé Haiti (Chapter 6), currently serving as a senior instructor at the University of Oregon and at Oregon State University, is teaching Entrepreneurship, Global Business and other management courses.

Many of the Global Champions highlighted in this volume have won awards for their work on sustainable development that has changed people's lives. This was not viewed as a goal or reason for their actions. It is, however, great that their efforts and impacts have been so recognized. For example, among Malala's (Chapter 7) many awards are *Time*'s 100 Most Influential People in the World and the Nobel Peace Prize. Hanyuan Lui's numerous awards include the Most Social Responsible Chinese Entrepreneur and the China So Yuan Philanthropy Award. Mahendra Peiris's (Chapter 4) innovations in sustainable farming earned him the Presidential Green

Award in Sri Lanka. Md. Tauhid Bin Abdus Sakab (Chapter 5) was awarded the Exporter of the Year Award for his leadership in promoting sustainable growth in Bangladesh. In the United States (Chapter 9), Alan Bryan at Walmart received the Lead by Example Award from the National Association of Women Lawyers, while Craig Stillman at Verizon was given a Leadership in the Promotion of Diversity Award from the Law and Education Empowerment Project. The Centre for Science and Environment and Peter Morgan (Chapter 3) are each recipients of the Stockholm Water Prize. And the list goes on.

Implications for educators

The myriad of examples, challenges and success stories in this book related to addressing the SDGs, offer numerous materials and ideas for educators across a range of fields. For example, entrepreneurship, management, business ethics, law, technology, international development, negotiations, finance, government and public policy, the social sciences, the natural sciences and the humanities are all areas addressed in some of the case studies that can be instrumental in class discussions. They can be used in existing courses or be the impetus for the development of new offerings or new modules in existing courses. The cases also demonstrate the interdisciplinary nature of SDG-related issues and the value of having business faculty working with those in the sciences to bring about meaningful research and programs.

The case studies also highlight the value faculty research can have on sustainable development. Collaborating with those working in the field and validating and publishing key challenges and findings can help motivate others and show skeptics what works and what does not in seeking to attain the SDGs. As noted earlier, the specific characteristics of programs and regions are expected to differ by location. Knowledge about how Global Champions identified and utilized the perspectives of local individuals, business leaders and other stakeholders can be valuable to others and help to create innovative programs across a range of geographic areas. Such details can also provide guidance to faculty in seeking funding from government agencies and foundations for new projects and research on sustainable development.

Global Champions of Sustainable Development is the first in the Routledge/PRME two-book series on how nations and communities are addressing the global development agenda promulgated by the UN SDGs. The second book, *Struggles and Successes in the Pursuit of Sustainable Development*, will continue the conversation and provide best practices and inspirational stories on how best to advance the SDGs.